Woman to Woman
MENTORING

How to Start, Grow, and Maintain a Mentoring Ministry

Ministry Coordinator's Guide

JANET THOMPSON

LifeWay Press®
Nashville, Tennessee

Published by LifeWay Press®
© 2000 • Janet Thompson
Fifth printing 2007

No part of this work may be reproduced or transmitted in any form or by any means, electronic or mechanical, including photocopying and recording, or by any information storage or retrieval system, except as may be expressly permitted in writing by the publisher. Requests for permission should be addressed in writing to LifeWay Press®, One LifeWay Plaza, Nashville, TN 37234-0175.

ISBN 0-6330-2950-5
Item 001114643

Dewey Decimal Classification: 248.843
Subject Heading: WOMEN\CHURCH WORK WITH WOMEN

Unless otherwise noted, Scripture quotations are from the Holy Bible,
New International Version, copyright © 1973, 1978, 1984 by International Bible Society.

Verses marked TLB are from The Living Bible
Copyright © Tyndale House Publishers, Wheaton, Illinois, 1971.
Used by permission.

Scripture quotations marked NKJV are from the New King James Version
Copyright © 1979, 1980, 1982. Thomas Nelson, Inc., Publishers.

To order additional copies of this resource: WRITE LifeWay Church Resources
Customer Service, One LifeWay Plaza; Nashville, TN 37234-0113;
FAX (615) 251-5933; PHONE 1-800-458-2772; E-MAIL *orderentry@lifeway.com*;
order ONLINE at *www.lifeway.com*; or visit the LifeWay Christian Store serving you.

Printed in the United States of America

Leadership and Adult Publishing
LifeWay Church Resources
One LifeWay Plaza
Nashville, Tennessee 37234-0175

Contents

Service Opportunity Descriptions Index 4
Dedication 5
Acknowledgments 6
About the Author 7
Introduction 8
Let's Keep in Touch 10

Section 1: The Vision
Chapter 1 Why Me? 11
Chapter 2 Why You? 21
Chapter 3 You Have Your Story—Now Where Do You Start? 25

Section 2: Preparation and Planning
Chapter 4 You Need to Have a Plan 39
Chapter 5 Learn by Doing 48
Chapter 6 It's Coffee Time! 54

Section 3: The Ministry
Chapter 7 The Orientation Coffee 68
Chapter 8 The Coffee Is Over, Now You Pray 89
Chapter 9 The Kickoff Night 99
Chapter 10 Six-Month Potluck Celebration 106

Section 4: Growth and Maintenance
Chapter 11 Advertising the Ministry 111
Chapter 12 Ways to Enhance the Ministry 121
Chapter 13 Recruiting Help 131
Chapter 14 When Is It Time to Give Away the Ministry? 163
Chapter 15 Who Will Be the First to Testify? 183
Chapter 16 What Other Churches Are Saying 202
Chapter 17 Let Go & Let God! 211

Section 5: Forms
Discussion 219
Forms Index Alphabetical by Title 220
Forms Index by Form Letter 221
Forms A-X 222

Service Opportunity Descriptions

Helper Positions
Orientation Coffee Hostess 137
Greeter/Hugger 139
Name Tag Scribe 141
Registrar 143
Photographer 145
Photographer's Assistant 147
Resource Guide 149
Hospitality Floater 151
Prayer Day Team 153
Phone Communicator 155
Prayer Warriors 157
Information Table Representative 159
Prayer Chain Shepherd 161
Prayer Chain Light 162

Administrative Team Positions
Assistant/Apprentice 169
Training Leader 170
Hospitality Shepherd Coach 171
Prayer Warrior Shepherd Coach 172
Prayer Day Shepherd Coach 173
Special Events Shepherd Coach 174
Financial Shepherd Coach 175
Publicity Shepherd Coach 176
Prayer Chain Shepherd Coach 177

Coordinator/Shepherdess Positions
Spiritual Shepherdess 178
Ministry Relations Shepherdess 179
Recruiter and Servant Coordinator 180
Worship Director 181
Phone Coordinator 182

Dedication

I dedicate this material first and foremost to my Lord and Savior. I am grateful that He asked me to, "Go and feed My sheep." I trust that this resource falls into obedience with that call. I put this book before you, Lord, for your approval and sovereign use.

Secondly, I dedicate this material to all the women who also hear the Lord's call to go and feed His sheep and have the courage to step out in faith and start a Woman to Woman Mentoring Ministry in their churches. I compiled this resource just for you, and I wish you Godspeed in your journey.

Gratefully, I dedicate this material to my husband, Dave, who supports me in prayer, encouragement, and love.

Acknowledgments

This material would not be in print today if it were not for the insight, encouragement, work, support, and love of the following people. I extend a heart full of gratitude and blessings for assistance in this act of obedience to our Father.

- Emmie Ensign and Kristen Martinez Pederson who asked me to be their mentor.

- Pastor Brad Sprague who shared my vision and passion for a women's mentoring ministry.

- Pastor Doug Slaybaugh who encouraged, supported, motivated, cheered me on, and repeatedly advised, "You need to put this ministry into a kit so other churches can share in the blessing." Thank you, Pastor Doug, for your persistence and faith in me.

- The entire Administrative Team and all the former, current, and future members. Your dedication, selfless giving, and servant attitude allowed the ministry to grow and flourish so that hundreds of women could experience the blessings of a mentoring relationship.

- Jane Crick, our ministry Publicity Shepherd Coach and editor of the ministry newsletter, *Beyond Coffee … Encouraging Words for M&Ms*. Jane designed the cover and ministry forms for the original kit. Thank you for your willing heart that always responded, "Sure!" to any request.

- All the many wonderful women who were willing to be vulnerable and open to allowing the Lord to work in their lives through a mentoring relationship. M&Ms, you are the ministry!

- The mentors and mentees who openly share their testimonies to encourage the women of our ministry, as well as you and the women of your church.

- My husband, Dave, who wore many helper hats during my writing process. To name a few: proofreader, editor, computer guru, chief cook and bottle washer, keeping the house running while I labored to meet deadlines. As a devoted Christian husband, Dave put my needs before his. I love you.

- My family who loved and encouraged me even when they did not understand what I was doing "up there in the office."

- Lena Campbell and Rhonda Andrews who gave me the gift of their time and talents to proofread and edit my original manuscript.

About the Author

JANET THOMPSON is the founder and director of AHW Ministries, also known as About His Work Ministries. In addition to her work as an author and speaker on topics relevant to today's Christian women, Janet has been "about His work" as a lay minister starting and leading the Woman to Woman Mentoring Ministry at Saddleback Church in Lake Forest, California. The Woman to Woman Mentoring Ministry was founded in January 1996 and continues to grow as hundreds of women experience the blessings of becoming Titus 2 women.

In order to share the Saddleback Church ministry with other churches, Janet wrote and self-published the kit, *Woman to Woman: How to Start, Grow, and Maintain a Mentoring Ministry*. As hundreds of churches used the original kit to start mentoring ministries, thousands of women around the world committed to walk beside each other in woman to woman mentoring relationships.

Janet has a Bachelor of Science degree in Food Administration from California Polytechnic University, a Masters degree in Business Administration from California Lutheran University, and a Master of Arts degree in Christian Leadership from Fuller Theological Seminary. She is also a CLASS (Christian Leaders, Authors and Speakers) graduate.

The Lord has blessed Janet with many life experiences. Janet and her husband, Dave, have four children and three grandchildren. They are now enjoying the season of life known as the empty nest or, as Janet calls it, "parent's time to rest." Dave is a manufacturer's representative in the golf industry and a helpmate/partner with Janet in AHW Ministries. They make their home in Lake Forest, California.

Introduction

10-20-16

The purpose of this material is to share the joy of a ministry that has truly blessed the lives of many Saddleback Church women. I dedicate this book to each of you following the call to start a Women's Mentoring Ministry in your church. You have sensed that women need to learn from each other, and you want to create a vehicle in your church for this to happen naturally.

I started the Woman to Woman Mentoring Ministry at Saddleback Church in January 1996. It was immediately apparent that the women of the church were looking for a way to establish closer relationships with each other. There was also a definite lack of role models in the lives of many new believers. Today, these women continue to respond to the invitation to learn from spiritually older women who can teach and guide them in the Christian way.

I have watched lives change. I have heard hundreds of testimonies of mentoring relationships enhancing not only the women's lives, but also the lives of their families. I longed for women in other churches to experience what we were seeing happen among the women of Saddleback.

On July 9, 1996, I was fasting and praying for the challenges and decisions facing my family. I keep my journal by me on fasting days because the Lord always speaks to me. On this particular day I wrote in my journal: "Answer from God: 'Put together a Mentoring Ministry handbook for publication. Focus on easy steps.' My mental response was, 'Lord, I really have my hands full growing and leading our ministry. I do not know how or when I would find the time to put it all down on paper.' " However, the Lord wanted the story told, and He found the time and the vehicle for me to get it into your hands. I hope that you enjoy reading the how-tos of starting, growing, and maintaining a Woman to Woman Mentoring Ministry in your church, and that you will soon put the steps into action. I also hope to inspire and encourage you by the ups and downs, highs and lows, setbacks and full-speed-aheads, I encountered in the journey I lovingly share with you. You and I are examples of God's incredible grace and sense of humor. He can work such magnificent feats out of the meager offerings of ourselves that we give Him. If we dedicate ourselves and our ministries to the Lord, He will receive the glory.

This resource is designed as an interactive tool for you to mark points to remember and make notes in the margins. Each time you see an ⟶ it is an indication for you to stop and write a response in the margin. I encourage you to respond to the activities as you come to them. If you do, you will find the material that follows will make more sense. So, before you start reading be sure to have your highlighters, pens, pencils, Post-it notes, and paper clips ready!

Even though I cannot be there with you physically as you start this exciting venture for the Lord, I would like to pray with you. I request the Lord's assistance before I start every project, speaking

8 *Woman to Woman Mentoring: Ministry Coordinator's Guide*

engagement, writing session, conference, meeting, orientation coffee, training. My intention is to pray before every event in my life, including getting out of bed in the morning. I would like to say I achieve that goal one hundred percent of the time. Being human, I often fall short, but I never give up on the goal. You and I both know the power of prayer. Bathe your ministry in continual prayer. Pray that the Lord will control the ministry and develop it at His will and that you will be in concert with His will. Let's pray together.

> Lord,
> You are so awesome in Your ways. You taught us how to teach each other. You sent Your Son, Jesus, to earth to be our role model—our mentor—and we will spend the rest of our lives trying to follow His example. You tell us in Your Word that You want us to transfer our knowledge to others. As Christians, part of the Great Command of loving one another as ourselves is helping them learn from our experiences and our hard-learned lessons.
>
> Lord, I pray today for the sister in Christ with whom you are letting me share the experiences and joys of starting a Mentoring Ministry for the women in her church. [Heather Teis]
>
> Lord, I thank You for her and her willingness to follow Your call. I thank You that she is seeking guidance in an area that might be new to her. I thank You that You trust both of us with this vital mission of directing women in our churches back to the basics of being examples and role models of godly women for the next generation of believers. You are uniting the two of us through this material, as we strive to bring the Christian values back into the hearts of women, families, and homes.
>
> Lord, please give my fellow servant clear vision and wisdom. Let this not seem like an overwhelming task to her but instead a call that is facilitating her to do what we as women do best—be encouragers to each other. Give her energy and bring those into her life who will assist her in this great feat that will definitely impact both her church and the lives of so many women in her church.
>
> Lord, please let her family and church family be supportive. We know this is a ministry You want—one that brings women back into the Titus 2 command that You gave us almost 2,000 years ago. Give her patience and love for all the women she will be encountering. Give her the desire to persevere when she wants to give up. Give her joy and happiness in fulfilling her assignment. Thank you, Lord, for this willing, servant's heart. Amen

Always keep in mind, "Not my will, Lord, but thine." He will do extraordinary work through ordinary people. We have the opportunity to see miracles happen in our lifetime and to be part of the transformation of lives. Have fun and live in peace as you go About His Work.

Blessings and love to you,

Janett Thompson

Other Helpful Resources

DVD

The DVD included in the *Woman to Woman Mentoring: Leader Kit* is designed to be informative, encouraging, and inspirational. It contains materials for the Mentoring Ministry leadership as well as segments to be used with mentors and mentees. More specific information about those segments can be found in the *Woman to Woman Mentoring: Training Leader's Guide*.

Following is a breakdown of the segments in the order they appear as well as the length for each:

Promotional Segment: Invitation to Orientation Coffee	2:30 min.
Segment 1: Overview	10:43 min.
Segment 2: Orientation Coffee	26:46 min.
Segment 3: Prayer Day	10:09 min.
Segment 4: Kickoff Night	10:06 min.
Segment 5: Mentor Halftime Refresher	8:58 min.
Janet's Message to Mentors	3:33 min.
Segment 6: Six-Month Potluck Celebration	13:21 min.
Celebration Message from Janet	3:55 min.
Segment 7: Three Generation Testimony	9:00 min.

CD-ROM

The CD-ROM included in the *Woman to Woman Mentoring: Leader Kit* contains messages of encouragement and training for the mentor from Janet Thompson. Ministry leaders have permission to duplicate these messages for the mentors in their ministry.

For information about other items on the CD-ROM, see page 219 in this Guide.

Women's Ministry

For more information about women's ministry products, services, and events offered through LifeWay Christian Resources, check our web site at *www.lifeway.com*. We would love to hear the testimonies that result from your Mentoring Ministry. You can email those through our Web site. If you are interested in receiving Janet Thompson's newsletter, please specify in an email also. To order additional copies of the *Woman to Woman Mentoring* resources or other women's ministry resources: WRITE LifeWay Church Resources Customer Service, One LifeWay Plaza, Nashville, TN 37234-0113; FAX order to (615) 251-5933; PHONE 1-800-458-2772; e-mail orderentry@lifeway.com; order ONLINE at *www.lifeway.com*; or visit the LifeWay Christian Store serving you.

CHAPTER 1

"Speak tenderly ... and proclaim to her that her hard service has been completed, that her sin has been paid for, that she has received from the Lord's hand double for all her sins. A voice of one calling: 'In the desert prepare the way for the Lord; make straight in the (wilderness) a highway for our God' " (Isaiah 40:2-3).

Why Me?

THE CALL

"Go and feed My sheep," was the call I heard from the Lord to start a Women's Mentoring Ministry at my home church in Lake Forest, California. Through a series of what can only be God's sovereign directions, He carefully and methodically directed me to the fulfillment of that initial call. I want to share that encounter with you, because if you are reading this book you too may have heard a call. However, you still may be unsure as to whether or not *you* are the one to fulfill it.

Let me be bold enough to say, "It is you." Once the Lord reveals an area of need where you can be of service, He will next give you the passion for it. That passion will be very personal. While you can get others interested and enthused, it is your personal passion that will carry you through the process from beginning to completion.

You may still be thinking: *Yes, but I know so little about how to do this. I am barely known at church, and I really have no idea how to begin. There are others who are so much more capable than I am. I will give this material to them. They would do a much better job at it than me.*

Don't do it! Do not give this material away until you have first put it into practice at your church. I turned the writing of this resource completely over to the Lord. I said, "Lord I will be the fingers on the keyboards, let it be Your words I type."

Without even knowing who you are, I can say to you: "You have picked this book up for a reason. You may not know why now, but God does. He will help you utilize and customize it to your own church circumstances, and He will provide you the tools and skills to implement it."

Here is a prayer that I prayed when I first started the Woman to Woman Mentoring Ministry at Saddleback Church. Let me pray it with you now.

Chapter 1: Why Me? **11**

> Lord,
>
> I do not know why You have chosen me to start a Women's Mentoring Ministry at my church. I feel so unworthy, and I really do not know how to begin or where I would even find the time. It seems like such a big job, but if this is truly what You want me to do, I will surrender my will, my talents, and my gifts to You. I turn this ministry over to You, and I will be Your vessel.
>
> Use me Lord, and help me to always remember that this is Your ministry not mine. Please give me the energy, the strength, the patience, the persistence, the desire, and the drive to do Your work. Please bring into my path those who would encourage and support me and women who would be willing to help me start such a ministry at my church. Please, Holy Spirit, speak to those women who are hungering for mentoring relationships and give them the courage to participate.
>
> Lord, please bless me with peace and courage to take the initial steps to fulfill this job that You have given me. In Your precious holy name I pray. Amen

Put the task of orchestrating this ministry on the Lord's capable shoulders, where it belongs and actually originated.

[Handwritten note: 10-20-16 I wonder if Heather prayed this!]

We need to put the task of orchestrating this ministry on the Lord's capable shoulders, where it belongs and actually originated. Perhaps my personal story will encourage you.

MY STORY

The Lord gave me the call to ministry in December 1993. Like the old Army poster, He said loud and clear, "I want you!" You may be asking yourself right now: *Why doesn't the Lord ever talk to me that clearly?* Or, *I've been praying and praying that the Lord would tell me what I should do, but I just don't seem to get an answer. Why did He tell her and not me?* I used to ask myself those same questions, until I realized that often He was talking to me in the ordinary circumstances of my day, or through other people. The challenge was to stop long enough to see and hear Him. As we become responsive to the subtle messages He gives us, He moves us on to the more obvious—the ones that light up in neon before our eyes.

However, like most of us, I did not hear immediately that "still, small voice." It took a year for the Lord to get my full attention. In January 1993, I felt a nudge from the Holy Spirit to study His Word more in-depth. I asked the Lord, "Where do You want me to go to learn more about You?" I thought I heard him say, "Seminary." "School?" I protested. Upon receiving my MBA in 1985, I distinctly remember saying, "I will never go to school again. This is the last time!" Just to humor God, I decided to research a couple of seminary programs in the area.

When all the brochures arrived I said: "No way. Too expensive. Too much work. I am a Food Administration and Business major, and I have no business in seminary with people who know what they are doing." I added to my argument, "Lord, I just got married this year. I have a new husband and stepchildren to get used to, plus a full-time job. It is impossible to fit this into our schedule and budget. What other ideas do you have?" Have you ever noticed that when God wants you, He does not give up?

The year passed by with no further action on my part to pursue seminary. In December 1993, as I was going through the Christmas mail, I came across a large envelope from Fuller Theological Seminary. *I did not request information from Fuller Seminary,* I thought quizzically. I opened the envelope and pulled out the cover letter addressed to me. The first line was thanking me for my interest in Fuller's Southern California, Orange County Extension program. I didn't even know they had an Orange County extension. The letter continued:

> At your request I am enclosing our application for immediate entrance to our program. Please complete all information on the form and mail to Sylvia at the Southern California Extension Office. The rest of the application materials for regular admission will be mailed to you at a later date. The enclosed form is to get you into class. If you help us with these aspects of the application process, we will be able to promptly complete your admission to Fuller and have you enrolled in classes for the upcoming [winter] quarter. We are looking forward to having you as part of our learning community. Thank you again for your interest. If you have any questions, please don't hesitate to call. Signed, In His service.

Included with the letter were the enrollment forms complete with highlighted areas where I was to sign. To this day no one at Fuller can explain how they obtained my name and address, or why I received the packet. God definitely had His hand in this one, and everyone I questioned about this miraculous occurrence confirmed that was their explanation, too. Divine intervention does get your attention. How could I ignore it? My husband said, "You don't! We will find a way to manage financially. You just need to sit down and figure out the activities you can cut back to make the time. I think it is pretty clear that God is calling you." I had the support of my husband and my family, but I still could not believe this was where God wanted me. My rational mind said, "I have a full-time sales career. What would I do with a degree from seminary?" The answer I got from God was, "Don't worry about it. When the time is right I will tell you. Will you step out in faith and trust Me, even if you don't know where I am leading you?"

I registered for classes late that winter quarter. I continued taking courses at night and on weekends, graduating in 1998 with a Master of Arts in Christian Leadership. I felt it was the only major relevant to my capabilities. I was sure God was not going to send me into full-time ministry or the mission field. How could He? My background was in business. Surely that was where He wanted me.

When God wants you,

He does not give up.

Chapter 1: Why Me? 13

"Go and feed My sheep."

One year into seminary, I began wondering what God's plans were for me. I saw an advertisement in *Today's Christian Woman* magazine for a Women in Ministry Leadership Conference being held in Portland, Oregon. I took note of it and put the magazine away. I did not want to go into Women's Ministry. The Lord knew I did not work well with women. I am not domestic, creative, or artistic. I worked in a man's world of business, and I was confident that was where the Lord would use me, if He chose to use me at all.

Several months later I again questioned the type of work available for women with a seminary degree. I wasn't trying to outguess God. I was just curious. I pulled out my *Today's Christian Woman* magazine and tore out the page advertising the conference. I found myself praying about it. I would have to take time from work, and it would conflict with a business meeting. It would be expensive to fly to Oregon and pay the hotel costs. I continued to pray and ask others to pray for me. That "still, small voice" answered and prompted me to go. I made plane and hotel reservations, sent in my conference registration, and got the time off work. However, I still went with the express purpose of researching opportunities available to women other than directing a Women's Ministry in a church. My plan was to network at the conference, and perhaps the Lord would help me understand why He had me in seminary. My intent was to convince God and myself that Women's Ministry was not my call.

Jill Briscoe was the keynote speaker for the conference, and I shared her sentiments when she confessed that she originally did not want to go into Women's Ministry. Like Jill, I had emphatically stated many times that I did not want to work exclusively with women. However, Jill went on to discuss how the Lord had led her screaming and kicking into full-time Women's Ministry, which she now dearly loves. Oh well, that was Jill and not me.

The Lord did speak to me at that conference in a very specific way, but not in the manner I had expected. On the third night, I was sitting at a table in a banquet room talking with some women, eating dinner, and enjoying the worship music. I sat back to relax and drink my coffee after dinner when I heard, *"Go and feed My Sheep."* I sat forward and looked around the table to see who was talking to me about sheep, but no one was speaking to me. In my mind I said, *"What sheep? Where? And what will I feed them when I find them?"* The voice came back to me again, more emphatic than ever before, *"Feed My Sheep."* I muttered under my breath an obedient, *"OK."* The rest of the evening I wondered what this meant, and what I had just agreed to do!

I called my husband later that night and told him I thought the Lord had spoken to me. Dave assured me that if it was the Lord, He would reveal the meaning to me in His time. That night we prayed that the Holy Spirit would give me the meaning of, *"Feed My Sheep."* The Lord was quick and gracious to respond to our prayers. The next morning I arrived at the opening session eager for another day of learning. As I settled into my seat, the speaker announced she would be basing her talk on the familiar Scripture in John 21:15-17 in which Jesus asks

Woman to Woman Mentoring: Ministry Coordinator's Guide

Peter three times if Peter loves Him. Three times Peter responded, "Yes, Lord, you know that I love you." Three times Jesus instructed Peter: "Feed my sheep."

I glanced at the agenda for the day. I let out a startled, "Wow!" The topic of the morning was "Shepherding Women." I received the message from the Holy Spirit immediately and realized the Lord was answering my prayer. I now understood that women were the sheep, and in some way I was going to be feeding them spiritually. I did not know how, where, or what I would feed them. However, like Peter, I loved the Lord, and past experience told me it would not be long before He would make it all clear to me.

I came home from the conference and told my family and small group about my experience. I asked them to pray for me to find my sheep and for direction as to what I should feed them when I found them. Within several weeks of the conference my flock began to take shape. The first bleating of sheep came as a message on my voicemail at work. It was from a woman in my company who had seen me wearing my cross necklace in a company training video. Emmie had recently rededicated her life to the Lord and wanted to get back into a sales position in our company. She was taking a sales course, and one of her assignments was to find a mentor. Emmie called me because I had a successful career in our company. Seeing me wearing a cross, she surmised I was a Christian. When she asked if I would be her mentor, I was both flattered and perplexed. I did not know what mentoring meant, nor how we would do it long distance. I said, "Let me do some research on mentoring. I am really not sure what that means. I will get back to you soon."

I immediately went to the Christian bookstore and bought a book on mentoring by Lucibel Van Atta, *Women Encouraging Women*, and read it in a week. I learned that *mentoring* means using the wisdom that comes from life's experiences to help others who are encountering similar experiences in their lives. Christian mentors share how God guides and supports, counsels and consoles, in both good and bad times. The book said Christian women mentors are role models of what a mother, wife, student, single, or divorced Christian woman looks like. Most people learn much better when they can see an example of what they are trying to learn. They need a visual pattern to follow.

I thought of the times in my life when I wished someone had been there for me. I thought of all the mistakes in decisions and lifestyle choices I might have avoided. I thought of what it would have been like to have someone in my life caring enough to keep me accountable and walking with the Lord, giving me counsel and advice from a Christian perspective and not that of the world. I am sure it would have prevented much heartache for God and me, as He watched me stumble along on my own.

Although I had not experienced the same problems as Emmie, I too had rededicated my life after a backsliding experience. I certainly could identify with what she was attempting to do in our company. I called Emmie and told her I now better understood mentoring and would consider it an honor to be her mentor.

10-20-16 Early in my Christian walk, God gave me a longing to want to help girls. I knew what it was like not to be loved + accepted, and even though I didn't realize it then, I wanted to give women what I didn't feel, growing up: to be loved + accepted. Now, 37 years later, the Lord is allowing me to do it. Of all places, in Las Vegas, NV.

Mentoring means using the wisdom that comes from life's experiences to help others who are encountering similar experiences in their lives. Christian mentors share how God guides and supports, counsels and consoles, in both good and bad times.

my thoughts!!

Chapter 1: Why Me? 15

I wrote Emmie's name on a page in my prayer journal titled "sheep" and thought perhaps feeding meant *mentoring*. God then created a series of events confirming that feeding did indeed mean mentoring. Some might call these coincidences. I believe it was God working through the process of getting me just where He wanted me ("God-incidences"—miracles happening in my life, like the ones that got me into seminary and to the Women in Ministry Leadership Conference).

When I wrote the first draft of *Woman to Woman Mentoring*, I had not included the process by which He worked the following God-incidences. In my quiet time, the Lord chastised me with this verse, "Seek the Lord and His strength; seek His face evermore! Remember His marvelous works which He has done, His wonders, and the judgments of His mouth" (Ps. 105:4-5, NKJV). I need to share with you all of "His marvelous works," because He is probably working them in your life right now, too. You do not want to miss the message He is sending you. So, let me tell you of the many God-incidences that continued to happen.

Several weeks after returning home from the Oregon conference, one of my daughters who led a young women's Bible study asked if I would lead the group for her the next week. I asked if she was sure the girls would want me. I suggested she call them to see how they felt about it. I assured her it would not hurt my feelings if they were not comfortable with me leading the group. As I heard her making the calls, I was praying, "Lord, let Your will be done here. I would be happy to help out, but if the girls do not want me to come, let me be humble and not take it personally." As I turned it over to God, I knew that whatever He wanted to happen would be OK with me. I could hear from my daughter's end of the conversations that the girls thought it was a great idea. My daughter came into my room smiling after she called everyone. The girls said, "Your mom is going to lead us? That's great! I'll be there for sure." Their unanimous, positive response surprised both of us. I still had my doubts if they would come, but that Monday night found us with 100 percent attendance. That was something that rarely happened, and the girls were eager to start the study.

When we finished the study, they asked me if I would continue to meet with them as part of the group. My daughter would still lead, and I could be the adult advisor. They liked that I knew who Chuck Colson was when his name came up in the study, and I could tell them about Watergate. They also appreciated that I was willing to share with them my life experiences, many of which were the same ones challenging them. This was such a shock to me. All the weeks they had been meeting at our house, I had made it a practice to stay out of their way, thinking they wanted their privacy to discuss personal issues. One quarter, I purposely took a class the night they met so I would be out of the house. Asking me to be part of their group was my first clue that the younger generation was reaching out for guidance from the older generation.

We hear so much about the generation gaps. When our kids hit the teen years we get the idea as parents that they do not want us around. Feeling a bit rejected and useless, I think we determine they will never need us or want us

Woman to Woman Mentoring: Ministry Coordinator's Guide

around again. That is not true. The girls, all in their late teens and early 20s, asked me to be part of their lives. From that night on, I began to meet each week as a member of the group. The Lord was positioning me for the next revelation. One Monday night, one of the girls brought her friend, Kristen, who was home from college for the summer. Kristen was the last to leave that night. As we chatted about her plans after she graduated from college the next year, she suddenly changed the subject and began talking about how badly she wanted a mentor in her life for the summer. Then she looked straight at me and said, "Do you know of anyone who would mentor me? Or, would you consider mentoring me?"

There was that word mentor again. Within two weeks, two women I did not know had asked me to mentor them. My reading had conveyed to me that a mentoring relationship was a fairly personal and vulnerable relationship. Neither of these women knew me personally, yet both of them, without hesitation, were boldly asking me to fill that role in their lives. Does that seem unusual to you? It did to me. This was not a coincidence. The Lord wanted to make sure I got His message loud and clear. In response to Kristen's request, my mind said, "OK, Lord, I get the picture. For now, feeding does mean mentoring."

I showed Kristen Women Encouraging Women and told her the story about the Lord speaking to me at the conference, and then Emmie wanting a mentor. I said I thought that I was beginning to understand what the term mentor meant, and that I would love to mentor her. We began our mentoring relationship the next week.

A short time later, a woman from my small group at church called and asked me to be a Barnabas in her life. She was starting to mentor a young woman, and she really felt she needed a Paul/Barnabas relationship for support. Several weeks later the wife of a gentleman in our small group said that she would enjoy having a mentor. She was struggling with how to raise children in a Christian home since her family members were not Christians. She needed some direction. I began to wonder if the Lord had a plan for me beyond being a mentor. It seemed there were a number of women needing a mentor. In fact, there were herds of sheep needing feeding, and one shepherd was not able to do it alone. I sensed that the Lord wanted me to use my personal mentoring experiences and leadership training from the business world to encourage and perhaps teach other women how to be mentors. Could He be telling me to start a Titus 2 ministry?

How would I go about starting a ministry like this? Whom would I talk to at church? What would it involve? How much time would it take? Who would help me? I am sure these are some of the same questions going through your mind. As I → as Heather if they were. look back over my prayer journal from that year, I asked these and many more questions of the Lord all summer. It seemed like a great idea, but I was not sure I was the one to do it. In fact, I was pretty sure I was not.

When "Not me, Lord!" thoughts started coming into my mind, the Lord intervened again and God-incidences started coming fast and obvious. First, the Lord placed our pastor to young adults at the gym at the same time I was there.

Chapter 1: Why Me? 17

It was a Friday morning in August, and I had just finished my workout. Like most women, when I am sweaty and grubby the last thing I want to do is see someone I know. As I saw Pastor Brad approaching, my first thought was, *I hope he does not recognize me, and I can avoid the embarrassment of being seen with no makeup and my unfashionable, after-workout hairdo*. It was working. He was walking right by, and it's no wonder since I am less than recognizable at these times. Just as he was almost past me, to my own astonishment I heard myself call out, "Pastor Brad! Hi!" He looked at me with a question mark outlined on his face, and I could see him trying to come up with some type of knowing response. He actually only knew me through the "Thompson kids" he pastored at church. So I helped him out and said, "It's Janet Thompson!" What was I doing? I was even giving him name recognition, and it worked. He now knew who I was. I let him off the hook by saying something about how glad I was that he did not recognize me. I hoped I normally looked a little better when he saw me at church.

As we began to talk, Pastor Brad mentioned that he felt many young women in the college, career, engaged, and singles groups were in need of mentors. Several young women had already asked him where they could find one. Pastor Brad said the Lord had been laying on his heart a need for a Mentoring Ministry for women at Saddleback Church. Being a male pastor, he knew it was not his place to start one. I told Pastor Brad that I too was feeling this calling. We agreed that I would contact him at the church, and we would share our visions.

Why was this a miracle, and why do I think it was intervention from God? Because that August day was the only time Pastor Brad and I ever saw each other at the gym. Pastor Brad later told me that he had not been in the gym for three months prior to our meeting, and had not been back since. Our meeting was not coincidence. The Lord knew that I had been letting the fact that I did not know who to talk to at church, or where to even begin the process, detour me from taking action. He put the person who was the closest to sharing my awareness of the need for this type of ministry directly in my path. He prompted me to initiate the conversation with Pastor Brad. That was not me speaking up, that was the Holy Spirit in me knowing that now was the hour of action.

Driving home from the gym that morning, I began to see a Women's Mentoring Ministry taking shape, and ideas came into my mind of how to start one. You would think that one God-incidence a day was sufficient, but He planned another one. That same day I had lunch with a friend from another church who shared, "I brought this book for you to read. I thought it might be of interest to you." She knew nothing of the morning's events. She pulled out a book entitled *Women Mentoring Women: Ways to Start, Maintain, and Expand a Biblical Women's Ministry* by Vickie Kraft. In that moment, I understood that I was not to feed all the sheep myself. I was to help nurture other women shepherdesses who would also go out and answer the Lord's call to, "Feed My Sheep."

In August 1995 I started the process of launching a new Women's Mentoring Ministry at Saddleback Church. Pastor Brad told me that the first step was to

18 *Woman to Woman Mentoring: Ministry Coordinator's Guide*

meet with the Pastor of New Ministries, Doug Slaybaugh. After I explained my vision, he handed me a "12-Step Planning Guide to Developing a Ministry at Saddleback." He then instructed me that I would have to complete all 12 steps before we could launch the ministry. I had originally thought that fall would be a great time to kick off the ministry, but after looking at the 12 steps, I was not sure what year that would be!

Undaunted, I quickly completed the 12 planning steps. We next agreed that I would do a test group and try out my ideas for the ministry on a small scale before opening it up to the entire church. Pastor Doug said I was going to have to network to find women to participate in this trial group. There was a word I recognized from the business world! I had built my sales career by networking, but this was a new field for me. I was not sure where to start. Pastor Brad suggested I begin with the college/career group and the Edge of Commitment engaged couples group. He happened to be the pastor for those two groups and gave me time on their next meeting's agenda.

It is a good thing Pastor Brad prompted me, because I might have procrastinated with this step. I started thinking things like, "What if he and I are both wrong and these young women are not interested in having older women in their lives. Maybe my daughter's group was the exception." Pastor Brad kept me accountable by setting the dates for me to present, and I went. The young women were very receptive. After I spoke, many of them came up and said that this type of ministry was an answer to their prayers. I received the names of 15 women interested in having a mentor.

Next, I went to the Women's Word Bible Study group, and 12 women said they would like to be mentors in a young woman's life. I felt the Lord was telling me I would have 10 mentoring relationships in this first experimental group, but I would have been happy with 1. I continued networking and talking about the ministry to every woman I met at church. I set a date of January 14, 1996, for the test Orientation Coffee. Then I prayed and waited on the Lord. Did I have any doubts that I was where the Lord wanted me? Absolutely not.

I prayed as I sent out 30 invitations to the Coffee, that the Lord would speak to the women He wanted to start this ministry. The Coffee was at my house, and as someone later said, "Women just kept coming through the front door!" Twenty women attended, and it was not a surprise to me that there were exactly 10 women wanting to be mentors and 10 women wanting to be mentored. January 1996, we started the new year with 10 mentoring relationships.

It seemed so unbelievable to me that the Lord was going to use me at my own church in a ministry for women! What a sovereign act of God to put Pastor Brad and me at the gym that August morning. Who knows how long I might have thought about starting this ministry? Since I did not know where to start, I might have just let that great idea from the Lord die without action. I think that is why the Lord had to make His presence so obvious to me in ways I could not ignore or call coincidence.

Chapter 1: Why Me? **19**

Is this what Heather has in mind?

With the Lord at the helm, you can do it! You can start a Woman to Woman Mentoring Ministry in your church that will change lives.

He did!!

The Lord continued to bless the ministry. On January 27, 1996, I gave a talk about the ministry at a quarterly Saturday morning fellowship time for women in our church. Twenty women responded that they would like to be in a mentoring relationship. It was not long before I had the names of 23 more women, and another Coffee planned for March 24, 1996.

I heard God continue to talk to me through other people and circumstances. One day it was a message on the answering machine. "Could you get a flyer ready for Sunday's SALT meeting (church core ministry meeting), and would you give a short talk on the new Woman to Woman Mentoring Ministry?" They were announcing the ministry at the meeting as a "New Ministry in the Making" at Saddleback. On the weekend of March 2, 1996, my ultimate vision became a reality—the Woman to Woman Mentoring Ministry was officially launched with an announcement in the church bulletin as *An Exciting New Ministry for Women!!*

I have only been the vessel that the Lord uses. With His help and the observance of His signs, I cleared my slate and He filled it. This is His ministry. I am just the willing conduit that He uses. I am so grateful that He is using me and that I have a husband who is supportive and encouraging.

The Lord is blessing the Woman to Woman Mentoring Ministry in spite of my lack of confidence and no previous experience at ministry. Our Woman to Woman Mentoring Ministry originated and is still led strictly on a lay basis. If you are already on staff at your church or you have been active in serving, moving through the procedures of your church may go faster. Saddleback is a large church, but the size of your church should not prohibit you in any way from incorporating this type of ministry into your women's program. I will give you steps in this kit on how to specifically work within a large- and small-church structure.

I hope by now, no matter what your role in your church, you are confident that with the Lord at the helm, you can start a Woman to Woman Mentoring Ministry in your church that will change lives. You may be thinking that you have not seen all the miracles in your call to ministry that I did. The Lord reveals Himself to each of us in His own unique way. He chose to motivate you in the way He felt would be the most effective. You may not need as much prodding as I did. You may be very eager to move on to the next step.

Let me talk about one more thing. What about the possible attacks from Satan? Let me say probable attacks. You and your family are going out on a limb for the Lord, and there is no question Satan is going to try to stop you. Rejoice if he does, because that probably means you are right on target with your ministry and the blessing of many lives.

You will receive blessings too—not by the world's standards all the time, but by God's. Cards, letters, and phone calls from women sharing how their mentoring relationships have changed and enhanced their lives will remove much of the sting of an arrow from Satan. Clothed daily in your godly armor, fight back with the one offensive piece—the sword of the Spirit. Fight with God's own words: "One generation shall praise Your works to another" (Ps. 145:4, NASB).

CHAPTER 2

"Whenever God gives one of us a vision of ministry, He also enables us to complete it successfully." Lucibel Van Atta [1]

Why You?

THE CALL IN YOUR CHURCH

I knew no one at our church who was interested in being a mentor or mentee, and I certainly had no idea who would help me organize the ministry. All I knew for sure was that the Lord had called me to *"Go and feed My Sheep,"* and I said, "OK!" Much to my surprise, God used that simple "OK" to mentor hundreds of "sheep" at my church and thousands of sheep at churches all over the world. How did the Lord take an inexperienced shepherd like myself and gather such a large international flock? Only through hours of prayer, listening to the Lord, and being obedient to His directions.

Perhaps you feel called to feed His sheep by starting a Mentoring Ministry at your church; or perhaps you recognize the need but are searching for a leader. You might be asking: "Who should start and lead our Mentoring Ministry?" It should be a woman who not only feels strongly about the need for mentoring in your church, but also has a *passion* to see that vision fulfilled.

If you sense the Lord is calling you, then you probably are the one. Warning—be watchful that you or someone else is not starting the ministry just because the church needs it or because someone asked you. A sense of duty or responsibility is not enough without passion and calling.

Be open to the possibility that this woman might be a very unlikely candidate. I certainly did not fit the ideal ministry leader profile. My interests were not in Women's Ministry. In fact, I had never even attended a women's retreat! I had been so busy with my business career that I had cultivated very few women friends. I always steered toward business groups—never anything exclusively for women. I was in a small group, but I had not participated in other church activities. Most people at church did not even know my name.

When searching for a Mentoring Ministry leader, pray first for God's guidance and provision. Second, begin networking. Talk about the church's desire to start a Mentoring Ministry for women. In advertising, describe it as an opportunity to start a new ministry at your church. Patiently wait and see who the Lord brings forward.

Chapter 2: Why You? **21**

The key to getting the ministry off on the right foot, and overcoming inevitable setbacks, is for the leader to know in her heart that this is where the Lord wants her. Starting and maintaining the ministry is going to be a time and energy investment. Hard work and disappointments may lead to giving up unless she knows the Lord is directing her. It is a labor of love for Him. Passion that endures is not something you can assign to someone.

Each story of a woman's call to this ministry will be different and may not be as direct as mine. However, the right woman will have a testimony of God leading and preparing her for the position. Be cautious of the woman who is positive that she is the one! Pray for discernment to distinguish between those who are self-directed and those who are God-directed.

I did not initially have a heart for women and their needs. However, as I was obedient to the Lord, He renewed my mind and changed my heart. Now they call me the "Mentoring Lady," and "the woman who has a heart for women!" I still look over my shoulder to see who they are talking about. Then I look up and give the Lord all the credit for my transformation.

The woman who leads the Mentoring Ministry may or may not be on staff. I am not on staff at our church. Staff members or lay leaders can use this material. If you are on staff, it should be easier and faster to access some of the church resources you will need. If you are not on staff we will discuss how to work within your church's policies and procedures.

When you have selected the woman to lead the ministry, whether it is you or someone else, the next step is to tell "Your Story."

Your Story

You have read "My Story." Now let's talk about yours. I am sure if you are reading this book you have a story. A story of why and how the Lord placed on your heart a need to start this type of ministry at your church. Your story is the reason behind your drive, desire, and passion. In the coming months, you want to be prepared to express that passion. Your enthusiasm will become contagious.

It is one thing to have a dream and a vision. It is yet another to share it with others. Until you can verbalize your motivation, others will have difficulty taking you seriously and helping you make it become a reality. Your story will help others catch the dream! Let me encourage you to take time to put "Your Story" on paper. This will serve three purposes:

Putting "Your Story" on paper will help you capture your hunches, ideas, dreams, and possibilities and put them into a concrete format for you and others to evaluate. By nature, women are feeling oriented, and many times we go with those feelings. We cannot always explain our feelings or how we are going to develop them. We just know something needs to happen. However, when we are asking others to support our ideas, they need to be able to understand our plan for implementing those feelings. There is a good chance you will need to interface with the men on your church staff, and any personality book is going to tell you that most men are fact oriented. Men usually cannot relate to a vision based on feelings or intuition. This is not to say that the male staff will not share your passion and vision. However, if they are going to get behind a new ministry, most pastors will want to know why you think it is necessary and how you plan to implement it. The more prepared you are to state your plans, even in your research stage, the more successful you will be at soliciting support.

2. **Putting "Your Story" on paper will help you define your own motivation.** It will be a journal of the steps you took in initiating the ministry and why you took those particular steps. Hopefully, hearing your own story will encourage you to begin immediately on the steps I am going to discuss for launching this ministry in your church. "Your Story" will also motivate you when times are tough and it really does seem like too much work. Reading your own story will rejuvenate your original enthusiasm when you find it waning in the difficult times.

3. **"Your Story" is your testimony, and the Lord will use it in some way—maybe numerous ways—to further His kingdom here on earth.** Just as the Lord is using "My Story" to write this book, speak to groups, and help others receive the blessings of a Mentoring Ministry in their church, He will also use yours. When people begin to ask you why you want to start this type of ministry, you will not hesitate to tell them from whence your strength comes. It is so important to always give God the glory for the initial idea and the ministry itself once it is in operation. Remember, this is not *your* ministry, it is His. "Ascribe to the Lord glory and strength, ascribe to the Lord the glory due his name" (1 Chron. 16:28,29).

Remember, this is not your ministry, it is His.

If you have difficulty writing, use a tape recorder. Find a way to get "Your Story" out of your mind and heart and into words. Here are some tips to help you get started.

- When did you first realize there was a need?
- In what form did that realization come?
- Have you heard other women mention the need for more women friends?
- Is there anything in your past that would have been easier to deal with if there had been a mature Christian woman in your life?
- Do you want to become more involved in service to your church but don't know where? Are you beginning to think more and more about the need that women have for each other?
- Are you burdened by the happenings in the lives of your women friends?
- Have you noticed that women just do not have time for each other?
- Do a number of your friends come to you with their problems or just to talk?
- Does the scriptural mandate that one generation should be there for the next convict you?
- Have you noticed how many single-parent homes there are and how many young women do not have wife and mothering skills?

Chapter 2: Why You?

- Is your church so large that it is difficult for women to meet?
- Is your church so small that cliques have formed?
- Have you always had the traditional women's groups and your enrollment is waning?
- Does your church have a number of young, new Christian women with many questions?

Have I jogged your memory enough? Can you now clearly remember what it was that triggered the feeling that there is a need for a Woman to Woman Mentoring Ministry in your church, and you are the woman to start it? Now have fun and give it expression.

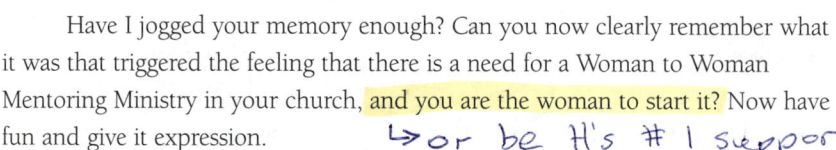
or be H's #1 supporter?

I am going to close this chapter right here, because if you are like me you may be thinking: *Janet is right. I should have my testimony ready, but I really want to know what she has to say about getting the ministry started. So I'll just keep on reading, and I will write my story later.*

Write the story of how God placed a Women's Mentoring Ministry on your heart.

You know how it is with later—it either never comes or it comes too late! Do not let that happen. I guarantee you that the Lord will use "Your Story" when you take the initial steps to introduce your idea to your church. Remember, it is the source of your passion and vision. The church is going to have to "buy into it" in order to know how to support you.

Yes, you have a story too. You did not just wake up one morning and decide to start this ministry. God has been working in your life. Think about it. Pray about it. Then begin to write the story of how God placed a Women's Mentoring Ministry on your heart. You will want to write out two stories. The first one will be the long story with all the details. This will be your testimony of how God has brought you to this point in your life. You also need a short version, similar to what we learn in evangelism training. We need to be able to give our testimony in three minutes. You will not always have the time or audience for your entire testimony. There may be times when you just share the part of it that applies to the situation.

Make some notes below and then close the book and start writing your stories. I will be waiting right here for you to finish. I guarantee you will come back to the reading of this book with new insight and enthusiasm once you hear your own story.

⎯⎯⎯⎯⎯⎯⎯⎯⎯⎯⎯⎯⎯⎯⎯⎯ Notes for "Your Story."

---

[1] Lucibel Van Atta, *Women Encouraging Women* (Sisters, OR: Multnomah Press, 1987), 34. — *@ beginning p. 21*

CHAPTER 3

"It is dangerous and sinful to rush into the unknown"
(Proverbs 19:2, TLB).

You Have Your Story—Now Where Do You Start?

TELL YOUR STORY

Have you had a chance to tell "Your Story" to anyone? Hopefully, once you wrote it or put it on tape, you could not wait to share it with someone. Better yet, perhaps someone has already asked you the source of your motivation. Talk about it to everyone you see. When there is a time constraint, give your three-minute version. Your enthusiasm will be contagious, and you never know who might be a source of help to you.

Let's take a look at some questions that might arise as you begin to share "Your Story" and new idea for a ministry. These questions could be show stoppers if you have not given some thought to the answers. They may even discourage you from talking about the ministry. No one likes being caught off guard. Let me share with you three questions I am sure you will encounter, and we will work through the answers together.

(1) What do you mean by mentoring? What is a mentor and what does she do? I am sure as you tell "Your Story" to people they ask, "What do you mean by mentoring?" Do you have an answer? In the beginning I heard this question continuously along with, "What is a mentor and what do they do?" Have you given thought to what mentoring encompasses, and what others might think it means?

Developing an understandable answer to this question actually helped me define the function of the future Woman to Woman Mentoring Ministry. I knew that my answer would be crucial to the success of the ministry. Why? Because it would help women determine whether or not a Mentoring Ministry was for them. It would also help me explain the concept of the ministry to those at church who would be approving its birth. You need to be ready to state the focus of your ministry and whom it will serve.

Can this ministry help and serve every woman in your church? Absolutely! But they are not going to know that unless they can identify with the purpose and

Chapter 3: You Have Your Story—Now Where Do You Start? **25**

function of the ministry. Let me give you an example of what I mean. Unless you have a church with a number of women who see themselves as the older, wiser, spiritually-mature woman, you may have difficulty finding women who feel knowledgeable enough to be the mentors. We have many mature women in Christ whose testimonies of their life's experiences and how the Lord carried them through would make them perfect mentors. However, this is what I heard from some of them, "I am not knowledgeable enough in the Bible to lead someone else." Or, "I don't know enough theology. I am still learning myself." This last statement came from a 72-year-old woman who had been a Christian most of her life. These women were being humble, but perhaps they were also expressing fear and insecurity. They were afraid that they might not always have the right scriptural answers. I discovered that many of the women thought they had to be Bible scholars before they could mentor someone else. They also felt they had to have lived perfect lives in order to be role models.

A Mentoring Ministry cannot function without mentors. It was apparent that I needed a definition for *mentor* that was not intimidating and that would not scare off women whom I knew would be perfect Christian role models. You will need to develop this definition also.

The definition of *mentoring* needs to be clear in advertising the ministry. I saw this as especially crucial at Saddleback, because we have many new believers. I anticipated that we would have flocks of sheep, but I was not so sure there would be enough shepherdesses. The other extreme of this problem can be the brand new Christian who wants to share what the Lord has done in her life. In her eagerness to share with someone else, she wants to be a mentor. You do not want to squelch her enthusiasm, and yet her newness in Christ would probably not offer the wisdom or maturity in Christ that would be of value in a mentor.

Let me help you develop some definitions that will prepare you to give an immediate and concise answer to the inevitable question, *what is mentoring and what does a mentor do?* Webster's Dictionary defines *mentor* as *a wise and trusted counselor.* Notice it says nothing about being an expert, old, or perfect. The Lord helped me see that all I needed to do was add one word to the dictionary definition: *a wise and trusted* Christian *counselor.* Adding the word *Christian* gave a depth of meaning to how we would define *mentor* and *mentoring* in our ministry. Now look at the Christian implication of Webster's three key words.

Wisdom would come from God within the Christian mentor, speaking through her. Her thoughts would be God inspired when she turned her life over to Him and allowed Him to teach her through her experiences in life. She would see that with Christ's help we learn from our mistakes as well as from the good decisions we make.

Trusted implies someone in whom we can have confidence to share our inner-most feelings and know they will not gossip or slander about us. We also trust the counsel they give us because we know their wisdom is God inspired.

Mentor:

a wise and

trusted Christian

counselor.

Counselor is a confidant. In mentoring, it is someone who can help you learn to always go to the one and only Counselor, the Lord.

You must be ready to convey this definition of mentoring to the women of your church. You need to assure them that we are continually in the process of learning and growing in Christ. We will never know it all. There will always be one more thing we can learn until the day we die. However, in order to help new believers grow, we have to be willing to share what we do know and what the Lord has done in our lives.

I was asked many times, "Are you sure you want this to be a Mentoring Ministry? Wouldn't it be better to call it a friendship or discipleship ministry?" I knew the answer without hesitating. God had clearly spoken to me. He wanted first and foremost a Mentoring Ministry that would incorporate friendship as well as discipling, but not narrowed down to just one of those functions. I think 1 Thessalonians 2:7-8,12 beautifully depicts this type of mentoring.

> We were gentle among you like a mother caring for her little children. We loved you so much that we were delighted to share with you not only the gospel of God but our lives as well, because you had become so dear to us. … encouraging, comforting and urging you to live lives worthy of God, who calls you into his kingdom and glory (1 Thess. 2:7-8,12).

The scriptural foundation commonly used for mentoring is Titus 2:3-5. Teach the older women to be reverent in the way they live, not to be slanderers or addicted to much wine, but to teach what is good. Then they can train the younger women to love their husbands and children, to be self-controlled and pure, to be busy at home, to be kind, and to be subject to their husbands, so that no one will malign the word of God (Titus 2:3-5).

This means one generation of believers, not necessarily chronological age of the generations. Many times it does turn out that the mentor is older chronologically than the person being mentored. We seem to have a natural respect for the experience and wisdom of our elders. It might seem awkward to both if a younger woman, though older in the Lord, was mentoring a much older woman. However, the age difference might only be a couple of years. Our motto in the Woman to Woman Mentoring Ministry is: "There is always someone older than someone else." That way no one feels put into the over-the-hill, older woman category.

(2) What is a mentee? Mentees are the women receiving mentoring. Who are those most likely to be the mentees? Again, because we are talking about a Christian audience, our answer is going to differ from the secular or business world. Regardless of chronological age, any woman who is a new believer is going to need a godly role model. She needs someone who will help her understand how to live as a Christian woman—mother, wife, daughter, sister, single parent, divorced, dating, remarried, widow, grandmother, career woman, neighbor.

"Teach the older women to be reverent in the way they live, not to be slanderers or addicted to much wine, but to teach what is good. Then they can train the younger women to love their husbands and children, to be self-controlled and pure, to be busy at home, to be kind, and to be subject to their husbands, so that no one will malign the word of God" (Titus 2:3-5).

Chapter 3: You Have Your Story—Now Where Do You Start?

Essentially, a mentee would benefit from mentoring at any stage of her life. If she did not experience a Christian home environment, she may never have seen these roles modeled. There may be no one in her family she can go to for Christian advice. Her decision for Christ may have actually alienated her from the family. Perhaps, like myself, she accepted Christ at an early age, later backslid, and has now rededicated her life to Christ. She may be having trouble finding God in the tragedies of her life and just need help getting back to Him.

(3) How do I know if I should be a mentor or mentee? Some women may feel they fall into both a mentor and mentee category. Here is how I defined the two roles in a flyer announcing the new Mentoring Ministry.

The Woman to Woman Mentoring Ministry asks God to help match women into one-on-one encouraging, supportive, friendship relationships.

Mentors: If you feel God's nudge to share in another woman's life by using what God has done in your life to encourage and assist her in the glorious walk of a Christian woman, God is calling you into mentoring.

Mentees: If you want to talk with another Christian woman who has been in your shoes and with God's help made it through and would like to support and encourage you in your Christian life, God is nudging you to seek out a Christian role model.

I also explain that mentoring relationships are two-way. Each woman may occasionally change roles, and the mentee may be mentoring the mentor through a tough day. Every woman will always want a mentor, but as Christians we need to give as well as receive. Maybe this time around the woman will be a mentor, and then the next time she can have a mentor.

I often say something similar to what Anne Ortlund wrote in *Disciplines of the Beautiful Woman,* as she talked about Jesus' command in Matthew 28:18-20, "All authority has been given Me ... Go therefore and make disciples of all the nations, ... teaching them to observe all that I commanded you; and lo, I am with you always" (NKJV). In reference to these verses Anne said:

"Discipling [mentoring] is what we're for, in this world! We're not for adoration and worship of God only, although that's number one. If that were all we're for, God could take us straight to heaven, where our worship would be undistracted. ... No, the reason he leaves us here a while is so that we can make a mark on others before we go.

And he commands us to be diligent and deliberate about making our lasting marks on others. That's our script in his play."[1]

How do you put all of this together to answer: *What do you mean by mentoring?* Your answer might be something like this: "The Woman to Woman Mentoring Ministry asks God to help match women into one-on-one encouraging, supportive, friendship relationships. The mentor is a Christian woman who shares and role models the Christian life with a sister in Christ who is spiritually younger."

If you are questioned further you might add: "Mentoring is often called spiritual mothering. Sometimes it might be discipling, other times it might be two Christian friends encouraging and supporting each other in living the life of a Christian woman. Mentoring is role modeling. It is using those "been there, done that" experiences in our lives to help other women through similar circumstances in their lives. It is sharing how the Lord helped us through it and offering encouragement and assurance that He is there for her too. Mentoring is coming alongside another woman and teaching her to go to the Lord and His Word for *all* the answers."

Most people seem to understand what I mean when I give this explanation, and I can see the relief in their eyes. Some of them will respond: "I can do that. I can be a Christian friend to another woman. I've certainly had a lot of experiences in my life, and God has been right there for me." The term *mentoring* is familiar in the business world and many of those same concepts are transferable to our Christian environment. In the business world, mentors usually have been in a business for quite awhile and are successful. They are knowledgeable about the specific business and probably are in a position that the mentees would like to be in someday. Mentors provide experience, knowledge, achievements, position, and, most importantly, a willingness to share all this with someone else. They encourage mentees to aspire to the mentor role themselves. We hope and pray that all the Christian mentees will someday become Christian mentors.

Mentoring relationships are two-way.

Do you understand now why it is so important to prepare your own definition of mentoring, mentors, and mentees? After you say it a few times, it will come naturally to you. You do not want it to be too wordy, but you do want to transmit an understanding of the concept. You need to be ready to give your answer at the time you receive the question. That is when the interest is highest, and the person asking will be the most receptive. The definitions you give need to be in your own words. What do you feel comfortable saying?

Take a moment to formulate your own personal response to the questions.

What do you mean by *mentoring*? ⟶

What is a *mentor*? ⟶

What is a *mentee*? ⟶

DO THE RESEARCH

Proverbs 13:10 tells us that a wise woman seeks advice and information from those who know more than she does. Obviously, you are a very wise woman because you are doing research, reading this book, and using the *Woman to Woman Mentoring* materials. This is a how-to book, so I assume you are searching for information on how others have established a Mentoring Ministry in their church. Good for you. That tells me you are earnestly trying to ensure that the ministry started in your church is successful.

==My prayer is that this material will speed up the process for you.== It does take time to do research, and that is time you could be spending operating the ministry rather than starting it. The research phase is an opportunity for the devil to have other things come into your life that begin to take up your time and cool down those passionate fires that put you into action. Hopefully, I can save you some of that time, and you can benefit from what I have learned.

Step 1: Research outside your church.

Why? Because when you start talking about this ministry in your own church, you want to move on it quickly. Before I generated enthusiasm, I needed to discover how feasible it would be for me to start this ministry. I wanted the ability to act on the enthusiasm immediately, and not put it on hold while I figured out how to do the ministry.

Call other churches in your area to see if they have a Women's Mentoring Ministry. If so, ask them to share with you about it. It is good to see what others are doing. Ask about what they have tried that worked as well as what did not work. Every geographic area has nuances and characteristics of their part of the country, and you might find some things that influence how you structure your Mentoring Ministry.

Much to my surprise, I discovered that very few churches in Orange County had this type of ministry. They all thought it was a great idea but had not started one yet. However, two churches I talked to did have mentoring ministries. One had a formal Mentoring Ministry, and the other was changing to more of a friendship ministry.

Step 2: Read books on mentoring.

I have compiled a ==Recommended Book List (Form D, p. 226)==. There is an asterisk by the books that I read in my research phase. Read as many books as time allows. They all contain a wealth of information about mentoring and present various authors' views and ideas. I think it is good to read a new book every couple of months even after the Mentoring Ministry is up and running. This keeps your ideas fresh and continues to renew your vision of mentoring.

Step 3: Work to better understand your church.

After you have compiled information from other churches and your own reading, it is time to take a look at the dynamics of your own church. Each church is different, and so are the needs of the congregation. A new ministry must fit into the overall mission and vision of the church.

For example, Saddleback Church is a large, seeker-sensitive church committed to the Great Commandment and the Great Commission. When I started

30 *Woman to Woman Mentoring: Ministry Coordinator's Guide*

the Woman to Woman Mentoring Ministry, our average attendance at church on a weekend was 13-14,000 people. We have an influx of new people and new Christians every week. If I structured our ministry with a yearly orientation meeting and matching, it would leave out the many women who start attending the church throughout the year. I knew an annual format would not work for us. Women who would benefit most from mentoring—the weekly new women attendees and new believers—would not be able to participate in a mentoring relationship when they most needed it. We would be missing the purpose of the ministry. We had to have a ministry that moved with the pace and purpose of our church. Therefore, I took what I could apply from my research and moved forward to see how we could adapt it to Saddleback. You will need to do the same. To assist you in this process, I have compiled a list of questions for you to answer. Ask yourself how these issues would effect a Mentoring Ministry at your church.

1. *How will the size of your church impact the ministry?* Women need women. Whether you are matching 10 or 100 women into mentoring relationships, lives are going to change and growth will take place. Unless your church is under 100 and maintains the same consistent congregation, I would offer more than one opportunity a year to join the ministry. However, you may only need to have two or three Orientation Coffees a year rather than the five we had the first few years. We now offer them quarterly. Small, frequent Coffees are better for matching because each woman gets ample time to introduce herself, and the women have an opportunity to interact and meet each other.

2. *Are all age groups evenly represented at your church?* It is good for you to know the age mix at your church and prepare for whatever adjustments you may need to make. Traditionally, mentors are older women. Do you have an even representation of all age groups at your church, or are there predominantly older or younger women? If you are at a traditional church, chances are you will have a larger number of older women than you would have at a church that caters to the younger generation. It is possible to have a Mentoring Ministry at either one of those extremes. We do not have a predominance of elderly women attending our church, although that is changing as the older "boomers" move into the 50-plus age range. The adjustment in thinking I had to make was that, for a while, we might have younger women mentoring even younger women. We probably would not have an abundance of the older women from which to draw for mentors. There might not be the traditional age span between mentors and mentees.

Today, more than ever, younger women are having many life experiences at an early age. If they have found the Lord during this time and learned to seek His council, they could be a wise mentor to a woman in her late teens or early 20s who is perhaps trying to find the right mate, right career, stay celibate while dating, etc. Therefore, if your church is like ours, you might start out with mentors who are young in age but old in the Lord. Perhaps someone in her 40s might be mentoring someone in her 30s. You need to be flexible in this area.

Chapter 3: You Have Your Story—Now Where Do You Start? **31**

Likewise, in a traditional church there will be more older generation women. Do not let age be a stumbling block. Remember our motto, "There is always going to be someone older than someone else" both in chronological and spiritual age. You will also find that age is not that important in the younger and older age groups. A 20 year old, though young, is still older and has experienced much more than a 16 or 17 year old. Similarly, after we get into the late 40s, age seems irrelevant in relationships. A 50-year-old, new Christian is probably not going to mind if her mentor is 45. You may need to share some of these thoughts if you face objections to not having the traditional older/younger ratio at your church.

There is always going to be someone older than someone else both in chronological and spiritual age.

3. **What is the range of spiritual maturity at your church?** When I started the ministry I was 48 years old, but like many women my age, in my mind I was still in my 30s. I was apprehensive as to whether or not I would find enough women who would be willing to say, "I am the older woman. I will be the mentor." I also knew that as an evangelistic church, we had a large number of new believers needing mentoring at all ages. An older woman might be a brand new Christian and need a mentor instead of being the mentor! It was apparent to me from the beginning that we would not interpret the "older women" teaching the "younger women" in Titus 2:3-5 with parameters of chronological age. Instead, we would have to carefully incorporate spiritual age.

I had no idea what age ranges or levels of spiritual maturity we would find in the women who would respond to the Mentoring Ministry. I did not see that as a potential concern. Announcing "Women of All Ages Welcome" on the publicity opened the door to everyone. We then let the Lord take care of whether or not we had an equal balance of age and spiritual maturity.

Take a look around your church. What do you see? Are there a number of spiritually-mature women in your church? Approach them with your idea for the Mentoring Ministry and begin encouraging them that it does not take a Bible scholar to mentor someone. It is good to be aware of the dynamics of age and spiritual maturity at your church, but do not let that be a stumbling block that Satan can use to discourage you. The Lord will help you work it out. Just turn it over to Him and pray continuously for His intervention. That brings us to a question that others might ask, and you might actually be asking yourself.

4. **What if we do not have enough mentors respond? or, What if it is only new believers in need of a mentor who join the ministry?** There is absolutely nothing you can do to avoid either situation, so why try to control it or worry about it? When people ask me that question, I respond: "It's the Lord's ministry. I am sure He will work that out. I know He wants this ministry in our church. I can do nothing but pray about it and leave the rest to Him." Every time you say this, you will feel the burden of that worry lift off your shoulders. He really has worked it out for us. It still amazes me that at every Orientation Coffee we have enough women who are willing to be either a mentor or a mentee, or both, and we can always make equal matches. You may have a woman who is both a mentor to a younger woman and a

32 *Woman to Woman Mentoring: Ministry Coordinator's Guide*

mentee with an older mentor to guide her through the challenges she is facing with middle age. Perhaps you can encourage a mentor to mentor more than one woman.

Let me assure you that God has not only worked out the details at our church, but also at numerous churches who have started Woman to Woman Mentoring Ministries with some fear and trepidation. But read what Becky Burns at Henderson Hills Baptist Church in Edmond, Oklahoma wrote to me after they experienced their first Orientation Coffee.

> Hi, Janet. Just wanted to thank you for your prayers last Sunday and preceding that day. We had an incredible day and an especially incredible prayer day. We saw God move where we knew it had to be Him because there was no way it would work out. We were able to match every woman … we made 33 matches. Numbers aren't what count but we are thrilled to have that many women committed to growing in the Lord together.

Do not lack faith in this area. You have to operate completely in faith, because there is absolutely nothing you can do to control it. As you start to advertise the new ministry, pray for those women the Lord wants to be a part of the ministry. Ask everyone you know to pray for the ministry and for you. Then marvel at the miraculous work the Lord will do.

5. **Is this a recognized need by the women at your church, or will you need to do some education first on the value of mentoring?** It is easy to research this. First, talk to every woman you come in contact with at church. If you hear as I did, "We need something like this so badly at our church. It is so great that the Lord has put it on your heart," you know you will be filling an established need. Write down the names and phone numbers of all the women who express interest. Assure them that you will let them know if you get this ministry started.

I mentioned to you in "My Story" that I also did some networking at the suggestion of Pastor Brad. I first went to the groups he pastored which were the college, young adults, and engaged couples groups. In a very short, five-minute message, I shared with them the idea of a Mentoring Ministry and asked how many women present would participate if I got one started. I asked them to give me their names and phone numbers and any suggestions they had. From these groups, I received the names of 15 women who would like a mentor. Next, I went to the women that lead the Women's Word Bible Study and asked them if I could do the same thing at one of their meetings. These were women doing an advanced study of the Bible and would be a good potential source of mentors. From this group, 12 women said they would like to be mentors if the ministry became a reality. I wrote down their names and phone numbers and concluded that there was an interest in this ministry at Saddleback Church.

Where are the younger and older women in your church? Sunday School classes? Young adults groups? Young married groups? Senior adult groups?

Women's Bible study groups? Missionary support groups? Do not rule out mixed groups of men and women. Ask for a few moments to address the women of the group. When you do this survey be sure to say, "*If* I start this ministry ..." This is only a market test, and you do not want anyone disappointed if it does not come to fruition. Nor do you want to leave them expecting it to start the next week.

Present the idea to groups where there are new Christians, which is where you are more likely to find those wanting to be mentored. Go to the groups that are focusing on spiritual maturity because that is most likely where you will find future mentors. If you have the opportunity to be the featured speaker at a women's gathering in your church, do it. You can talk about the concept and value of women mentoring and encouraging each other. However, do not let waiting for a speaking opportunity delay you in starting the ministry.

Starting small is a good idea. I started without publicity and only networked. That allowed me to work out a lot of the details on a small scale before I took it to the entire church. Let me assure you that if the Lord has put mentoring on your heart, there is a need in your church—if there are women in your church, there is a need for a Mentoring Ministry! Today more than ever before, women need each other.

If there are women in your church, there is a need for a mentoring ministry!

Has anyone before you tried to start this type of ministry at your church? If so, what were the results? Ask questions of the church staff to see if they know of a previous Mentoring Ministry or attempt at one. If there was such a ministry before you, find out as much as you can about how it operated and why it did not continue. This is very valuable information. You will know what did and did not work at your church in the past, and it could prevent you from repeating the same mistakes. As I began networking the ministry, I heard on more than one occasion, "They tried to get a Mentoring Ministry started here about five years ago, but it never got off the ground." No one I asked could remember who tried to start it or why it did not work, so I was not able to learn from anyone else's experiences. However, the church staff was quite cautious about trying a Mentoring Ministry again, although they readily agreed there was a need for one at our church.

Talking to people about the concept of the ministry was very helpful. One day I saw a lady from the church working out at the gym we both attend. As usual, when she asked me what was new, I began to share with her my desire to start the Mentoring Ministry. (You tell "Your Story" every chance you get.) She mentioned the failed attempt five years ago, and then she said, "I have the names of all those women who were interested at that time. Give me a call at home and I will give you their names and phone numbers." Here is where follow-through on your part is very important. I did call her. She gave me the names and phone numbers of 35 women. She herself was a mentor at our first Orientation Coffee. I now had names of women to contact who might still have an interest. The mention of the failed ministry attempt never daunted me. It obviously had not been the right time. That certainly did not mean that there was not a need and a desire today.

I did learn from knowing about the previous attempt. I did not take personally any hesitancy or cautious attitude I received at the church. I knew there was not a lack of confidence in a mentoring program or in me. For whatever reason, the church had a bad experience in the past, and it was understandable that they would want to proceed very carefully and slowly. It was good for me to know this. The Lord reminded me that I could fail, too, if I did not do a thorough job of planning and preparing. It kept me patient, which is something I normally am not. I want results right away and do not always like to take the methodical steps to ensure something is successful and lasting. As I took my time to do research, formulate a plan, and determine the need, I thought of the sound advice in Proverbs: "Plans fail for lack of council" (Prov. 15:22).

If no one before you has ever tried to start a Mentoring Ministry in your church, congratulations. You are the pioneer, and you get to be the trailblazer. However, if there was a bad experience in the past, do not let it discourage you. I certainly was not going to let the earlier failure quiet the call I heard from the Lord. Do, however, be cautious and try to avoid the pitfalls that others may have encountered.

"Plans fail for lack of council" (Prov. 15:22).

If you are not on the church staff, who will you be working with on the church staff? Who will be your contact person that helps you get the ministry approved and operating? To whom will you tell "Your Story"? You may already know the answer to these questions at your church, or you know the person to ask. However, if you are like I was, this can be a big stumbling block in your mind. As I wrote in "My Story," not being involved in service to our church at that time, I saw this step as a bit intimidating. How would I, an unknown church member, walk into the church office and announce that I felt God was leading me to start a ministry with the potential of involving thousands of women? Where would I go? How would I begin? As I described in "My Story," this step was a hurdle for me. I had the vision, but I really had done nothing about it. Would I have pursued my vision if the Lord had not put Pastor Brad and myself at the gym at the same time that hot August morning? I cannot answer that. I would like to hope so. The important point here is that if you are not in a decision-making position or already on staff in your church, you need to form a liaison with someone on staff soon. It might be someone on the church staff who works with women's groups or young adults, college, and young career groups. I guarantee that staff members ministering to young women have sensed the need in these women's lives for Christian role models. They will readily understand the purpose and need for a Women's Mentoring Ministry. Seek out a staff person and make an appointment to meet with him or her. If your church has a Women's Ministry, that is the logical place for a Women's Mentoring Ministry. Make an appointment with the woman directing the Women's Ministry at your church. At all of these meetings, share "Your Story."

This essential step could happen readily for you as it did for me, or it might take longer. Your ministry may not receive the necessary support and recognition

Chapter 3: You Have Your Story—Now Where Do You Start? **35**

if there is not someone helping, encouraging, and supporting you from within the church. If you do not immediately know who that might be, start networking and asking questions. Make appointments to meet with the people you think are the most likely to understand your vision and "Your Story." If they are not the right people, they should be able to point you to someone who is. When you find the right support person, you should be on your way to interfacing with the church. It is now time to put your vision into action. You also want to pray that the Lord will help you communicate clearly and be open to suggestions and advice that you might be about to receive.

When you find the right staff person, what do you say? You want to set an appointment for the two of you to get together. At this meeting you will tell "Your Story" with great enthusiasm and passion. It is good to also have "Your Story" in writing to leave with him or her. Be prepared to share your ideas and plans for the new Women's Mentoring Ministry. You might want to have this resource with you to help explain where you received your ideas and show some of the forms you will be using. The more this staff member can see that you have thought through the steps of starting the ministry and are sincere in your desire to see it to completion, the more receptive he or she will be. You might find the person you are meeting with will have already noticed that your church is in need of this type of ministry. It is still useful to share any comments people have made to you about their interest in participating in the Mentoring Ministry.

You might also find there is a definite format for starting a new ministry at your church. At my first meeting with the pastor to new ministries, I naively went in armed with a flier for the weekend church bulletin announcing the new Women's Mentoring Ministry. Everything I had read said that fall and spring were good times to kick off women's programs. It was late August, so September or October sounded great to me. I had visions of the Women's Mentoring Ministry being announced from the pulpit and hundreds, maybe even thousands, of women flocking to join. I received appreciation for my enthusiasm and passion for starting the ministry, but I had more homework to do before we announced this ministry to the church. I would need to proceed very methodically before I could officially announce the ministry to the congregation. Then Pastor Doug handed me Saddleback's "12 Steps to Start a New Ministry" and explained that I would have to work through each of the steps and report on each one. As I left that meeting, I wondered whether I would be ready by fall of the next year!

I did not want this procedure to set me back. I smiled, took the forms, and assured him that I would work through them as quickly as I could. We agreed to periodic meetings to see how I was progressing. While I saw my time frame becoming very delayed, I remembered that all things happen in God's time. The Lord was probably telling me I had more work to do.

In the next chapter, I will share the 12 steps. Once you read them and work through them yourself, I think you will see why they are so valuable to complete.

NAME THE MINISTRY

You are welcome to use Woman to Woman Mentoring Ministry as the name of your ministry. Arriving at a name was a very important and fun part of the process. The name needs to catch women's attention and transmit to them the focus of the ministry. Determining a name for the ministry is necessary before you can start publicizing it. I had not given a lot of thought to this step. Other churches had used Heart to Heart, which was also the name of a quarterly women's fellowship meeting at Saddleback. That name would not work for us. Other names I found were Encouraging Hearts and Titus 2. Encouraging Hearts was a great name, but I thought it would be too close to Heart to Heart. Titus 2 was not appropriate for us because we have a number of seekers, unchurched, and new Christians attending, and they might not know what Titus 2 meant. They would not understand that this was a ministry for them.

One day in the beginning of my ministry journey, I was discussing with Pastor Brad my lack of a name for the ministry. I ran through the above names with him and all the reasons they were not right for our ministry. I expressed my desire that the name clearly transmit the meaning of the ministry when placed in the church bulletin for the congregation to read. There is not usually much room allotted in the bulletin for a description of each ministry. Women reading the title in the bulletin would not have someone there with an in-depth explanation. My goal was for women sitting in church to know exactly what the ministry represented when they read the announcement in the bulletin. Pastor Brad listened to me explain my dilemma. When I had finally run out of breath, he said that he had an idea and had actually written down a name. That surprised me. I guess it had never occurred to me that a man could possibly come up with a name for a Women's Ministry. However, when I heard Pastor Brad say, "Women to Women," I knew we were getting close. I liked it. In fact, I was wondering why I had not thought of it myself. However, as I said it over in my mind, something was still not quite right. Then I realized it was the word *women* that bothered me. *Women* means more than one and could convey the idea of a ministry for a group of women. Using the singular, Woman to Woman, gets across the concept of the one-on-one relationships that would be developing. I explained my thought process to Pastor Brad, and he agreed. We prayed about it and both had peace with the name Woman to Woman Mentoring Ministry. I added *Mentoring Ministry* to the name for reasons of clarification. Again, I wanted women to know clearly from the name what they would be doing in this ministry. Woman to Woman Mentoring Ministry became the official name for the ministry, and you can certainly use it at your church, too.

I would suggest that if you choose to give your ministry a different name, you go through the same procedure:

1. Determine what message you want to convey in the name.
2. Make it self-explanatory. When people see or hear the name they should be able to know clearly what happens in your ministry.

Chapter 3: You Have Your Story—Now Where Do You Start?

3. Include others in the name-finding process and solicit their ideas.
4. Research names other churches in your area have used.
5. Pray, pray, pray about it.

When you have the name the Lord wants you to use, you will have complete peace. I never looked back or ever considered changing the name. No one questioned the name once we began to use it; however, several times it appeared in the bulletin as Women to Women. When I called to ask them to change it, I took the time to explain why I used the word *woman* instead of *women*. This helped them understand the significance and importance of using the correct name. I felt we had the Lord's blessing with Woman to Woman Mentoring Ministry, and you want to feel that with the name you select, too. "The Lord's blessing is our greatest wealth. All our work adds nothing to it!" (Prov. 10:22, TLB).

STAY FOCUSED ON WHOSE MINISTRY IT IS

It is so easy to refer to this as *my* ministry. Especially when people come up to you and say things like, "How is your ministry going?" Or, "I hear great things about your ministry. You must really be proud." Red flags should immediately start going up when you hear these kinds of things and if you hear yourself taking credit for the success or praises you are receiving. Yes, you and I have put a lot of work into our ministries, but we are just the vessels the Lord has graciously chosen to use. We are only doing what we committed to Him to do.

I found it so easy to unconsciously become proud over doing the Lord's work. I therefore developed some responses to give to good-hearted well-wishers and encouragers. Feel free to use them. They are: "The Lord's ministry is going great. It really feels good to know I am in His will." Or, "Oh, I can't take all the credit. This is not my ministry. I am just the fortunate vessel He graciously chose to use. The glory and thanks definitely go to the Lord. Please pray for Him to continue blessing the Woman to Woman Mentoring Ministry."

Whatever you say, say it in love and not to rebuke the other person. Let your words be a testimony that with God's direction they, too, could be a vessel to do His work. Ask those around you to help you with this. I tell every new group of mentors and mentees that all the credit for the ministry goes to the Lord. I assure them that this is a ministry designed for them, not me, and the head of the ministry is the Lord. I try not to talk about *my* ministry or *my* ministry team. I asked my husband to let me know if he hears me using the *my* word on the phone, at church, in conversations, or at speaking engagements. It only took him telling me a couple of times before it became a habit to refer to the ministry as: "The Lord's ministry, which He has blessed with many willing hearts."

This is not my ministry. I am just the fortunate vessel He graciously chose to use.

---

[1]*Disciplines of the Beautiful Woman*, Anne Ortland, 1998, Word Publishing, Nashville Tennessee, page 65. All rights reserved.

CHAPTER 4

"Plans go wrong with too few counselors; many counselors bring success" (Proverbs 15:22, TLB).

You Need to Have a Plan

PREPARATION IS A PROCESS

By reading this book, you are seeking counsel from someone who has "been there, done that." I have the opportunity to mentor you, and you can learn from my mistakes and my victories. When we kicked off the Woman to Woman Mentoring Ministry at Saddleback, it was a tremendous success from the beginning and has continued to grow at an unbelievable pace. So relax and take the next steps to building a basis for a successful ministry that will outlive you.

When you complete the research phase, it is time to formulate a plan of action. However, it is best to finish reading this book and incorporate the ideas I describe in upcoming chapters before you actually develop your plan. Then make the necessary modifications to customize it for your church.

When I started the Woman to Woman Mentoring Ministry in 1995, the development of a new ministry at Saddleback involved a 12-step planning process. I have to admit, when I first saw the 12 steps it looked foreboding and time consuming; however, I did appreciate the organization and thought that had gone into preparing it. Today, I truly appreciate the value of having taken the time to think through the various planning steps before I started publicizing the ministry.

The remainder of this chapter discusses the "12 Planning Steps for Developing a Ministry at Saddleback"[1] that was used at that time. You will have an opportunity to see how I utilized these steps in developing the Woman to Woman Mentoring Ministry, as well as discover ways to adapt them for your own use. Keep in mind that my answers were based on our specific circumstances and structure at Saddleback Church. Your answers may look different as you customize them for your ministry.

12 Planning Steps for Developing a Ministry
Phase 1

The first part of the planning process is "Qualifying a New Ministry Idea." Now you will understand why you developed "Your Story," because this is the crucial place to tell it. This is where you are going to "sell" your idea. Every great idea needs backers, and the church staff is yours. You need them on your team. To support your idea, they are going to need to know your commitment to your vision and your plan to make it a reality.

As I sat at my first planning meeting, we went through Phase 1 of the process. I read Saddleback's goal in starting new ministries. *Goal:* "To meet the people presenting the idea and hear their story, their heart, and their perspective related to the ministry opportunity. Likewise, to introduce us (Ministry Development Center MDC) to them and affirm our support for their involvement in the ministry of Saddleback Community Church.

"The priority for meeting one is to the person/s presenting the idea. Therefore, it is very important in that even if one's idea goes nowhere after meeting one, the person/s presenting the idea, leave feeling like they have been heard with respect and dignity, and the door is wide open for future 'creative ministry impulses and/or insights.' "

Whether or not your church has a formal plan for new ministries, they are going to have similar goals to Saddleback. The church staff, whom you have determined you will be working with in your ministry, will want to know your goals and the source of your motivation and passion for the ministry. Sharing "Your Story" with them will answer many of those questions. If you are not on the church staff, they may also ask you the following questions. Be prepared to answer:

- How long have you been coming to this church?
- What attracted you to this church?
- What do you like most about this church?
- Have you had a chance to attend any growth classes the church has provided? (Purpose-driven churches will call these classes 101, 201, 301, 401, 501.)
- Have you had other ministry involvement outside or prior to this church? If so, what part did you find most satisfying?

Even if they do not ask these specific questions, I would suggest that you offer the answers. This will help them become better acquainted with you.

Next, you can present the plan you have developed as a result of working through the following 12 steps. You and the ministry will receive tremendous benefit from your thinking through the answers to these questions before starting the Woman to Woman Mentoring Ministry in your church.

Here are the 12 steps along with the discussion I submitted of my planning process. After each step, I have allowed space in the margin for you to answer the question as it applies to you and your specific church environment. Give some time to each step, and carefully think through how it applies to the ministry you

point in your
ons, and allow

elp you anticipate
citement and
this is the part that
potential ministry. I
the "doing" phase,

This is a strategic point in your ministry journey.

ion? Which of the five
each, fellowship/

nistry would be
certainly be
duct.

Your answer ─────────────────────────────▶

2. **Who do we serve?** *Who is our customer? Of Saddleback's Five Circles of People Groups, which group will this ministry serve most (a target group): the community, the crowd of weekend attendees, the entire congregation, the committed, or the core?*

My answer: The Woman to Woman Mentoring Ministry would utilize our committed and core women to minister to the general congregation and hopefully reach the weekend attendees' attention.

Your answer ─────────────────────────────▶

Phase 3
3. **What are their needs? What services will we offer?** *What are the needs of the target group we want to serve? Which of these needs should our ministry focus on? What kinds of support could we provide for these needs? What are the specific services we will offer?*

My answer: Our target group would be women seeking a confidential, one-on-one relationship with other Christian women who are more mature in their faith and life experiences and who could act as encouragers, listeners, supporters, and role models.

Webster's Dictionary defines *mentor* as *a wise and trusted counselor*. Titus 2:3-5 instructs the older women of the church to teach the younger women of the church how to grow and function as godly women, mothers, and wives. Examples of women who might seek a mentor would be women with emotional hurts, women from non-Christian homes, women without mothers or without Christian mothers, widows and single parents, single women, engaged women, women seeking a Christian role model, newly married women, women with young families, new believers.

I have mentioned the idea of mentoring to the Career and Edge of Commitment women at Saddleback, and 15 women gave me their names and phone numbers and expressed an interest in having a mentor. I see the Woman to Woman Mentoring Ministry as being twofold:

1. Creating an environment for women to be matched in one-on-one relationships. I have researched methods of doing this and talked with several churches that currently have this ministry in place, as well as one church that is just starting a mentoring program. They all started the matching process with a kick-off orientation tea or coffee (publicized in the church bulletin), inviting women interested in being mentored and women interested in being mentors. The format allowed time for intermingling and filling out personal profile forms to be used later for matching. All churches I have talked to say a natural pairing seems to take place at the orientations, with the profiles used to assist the women to find someone with common interests. Most of the women I have spoken to feel this would be an appropriate procedure.

2. The second area of the ministry would be to support and train the mentors in quarterly gatherings where they would have an opportunity to learn and share with each other. I would be willing to coordinate these with the assistance of a team, comprised of two mentors and two mentees.

The churches I have spoken with to date are: (I listed the churches and dates I talked to them). I contacted Focus on the Family to obtain their information on mentoring. They are sending me a cassette tape and brochure.

◄─────────────────────────────────── Your answer

4. **How will those services be provided?** *What will be our ministry strategy for providing services for the needs of our targeted group? What will be our operational plan? How will coordination and communication be handled?*

My answer: The mentoring relationships will have a suggested minimum time frame of six months. We will invite interested women to attend Orientation Coffees held in homes. There will be suggestions given as to how to start the relationships and maintain them, with a lot of flexibility encouraged by the participating women. The women will fill out Profile Cards and a Prayer Day

Team will pray over the cards and match women into mentor/mentee relationships. Mentors will come to quarterly training sessions to talk about
areas where they could use assistance, as well as to share testimonies and blessings with each other. While we are in the initial startup stages with a small group, I should be able to handle the calls myself. After we take it to the entire church, I would probably enlist the help of my team.

Your answer ⟶

Phase 4

5. **What kind of team is required?** *What are the various roles and ministry tasks that are needed to support this ministry? What type of team structure, qualities, and skills will be required for this ministry?*

My answer: I would need a support team of probably two mentors and two mentees, as well as myself. The team would pray over the Profile Cards in making matches, put on the quarterly meetings and Orientation Coffees, help with communication, etc. Four women in the startup group have agreed to be part of this team.

Your answer ⟶

6. **Will the ministry be led?** *What type of leadership structure, qualities, and skills will be required for this ministry? How will decision making be managed? What authority and responsibility will be assigned?*

My answer: Yes, the ministry will need leadership. Since at the moment I am the one with the initial vision, I am offering to be the ministry leader. The mentoring relationships should be fairly self-sufficient. However, there would need to be plans to perhaps have an Orientation Coffee several times a year for new women joining the church who would like to participate in a mentoring relationship.

Your answer ⟶

Phase 5

7. **How will the ministry be supported?** *How will the team be supported by its leadership, volunteers, and church staff? How will this ministry receive the direction and support needed to grow? How much direction and support will need to be provided by the church leaders and staff?*

Chapter 4: You Need to Have a Plan   **43**

My answer: There might need to be some typing, copying, and mailing done by the church staff as well as help with putting notices in the bulletins, arranging for rooms to have orientation meetings, etc. I have already interfaced with the leaders of the Word Bible Study group, and perhaps there are other groups I could meet with to introduce the ministry. Use of announcements in the church bulletin would be vital. We would make an announcement of the ministry and pass out fliers at all women's activities in the church (retreats, Heart to Heart Cafe, Word Bible Study group, singles, young career groups).

I would hope to solicit both mentors and mentees willing to serve in the ministry. It could even be a service and activity they do together. Having Orientation Coffees throughout the year, rather than just once a year, will keep the ministry growing and continually allow the women of the church to participate.

⟵──────────────────────────────── **Your answer**

8. **What kind of training is needed?** *What kind of S.H.A.P.E.S* are required? How do those currently involved measure up? What development and training will be needed? How will ongoing development and nurture be handled? How will this skill training be provided? (*spiritual gifts, heart, abilities, personality, experiences).*

My answer: It would be vital that women involved in the ministry see the need to reach out to each other in encouraging friendships. We would need mature Christian women who would be positive Christian role models from which new Christian women could learn the joys of living a godly life. There would need to be a commitment to stay in the relationships for the time suggested. Most of the mentors would probably benefit from ongoing training—quarterly meetings where both additional training and sharing could take place. I would do the majority of the training at first, then have guest speakers on various topics. We would also encourage the mentors to participate in this as they become more experienced. I have reviewed several books that I am also going to recommend to them. I will be available to assist them. If there are specific problem areas, we could call on the counseling and pastoral staff of the church to help us.

⟵──────────────────────────────── **Your answer**

9. **How will we expand the ministry?** *How will we recruit, orient, and train new ministry participants?*

My answer: After establishing the initial core group, I would like to introduce the ministry to the entire church, probably through the bulletin and a table on the patio. If the response warrants it, we could have Orientation Coffees quarterly to introduce women to the ministry and establish new mentoring relationships. I would also make myself available to meet with any group of women in the church interested in becoming part of the ministry.

Your answer ───────────────────────────────▶

Phase 6

10. What will be the process for feedback and evaluation? *How will success be measured?*

My answer: I will call the mentors monthly to see how they are doing and will encourage feedback and sharing at the quarterly mentors meeting. We might also have a biannual luncheon for all the mentors and mentees. It would be a time of sharing the blessings and the testimonies I know will be a result of this ministry.

Your answer ───────────────────────────────▶

11. What structure is needed for maintaining the ministry? *What organizational and operational structure is needed to maintain the intended?*

My answer: The individual woman-to-woman relationships are going to be fairly independent. The overall ministry would need to have a calendar of events planned out a year in advance to keep it growing.

Your answer ───────────────────────────────▶

12. What is our vision for growth? *How will the ministry grow into new groups and services that include a strategy for new leaders?*

My answer: I am sure that there will be women who come out of these relationships with a stronger sense of belonging to the church. Part of their individual relationships might be doing something together in the church (i.e., joining the Word Bible Study, participating in the crafts or drama ministry, or team teaching nursery Sunday School). The list is endless as these women grow closer together and closer to the Lord. I am sure that women who were initially mentees will mature through their mentoring relationships and be ready to be mentors the next time. I would also imagine that women with leadership abilities will grow through the training and eventually be able to replace me or, at minimum, enhance my efforts.

Your answer ───────────────────────────────▶

This is a foundation of ideas, suggested applications, and structure for the ministry.

Ministry Mission Statement

I would add one more step to this 12-step planning process. I guess that would make it step number 13. Actually the 13th step is a summary of several of the above steps. You need to write a mission statement. It is good to write down ministry parameters and goals in a mission statement for use as a reference for everyone in the ministry. You want each woman who joins the ministry to have a copy. We print it on our Coffee Programs and in our quarterly newsletter. It describes the purpose, goals, and spiritual foundation of the Woman to Woman Mentoring Ministry. A mission statement is especially helpful when making decisions, adding new phases, and experiencing times of rapid growth. It gives you guidelines and boundaries to assist in determining that everything you do is in agreement with your mission statement.

I did not actually write a mission statement until after the first year. The goals and direction of the ministry were in my head, but it should have been down on paper for all to see. I would suggest that you take time right now, if you have not already done so, and design a mission statement.

Pray about it before you start, and be comforted that it is not written in stone. You may modify it later, but for now you will have a foundation and guidelines to come back to when you question whether or not you should do something in the ministry. After reading our Woman to Woman Mentoring Ministry Mission Statement, take some time to design one for your ministry.

Woman to Woman
Mentoring Ministry Mission Statement

To give the women of Saddleback Church the opportunity
to experience joy and growth in their Christian lives by participating
in one-on-one supporting and encouraging mentoring friendships.

A mentor will be a woman who is a practicing Christian,
regularly attends Saddleback Church, and has the desire
to let her life be an example and godly role model.

A mentee will be a Saddleback Church woman
who is young in her walk with the Lord.

Women of all ages are welcome.

The scriptural foundation is Titus 2:3-5, where we are told
to teach and guide the next generation of Christian women
in how to live the life of a godly woman in Christ.

If you have gone through the above 13-step exercise, I am sure that you feel much more confident than you did before. You also have a definite plan of action to present to the decision makers of your church. If you are like me and are eager to just get to it and perhaps skipped your answers above, I encourage you to go back right now and fill in your thoughts. It is always fun for me to look back on my responses and see how right on I was in some areas, but how far off I was in others. For example, thinking I could handle all the necessary phone calls, or that the ministry could start the next month! It is not a problem if you do not have all the answers or are not sure how some aspects of the ministry will progress. I did not either. You will notice that in some cases I gave a very brief response because I had never seen a Mentoring Ministry in operation. I could not anticipate exactly what would happen. This is OK. You don't want the ministry plan to be so rigid that it doesn't allow for enhancement by experience. I only wrote what I *thought* would happen.

In the next chapters, you will see what actually evolved. I understood that new ideas would continue to evolve as we actually "did ministry." I graduated with my first degree from California Polytechnic University in San Luis Obispo. The motto at Cal Poly is "learn by doing." In other words, book knowledge is great, but you need to be able to apply it. That is how I felt at this point. I had a game plan, and hopefully so do you. This is a foundation of ideas, suggested applications, and structure for the ministry. Now it is time to seek approval to start. Then be ready to customize and modify as you put your plan into action.

In the following chapters, you will see what actually happened when I put my plan into action. Since I did not have a step-by-step guide to applying my plan as I am offering you, I learned as I went along. I will take you through the steps that I took and share my mistakes and victories and how the Lord blessed them all. Hopefully this resource will save you time, energy, and frustration, and as many have said, "You will not have to reinvent the wheel." Let the fun begin!

Be ready to customize and modify as you put your plan into action.

---

[1] Adapted from "12 Planning Steps for Developing a Ministry at Saddleback," (Lake Forest, CA: Saddleback Church, 1995).

CHAPTER 5

"The wise man is glad to be instructed, but a self-sufficient fool falls flat on his face" (Proverbs 10:8, TLB).

Learn by Doing

The Proverbs do not mince words, but really tell it as it is. Now that you have a plan, you are probably ready to announce the starting of a new ministry at your church in this Sunday's bulletin. I know I was. *What more could we possibly need to do?* I asked myself. But Pastors Doug and Brad kept pulling in the reigns. As I tried to charge forward, they would remind me that there was no rush.
They continually warned me not to start the ministry with a great deal of fanfare and then crash and burn because of an issue I had failed to take into account.

Men are from Mars, Women are from Venus, so the book title says. That was a good reminder to me that men and women do not think alike. Pastor Doug and Pastor Brad are more detail- and structure-oriented than I am. For example, I would make statements like, "I know that if we get a group of Christian women together in a nonthreatening, pleasant environment, invite in the Holy Spirit, and give the ladies a chance to interact, bonding will take place at the initial meeting." My research revealed that some women would match themselves at the first gathering. Given the opportunity to interact and get to know each other over a cup of coffee, a lot of matching would take place on its own. This was hard for the pastors to understand. They could not imagine that women, who in some cases might be strangers, would be vulnerable so quickly with each other.

It was also hard for them to comprehend that we could match women just by praying over their Profile Cards. After all, we would be placing two women who possibly did not know each other well into a relationship that had the potential to become very close and intimate. Pastor Doug said, "It's kind of like setting them up for a blind date!" As much as I tried to assure Pastor Brad and Pastor Doug that this was how other churches were doing it, they continued to have troubled and perplexed looks on their faces. They said men would never do that. I tried to assure them that women would. My response was, "Women do not need the head knowledge before they can apply the heart knowledge." We finally came to a compromise. They were not saying my plan would not work. They just needed to see it tangibly happen first, which I agreed was fair. Pastor Doug suggested I network further among the women of the church and find five or six interested in being part of a test group to try out my ideas. The results of this group would determine when (or if) we could take the Woman to Woman Mentoring Ministry to the church. In this first test group, the mentors and mentees would reconvene in three months to evaluate how the mentoring relationships had worked for them. The test Orientation Coffee was not in my original plans, but I could definitely see the wisdom in it. Now that I have seen the benefits, I am going to suggest that you do the same. Although you may be following the steps in this book faithfully, your church and the women of your church have their own unique characteristics. First Thessalonians 5:21 says, "Test everything. Hold on to the good."

The learn-by-doing test Orientation Coffee gives you the opportunity to make adjustments as needed. It gives you practice going through all the steps on a smaller scale—like a dress rehearsal (which is what we actually called it). Even if you have presented a well thought out plan, your church might be hesitant to start a Mentoring Ministry. The Dress Rehearsal Coffee will help alleviate their concerns. Ask permission to try your ideas on a small scale first, then offer to report on the results. You will learn a tremendous amount during this trial period and gain confidence in yourself and your plan. The following verse helped me to accept this part of the process: "We can make our plans, but the final outcome is in God's hands. We can always 'prove' that we are right, but is the Lord convinced? Commit your work to the Lord, then it will succeed" (Prov. 16:1-3, TLB). Recommit the ministry to the Lord and begin to look for women to be a part of your test group.

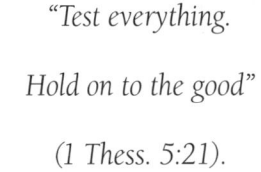

"Test everything. Hold on to the good"

(1 Thess. 5:21).

THE "DRESS REHEARSAL" ORIENTATION COFFEE

I would like my ministry experience to be a "been there—done that" mentoring role model for you. However, you still need to become familiar yourself with how to put it all into practice. If there is not an initial committee to help, do not take on more than you can handle in the beginning. As you get rolling and women join the new ministry, I guarantee that help will come. Take the how-tos in this book and conduct a practice run with a small Orientation Coffee for starters.

I would not recommend that you immediately take on the whole church unless you have a small, consistent congregation, and you know that one Coffee may accommodate all the interested women. Get ready though—once the word is out about the fun and blessings of mentoring, lots of woman are going to want to join. If you have a mid- to large-size church, there is no question that you should start out slowly. There will continue to be the woman who "couldn't make this Coffee, but would love to come to the next one." So start humbly, and the Lord will help you successfully grow to the size He has planned for your church.

We continue to use Orientation Coffees to introduce women to the ministry. Our first Dress Rehearsal Coffee format has remained the same. We have enhanced the methods and learned a few things, but the principles have not changed.

Are you ready to begin? Get out your highlighter and a pen. It's time for you to go to work again, applying the steps to your individual church. You will be able to see how the work you have done thus far has prepared you to take that leap of faith and begin to plan for your Dress Rehearsal Coffee. As we begin the process, I will be reviewing several points made earlier so you can understand why the format we have used has worked so fabulously. Are you ready? Let's embark on a journey that will change lives—starting with yours!

Keep It Simple!

In brainstorming ideas for the first Orientation Coffee with several women in the church, I could see how this could quickly get out of hand. I envisioned inviting women over to my house for a cup of coffee and cake and providing them an opportunity to learn about the Woman to Woman Mentoring Ministry and meet each other. However, one day as I sat in Pastor Brad's office describing my vision to him, he invited a woman from the church staff to come offer her input. She thought a Mentoring Ministry was right on target with the needs of the church, and then I could see a look of excitement in her eyes as ideas unfolded. Her eyes sparkled as she described the beautiful home of a couple in the church who offered their house for such occasions. Pastor Brad then began to share her enthusiasm as he described the view from the patio of this spectacular home on a hill overlooking the city. Soon they both had us visually out on the patio that surrounded the house, having coffee out of fine china tea cups, with linen napkins atop lace-covered tables. Tuxedo-clad male church staff members poured coffee out of sterling silver coffeepots, while violins played softly in the background. The atmosphere was elegant, with women dressed for afternoon tea.

This sounded lovely, but a flashing neon sign in front of my eyes said, "**Tilt!**" What they were describing would take a lot of time, money, and help—none of which I had. It would be perfect if we were only going to do one Coffee a year, because it would take me at least a year to put something like that together. It also sounded much too formal for the atmosphere I thought most conducive to women meeting each other for the first time. I politely thanked them for their ideas, and then started to work on plans for a much simpler Coffee. You want this first Coffee to be something you can do by yourself if helpers do not surface. Have it at your own home so you will not have to worry about coordinating food and supplies somewhere else. You will be more comfortable and organized in your own home for this first Coffee. Then you can see what develops from there.

Start With a Committee of One

Keeping it simple and doing a test group allows you to start the ministry by yourself if that is necessary. Ask friends and family members to help you with the first Coffee. You can give them the service opportunity descriptions found in Chapter 13, "Recruiting Help." Then start recruiting helpers at the first Coffee. Once women become aware of the ministry, they will begin to serve.

"We can make our plans, but the final outcome is in God's hands. ... Commit your work to the Lord, then it will succeed" (Prov. 16:1-3, TLB).

Pick a Time

Pick a time of year for your first Coffee that is not hectic with activities. Good times are January, February, early March, middle of September, and October. I started ours January 14, 1996, and it proved to be a great way to start the new year.

Find Women to Attend the First Coffee

Remember the groups at church you visited in the research stage—the college and career groups, the engaged couples' group, the women's Bible Study groups, and the Sunday School classes? Here is where you use the names and phone numbers of those women who expressed interest in a Mentoring Ministry. You have also been writing down names and phone numbers of anyone who expressed an interest when you mentioned the new Mentoring Ministry you were starting. Your initial efforts now begin to be fruitful. These are the women you can contact and invite to your first Orientation Coffee. Following is a sample letter to send them.

> *Dear Sister in Christ,*
>
> *Your interest in the Woman to Woman Mentoring Ministry and expressed desire to participate in a mentoring relationship is exciting. I would like to invite you to attend an afternoon Coffee at my house to learn more about the Mentoring Ministry and to share ideas on how to make it meaningful to your life. I feel that a mentoring relationship would bless many women in our church, and it seems that God has also put this mission field on your heart. I thank God daily for all of you—those who would like to be mentors as well as those who have acknowledged a deep desire to learn from another Christian woman.*
>
> *The details of the Coffee are:*
> DATE: Sunday, (date)
> TIME: 2:00 p.m. until 6:00 p.m.
> PLACE: Address
> PLEASE RSVP: Phone number
>
> *If you know of other women at our church who would like to come to the Coffee, please feel free to invite them, and/or give them my phone number. I write this letter to you with excitement and anticipation of all the Lord has planned for the new friendships, experiences, and the witness that will be a natural outcome of this Mentoring Ministry. I will be in prayer for all of you as you pray about being a pioneer in this call to Christian women of our wonderful church. Until we meet, may God's richest blessings be on you and your families.*
>
> *In His Service,*
> *(Your Name)*

Send this letter out three weeks before the Orientation Coffee so women can get it on their calendars. However, I learned, and continue to learn, that an RSVP is not a courtesy often practiced today. Most people want to hold their options open to the last minute and are hesitant to say yes too soon, in case a better opportunity comes along. Consequently, the week before my first Coffee, less than half of the women had responded. Feeling like I needed to have some idea of what to expect, I began making phone calls. Lesson number two, many people do not return phone messages left on recorders. Finally, I just had to leave it up to the Lord and say, "Lord, whomever You want to attend will be there. Whether it is 5 or 15 will be up to You. I have done my part to let them know." Exactly 20 women attended the first Coffee, and we started the ministry with 10 mentoring relationships—the exact number I had told Pastor Brad and Pastor Doug I thought the Lord would give me for the trial group. The Lord is faithful.

Hold the "Dress Rehearsal" Coffee

From this point on you will follow the directions in the next chapters. You will just be doing everything on a smaller scale for this test group, and the relationships will last only three months so that you can evaluate them sooner. This gives you the opportunity to make any necessary adjustments before announcing the new ministry to the entire church. You also will have recruited helpers to handle a larger crowd. That is why I encourage you to start the ministry whether or not you initially have help. You are not going to find helpers until women know about it.

I really had no idea what to expect at this first Coffee, and neither did the women who were coming. You are going to learn from this together. However, you do want to create a relaxed, homey atmosphere where women will be at ease in this new experience. It is not appropriate to be pretentious or elaborate. They need to feel comfortable and welcome.

Be Ready—The Word Is Out

Soon after our first Coffee, I began receiving phone calls from women wanting to know how they could get into the Woman to Woman Mentoring Ministry. When was I going to have the next Coffee? I still had not made any public announcements at church. Our status continued to be a "Ministry in the Making," and so will yours. But what a great problem to have—a waiting list. Word was out. Women were starting to talk about their mentoring relationships and others wanted to know how they could be involved too. If this happens to you, take down names and phone numbers as you did in the research step, and tell them you will call with the date of the next Coffee.

Have a Six-Week Check-In

Have the first test group of mentors return for a six-week check-in meeting. For us it was apparent that the women's mentoring relationships were impacting the

52 *Woman to Woman Mentoring: Ministry Coordinator's Guide*

lives of both the mentors and the mentees. I felt ready to have another Coffee, and my waiting list now had 20 more names on it.

If you feel confident about the first Coffee and the response at the six-week meeting is positive, take a progress report to the church and seek permission to start planning your next Coffee. However, if your agreement with the church was to wait for the test group to complete their three-month relationships, then be patient and wait.

Close the "Dress Rehearsal" Group

At the end of three months, gather back together the mentors and mentees. Ask them to share with you their perception of the process and their experience in their mentoring relationships. Give them the M&M Questionnaire (form J, p. 232) to answer. If the results show areas you feel need adjustment, start making those changes now. That is the purpose of this initial test group. Be sure to let the participants know you need their honest input so you can improve the ministry for the future.

This is also the time to ask for assistance. Share with them Areas of Opportunity for Service (form V, p. 247), and the positions you need filled for the next Coffee. What better source of help than women who have experienced the blessings of a mentoring relationship.

I approached Pastor Doug with a six-week "blessing report" and presented the idea of our first "official" Orientation Coffee in March. He agreed it was time to plan the next Coffee. I was elated. We would again meet at my home on March 24. This time, I was able to put an insert in the church bulletin announcing a "New Opportunity for Saddleback Women." That weekend the phone began to ring nonstop and the Woman to Woman Mentoring Ministry was a "real ministry" at last.

Let's get yours started, too. It's show time, or, should I say, Coffee time!

It's Coffee time!

CHAPTER 6

"Serve wholeheartedly, as if you were serving the Lord, not men" (Ephesians 6:7).

It's Coffee Time!

LET THE MINISTRY BEGIN

You have taken the steps to get the Mentoring Ministry approved at your church. Interest is being generated, and women are starting to call. It is time to plan your first "Learn-by-Doing Dress Rehearsal Orientation Coffee." Are you nervous? Excited? I was, too. I was also in awe. The reality of the ministry was such an answer to prayer. Finally, I was planning the first Coffee, and now, so are you.

My prayer for you now is that you enjoy the experience and the process. There is nothing that makes me more sad than to see a bride-to-be stressed and anxious about her wedding. Planning such a wonderfully exciting event should be a glorious celebration orchestrated by God. That is how I hope you feel about your first Orientation Coffee—you are the Lord's bride, and He has asked you to plan a glorious celebration orchestrated by Him. Since it is His celebration, let Him lead and guide you and put all your worries at His very capable feet. I am going to take you through the steps I learned to having a stress-free, enjoyable Orientation Coffee. As we discussed in the last chapter, I suggest you ask several of your friends or family if they will assist you with your Dress Rehearsal Coffee. Learn from my experience. If you try to do it all by yourself, it will exhaust you. Let's look at the answers to some questions you might have.

WHY A COFFEE?

I know you have been dying to ask this question since you noticed I keep referring to Orientation Coffees and not orientation teas or orientation meetings. You might guess that I chose to have Coffees because I am a coffee drinker and not a tea drinker. You would be partially correct. I do love coffee.

However, there really were other reasons besides my enjoyment that led me to have Coffees rather than teas. They are the same reasons I rejected an idea given to me early in the ministry planning stages. Remember me telling you about the suggestion that we have a formal gathering at a large regal home and the reasons I didn't want that atmosphere? I actually feel confident that this seemingly subtle differentiation of Coffees versus teas contributed dramatically to the quick success and growth of our Woman to Woman Mentoring Ministry.

Why do I make that statement? First, your church may already have tea events for women such as Spring Tea, Retreat Tea, Christmas Tea, or High Tea. If these are traditional events at your church, you do not want the confusion or competition of an Orientation Tea. Second, a tea sounds formal. It usually involves tea cups and saucers, lace table cloths, and finger sandwiches. I asked several friends what they envisioned if I said I was inviting them to a tea. Unanimously, they replied, "Tea cups and saucers, little sandwiches, women dressed in hats and gloves sipping tea out of china tea cups. Definitely a formal affair." That is not the atmosphere I envisioned for the Woman to Woman Mentoring Ministry. I saw the mentoring relationships as two women having their initial meeting in a casual, informal atmosphere, and then later getting together weekly and talking over a steaming mug of cappuccino or cafe latte at a neighborhood coffeehouse.

I spoke once at a conference of women where the average age was mid-20s. I asked them what came to mind when I mentioned a tea, and there was complete silence. Nothing came to mind, because most of them had never attended a tea. That reconfirmed to me that younger women, a group you really want to reach, probably would not come to a tea. I think we are more a coffee-out-of-a-decorative-foam-cup generation, than tea-out-of-a-china-cup era. With a coffeehouse on every corner in the Saddleback Valley, I felt we were a coffee group of women, and I would imagine your group is too.

This was difficult for some to understand, perhaps because traditionally women have teas. I would send in Orientation Coffee information for the church bulletin, and it would come out the next Sunday—you guessed it—Orientation Tea. When I went into the church office, everyone would ask me when we were having the next tea, or how was the last tea? Stay patient if this happens to you. Use it as an opportunity to explain why you have Coffees versus teas. Soon everyone will be using and understanding the correct terminology. Tea drinkers, do not be dismayed. If you want to have an Orientation Tea, go right ahead. We do always have hot water and tea bags available for those who want a hot cup of tea.

That's it!

It is His celebration. Let Him lead and guide you and put all your worries at His very capable feet.

WHY "ORIENTATION" COFFEE?

Adding the word *orientation* clarifies that it is an information meeting where they can come to learn more about mentoring. They can wait to decide if they want to commit to a mentoring relationship after they hear more about it. This takes the pressure off them and you. They know they will have a choice as to whether or not they want to join the ministry. You can defray most questions by encouraging them to come to the Orientation Coffee where you can give a detailed explanation to all the women at one time.

When the ministry first starts and the phone is constantly ringing, it is very time consuming to try and tell each caller all the details. Often they will try to determine in advance if they should be a mentor or mentee. Having an Orientation Coffee allows you simply to say: "Why don't you come to the Orientation Coffee and learn all about mentoring? We will give a complete explanation. You will have a chance to ask questions, and you can determine whether you want to be in a mentoring relationship as a mentor or mentee at that time." Then you continue giving them details of how to register for the Coffee. As we will talk about later, many women come thinking they need a mentor and realize they are the mentor, and vice versa. This is not a determination made without prayer and more information. (For brevity in this material, I will frequently refer to the Orientation Coffee as Coffee.)

WHY SUNDAY?

The answer to this question is, "Because it works." By process of elimination, it proved to be a day when the majority of women can attend. I considered Saturday, but honestly, Sunday worked best in my home, so I figured it probably was best for other people, too. Think about it:

- You want to include the women who work outside the home, so that eliminates weekdays.
- Saturday is often chore and catch-up day for the family, and the kids are involved in sports.
- Chances are the women attending are going to be leaving their children with their husbands who may have plans or have to work on Saturday.
- Sunday afternoon is relaxing for most people. If they have attended church, they are in a very good mindset to have coffee and chat with other Christian women.

I attribute a good deal of the success we have had with attendance at the Coffees to the timing. When I have randomly asked if other days would be better, most women respond that Sunday afternoons are perfect. Again, there may be some dynamics at your church that make Saturdays work best. I would highly recommend sticking with a weekend day. Then use that same day of the weekend and the same time for every Orientation Coffee. This provides consistency.

No matter what day or time you choose, there is always going to be someone who cannot attend. You are not going to please 100 percent of the people 100 percent of the time. Don't even try. Select a day and time when the majority of women in your congregation can attend. If a woman cannot make the currently scheduled Coffee, assure her that you will be having more Coffees throughout the year. She can try to get off work, or find a baby-sitter, or plan her vacation around a future Coffee. Most women can eventually attend an Orientation Coffee if they

You do not want to match anyone into a mentoring relationship that has not attended an Orientation Coffee.

have a strong desire. You do not want to match anyone into a mentoring relationship that has not attended an Orientation Coffee.

WHY 2:00-6:00 P.M.?

The time evolved as we grew in size. The first two Coffees at my house were from 2:00-4:00 p.m. As the Coffees increased in attendance we added 30 minutes, ending at 4:30 p.m. Coffees 5 and 6 were to end at 5:00 p.m., but with 86 women at the sixth Coffee, it ended at 6:15 p.m.! It is difficult to know how many women are going to attend. Therefore, it is better to schedule extra time. If you finish early, the women can leave or stay and visit with each other. This is better than having them leave because they have commitments, and you are running overtime.

I chose 2:00 p.m. as a starting time because people attending our last church service do not get out until 12:30 p.m. They need time to get the family home and have lunch before they come to the Coffee. Evenings are hectic, because everyone worries about work and school the next morning. Unfortunately, society has taken a rather laid-back position about arriving on time. Women arrived at the first Coffees as late as 3:15 p.m. At that point, you will see later, they have missed everything you have to say about mentoring. I did not want to be matching into mentoring relationships women who had arrived late and would not understand the concept of mentoring. It is also very disruptive when women continue to come in the front door after you have started the program.

For the first six Coffees, I assumed we would have to live with the problem of late arrivals. However, at the sixth Coffee it was raining. Late arriving ladies were shedding rain gear that prevented them from slipping in quietly. When I address the group, I usually position myself by the front door. You can picture the distraction of the door continually opening and shutting after we have started the program. After that experience, I decided we had to get firm on the times. Now, our fliers and voicemail messages announce that we start promptly at 2:00 p.m. and will not be admitting anyone after 2:30 p.m. It also states that we cannot match anyone who leaves before 6:00 p.m. This allows them to make plans and arrangements in advance or know that they need to wait and attend the next Coffee. During the initial welcoming phase of the Coffee program, I thank them for being on time and remind them that staying until 6:00 p.m. is required to be matched into a mentoring relationship. Announcing this at the beginning gives anyone who was planning to leave early the option of attending another Coffee or arranging to stay until 6:00 p.m. You will see later why it is so important that women stay for the entire Coffee experience.

WHEN IS A GOOD TIME TO LAUNCH THE MENTORING MINISTRY?

Winter and fall seasons are great times to start a Mentoring Ministry. January or February are good months, because the Christmas holidays are over and women are ready to start new ventures in the new year. The new year often spurs New Year's goals to grow spiritually or become more involved in church and ministry activities. After school is back in session in September, or early to mid-October, also are good launching times. The starting of the school year often brings with it the desire to learn and to experience personal growth. Many moms think of the school year as their time to become involved in things outside the home. Late October is not good because of the nearness of Thanksgiving and the Christmas holidays. Spring is traditionally a busy time of year to juggle dates around Easter holidays, spring school breaks, Mother's Day, Memorial Day weekend, and any spring women's activities at your church. I do not recommend launching a Mentoring Ministry in the late spring months because of full calendars and the summer months approaching. It would be difficult to keep momentum going over the summer. Early March might be another possibility. In selecting the months for your future Coffees, you need to be aware of busy seasonal times, as well as your church calendar of events. (Remember to conduct your "Dress Rehearsal" Coffee first. Pick any three month time span for it.)

HOW FREQUENTLY ARE COFFEES HELD?

Your objective is to provide women a frequent opportunity for placement in a mentoring relationship. Since everyone must attend an Orientation Coffee, you need to offer more than one a year. For the first three years, we held five yearly Orientation Coffees to assure that everyone had an initial opportunity to be involved. We currently have four Orientation Coffees a year and an all-ministry Christmas party. The number of Coffees you offer will depend on the size of your church, keeping in mind that it is better to have small, frequent Coffees. Unless your church attendance is under 100, I suggest a minimum of three a year. Mid-January to late February are good months for the first Coffee of the year. Based on when you have your first Coffee of the year, spread the others throughout the year accordingly. Cap off the year the first Sunday in December with a Christmas party.

HOW MANY ARE GOING TO ATTEND?

This seems like an especially important question since your Orientation Coffees take place in someone's home. It is good to know how many chairs you will need, how much coffee to prepare, etc. Let me warn you before you lose any sleep over trying to figure out exactly how many women are really going to show up—you will probably never know for sure.

I can tell you that if you are a woman like me who likes to be in control and know everything in advance, this could be the most nebulous and frustrating part of the ministry, if you let it. God really had to work with me on this. I had to accept that it was His ministry, and He knew how many were going to come. I did not need to know. I had to trust Him and have faith that He would provide for all our needs.

Since everyone must attend an Orientation Coffee, you need to offer more than one a year.

I know it sounds incredible that you would never have a firm number, but it is something you just need to be aware of and not stress over. I had to come to the realization, as I told you before, that people today do not RSVP. I learned a big lesson that I have practiced since the first Dress Rehearsal Coffee: Do everything you can to let the women know about the Coffees and meetings, and then leave the rest up to the Lord. It is His ministry. He will have the women attend that He wants, and He will be sure you can accommodate them. He has been faithful to us, and He will be faithful to you.

Let me share with you an email I received from River of Life Fellowship Church in Kent, Washington after they had their "first-ever Orientation Coffee." (That was the heading on the email!) They named their Mentoring Ministry, Women of the Heart.

> *God is so good! We had a wonderful turnout last Sunday in our fellowship tent for the first-ever Women of the Heart Mentoring Ministry Coffee. I had been believing God would send 30 women for the last several months. When we were setting up the chairs, my friend asked, "How many?" We learned long ago to always add one chair, so we set up 31. Guess how many Profile Cards I counted at the end of the day? You got it—31! Isn't God faithful?*
>
> *In His Service, Sue Brockett, River of Life Fellowship Church*

It would be easier for us to get exact head counts, but that is probably never going to happen. I teasingly threaten that reviving the old etiquette courtesies of our grandmothers' era is going to be the topic of my next book. Until then, I do continue through mentor trainings to reinforce that as Christians, courtesy is part of "loving your neighbor more than yourself." My hope is that the mentors will pass this on to the mentees.

Another attempt I made at bringing home this point was a poem I wrote for our ministry newsletter. Perhaps it will be helpful to you, too.

Your Response Is Kindly Requested
by Janet Thompson

You are such a tease,
When you forget your RSVPs.
The poor hostess never knows
If she'll have a crowd or no-shows.

It takes just a moment
To respond to the event.
And yet the worry spared,
Let's the hostess know you cared.

*It seems to be a lost courtesy,
And that really worries me.
Christian women could make a difference
By being willing to honor their commitments.*

*You know if it was you
Who needed to know how many or few,
You'd be pulling out your hairs
Wondering if you had enough chairs!*

*So when the invitation arrives,
Put it in a spot that cannot miss your eyes.
Then before the week is over give a ring a ding a ling,
And hear your hostess smile as you're RSVPing!*

SHOULD YOU EVER SET A LIMIT ON ATTENDANCE?

I have never turned anyone down who has called to register for a Coffee. How can you say no to someone who is calling you from a pay phone in front of the church saying: "Can I still come? I just saw the Orientation Coffee flier in the bulletin today, and I desperately need Christian women friends. How do I get there?" Are you going to say no to this woman even though you already have 54 on the RSVP list, and your hostess is really getting nervous? I don't think so. If you have truly said, "Lord, this is Your Coffee. Please bring to it the women who will benefit most at this time in their lives. We are only having this Coffee because You want us to. Lord, we put it completely in Your hands, and we will just keep the coffee and punch flowing." You know that Jesus would not say no to someone who wanted to come and improve her Christian walk with Him. It would not bother Him a bit if she had to sit on the floor. He might even tell us the story of His good friends Mary and Martha, and the time He went to their house for dinner. I think Mary was actually sitting on the floor herself.

Let me tell you a story that reinforces the open registration policy. As I was leaving the house on my way to an Orientation Coffee, the phone rang. This was before I had voicemail at church, and I had used my home phone number in the bulletin. The phone had been ringing all morning, and I decided to answer it one more time before I left. There was a very young sounding voice on the other end asking me when the Coffee started. I told her it started at 2:00 p.m., as I glanced at my watch and saw it was already 12:30 p.m. She said, "OK," and started to hang up. I really needed to go myself, but I quickly asked, "Do you want to come?" She said she wasn't sure. Then I asked if she knew how to get there, and she said she did not. I gave her directions and hung up without ever getting her name. She sounded so young. I thought she might feel intimidated, but I dismissed the thought and left.

At 1:45 p.m., the first person arrived at the front door of the Orientation Coffee home. It was not a face I recognized, nor was her name on the guest list. I greeted her and welcomed her into the house. She then asked if there were going to be any children attending today. I told her there would not be any kids. She said her 15 and 12 year olds were in the car, but she would see if they wanted to go to the movie across the street while she attended the Coffee. About 15 minutes later she returned stating that the kids were at the movies. Later in the sharing part of the Coffee this woman, whom none of us knew, stood up and told a story that had us all vacillating between laughter and tears. Her name is Jane, and here is a summary of what she said:

"I am a single mom who really did not feel I needed to go to church. My kids have been coming to Saddleback Church with their dad on his weekends with them. I would never go when they asked me to take them on the Sundays they were with me. They kept after me so much that finally today I gave in and told them I would take them. As we drove up the long entrance to the church and I saw all the people directing traffic I said, 'This isn't church. This is more like Disneyland.' When we got into church and I saw all the smiling faces and everyone laughing, I told my kids again that this could not be church because everyone was having too much fun. Then my 15-year-old daughter saw the flier for the Woman to Woman Mentoring Ministry Orientation Coffee which said to come if you wanted to make Christian friendships with other women in the church. My daughter said, 'Mom this is just what you need—friends. They are meeting today, and you should go. You need friends.' I told my daughter that I worked with women all day, and the last thing I wanted to do with my free time was be around women."

Jane went on to explain that when they arrived home from church, her daughter called me while Jane was in the bathroom. That was the young voice that called just as I was leaving. When Jane came out of the bathroom, her daughter said that the Coffee started at 2:00, and she had the directions of how to get there. Jane protested that it was already almost 1:00, but her kids would not give up on her. They managed to get Jane to come, even though she was very skeptical. However, once she arrived, it was as if nothing would stop her from staying. The fact that there would not be children could have been an excuse to leave. Jane said that once she met us, she wanted to stay and see what it was all about.

That Sunday was Jane's first time in any church in 17 years. What if I had said that I was sorry, but we could not squeeze another person into the house? After Jane met with her mentor, I received a call telling me how much she enjoyed her mentor and the church. She has been attending church and getting back into her Christian walk ever since that fateful Sunday. I saved a message Jane left on my answering machine telling me how blessed she had been by the Woman to Woman Mentoring Ministry and the church. I play it back when I need encouragement myself, and I have included it for you to read in Chapter 15.

My philosophy has been that if the Lord puts it on someone's heart to call about coming to the Orientation Coffee, they will always receive an encouraging welcome. As you might have expected, the Lord has constantly honored that. There always seems to be plenty of coffee, food, seats, and blessings. You and the Lord have worked too hard to get the ministry functional to turn anyone away. So, say to those who call to register, "Yes, we would love to have you come, just be sure to arrive by 2:00."

WHY ARE ORIENTATION COFFEES IN HOMES?

Homes are homey. I know that sounds redundant, but there is a certain warmth and friendliness that is innate in our homes and not reproducible in a meeting room or classroom at church. In a meeting room you would probably have women sitting in rows on folding chairs or seated around tables. There is not much opportunity for interaction in that type of arrangement. Of course, if your church has a cozy fireside room, or a room set up like a living room, that would be perfect. We do not have that option, so we choose to use homes.

In a home, there is a tendency for women to sit next to each other on a couch or in chairs grouped together in a conversational way. Most of us have our homes designed to encourage interaction and conversation. In a home, there is also more likelihood of women standing around the kitchen or living room chatting and talking with each other. Meeting rooms signify meetings, committees, and business. Homes usually mean entertaining, warmth, and friendliness. You want the women to feel comfortable getting to know each other in a relaxed, unrestricted, informal atmosphere. Most women are going to feel comfortable in a home setting, because even if we work outside the home, home is still our domain. Getting together for coffee and a chat in a home is much less foreboding than going to a meeting where coffee is being served. The first Coffee will probably be in your home. I actually had the first two in my home, but since I put out the offer for women to serve as hostesses, we have never lacked for a home.

WHAT SHOULD YOU SERVE AT THE COFFEE?

Obviously coffee will be on the menu. Some hostesses like to serve flavored creamers for a coffeehouse flare or heat up a cappuccino mix in a big coffeepot. You will need decaffeinated coffee for those who cannot have caffeine. I used to put out tea bags and hot water, but no one used them. It seems my intuition about us being more of a coffee generation proved to be true. Of course, your experience may be different. Hot apple cider with cinnamon sticks is always popular in the fall and winter months. Punch, lemonade, or a flavored iced tea is good for a cold drink, along with ice water, for the late spring and summer months.

My good friend Pam gave me a punch recipe that is low cost, easy, and delicious. Make it with equal parts of cranberry juice and 7UP®. I usually use sugar-free cranberry juice and Diet 7UP® for those who watch calories. It is very colorful in the punch bowl, especially during the holidays. One of our hostesses made a delicious punch with one bottle of pineapple soda to two bottles of ginger ale. Then she floated orange sherbet, vanilla swirl ice cream in it. Delicious!

Finger foods are best for refreshments. Those that do not require plates and forks are easy to eat while standing or sitting and balancing a drink. Popular items we have served have been cookies and brownies, bundt and loaf cakes, cheese and crackers, and cut up fruit. Do not overdo on the food, because the women really are not going to have a very long time to eat. We have found that women do not eat much in the afternoon.

If you feel you are going to have a large crowd, ask several of the helpers to bring a goodie. You will find that many times the guests arrive with a treat for the hostess. Do not worry a great deal about the food. There always seems to be plenty.

How Do You Finance the Ministry?

Each church will have its own philosophy about how to obtain funds for the ministry. If your ministry receives funds from the church budget, that may be your answer. If the budget allotment does not cover all your needs, you can charge a registration fee and collect it as women register in advance or at the Coffee. Five to 15 dollars would probably be appropriate. This would depend on whether or not this is a common practice at your church. We put out a donation basket at the Coffees and Christmas party and invite women to give what they can. We suggest a $10 donation per woman at the Orientation Coffee, but make it clear that they are welcome whether or not they can contribute. Put the donation basket on the registration table at the Coffee and make an announcement about it in the Program.

We have been able to meet all the financial needs of the ministry through donations and our church budget allotment. At first we gave most of the money back to the hostess to cover her costs for paper goods and food. As the ministry grew and the donations were more substantial, we obtained supplies in bulk and provided them to the hostess. Some businesses will donate or give a discount to a ministry.

Sue Brockett from River of Life Fellowship Church wrote to me how her Mentoring Ministry was self-supporting by charging a registration fee. She says, "So far, it also looks as if our ministry will be self-supporting. We collected $15 from each lady at registration, and will have about $50 left over after everything is paid. I have a basket labeled 'Ministry Donations' and will carry it to every function encouraging ladies to contribute. The church office sure appreciates it!" The registration fee can also be used to purchase the *Woman to Woman Mentoring: Mentor* and *Mentee Handbooks* for the ladies in the ministry.

SHOULD YOU HAVE RESOURCES AVAILABLE AT THE COFFEE?

I would highly recommend that you have resources available for the ladies to purchase at the Coffee. Form D is a Recommended Book List. Have books specific to the topic of mentoring at the Coffee and Kickoff Night. This makes it very convenient for them to immediately begin learning more about mentoring. During the Coffee program, I suggest that the ladies purchase one of the books to familiarize themselves with the concept of mentoring whether they are planning to be a mentor or mentee. They are far more likely to do this if you make it easy, as opposed to their taking the list to the local Christian bookstore. Try to have someone at the resource table who knows about the books and can answer questions and give suggestions. Her official title is **Resource Guide,** and you will find a description of her role in Chapter 13, page 149.

WHAT ABOUT THE HELPERS?

Chapter 7, "The Orientation Coffee," gives a detailed description of all the helper positions you will be recruiting in the future and the role each one takes in the Coffee process. It also has instructions on how to double-up positions and work with a skeleton crew of helpers at your first Coffee. I actually asked friends and family to help at my Dress Rehearsal Coffee.

Chapter 13, "Recruiting Help," discusses how to start recruiting helpers at your first Coffee and lists all the helper positions and a brief overview of what each does, followed by a Service Opportunity Description. Chapter 14, "When Is It Time to Give Away the Ministry?" lists all the administrative, shepherd coach, and coordinator positions, and their Service Opportunity Descriptions. As the ministry and Coffees get larger, you will fill the positions and recruit a **Prayer Day Team.** Remember, it is possible to start with just you, but try not to impose that stress on yourself.

WHAT IS A PROFILE CARD?

Form A is a sample of the Profile Card we now use. Print it on cardstock in a light color such as cream or light pink. Dark colors make it difficult to read what the women write on the card. Another thing that helps in legibility is providing the ladies with a pen and clipboard to use while filling out the card. This eliminates them filling it out in an ink color that is hard to read and gives them a hard surface to write on. The **Prayer Day Team** will thank you for taking these important steps.

I will go through the Profile Card line-by-line to explain to you why we ask certain questions and how we use the answers in matching the women. It would be helpful for you to have the sample Profile Card (p. 222) in view as you read the following descriptions.

- *Date and Coffee #*: This may seem obvious, but when you have had four or five Coffees they all begin to run together in your mind. This will be a future reference of which Coffee they attended.

- *Tape Photo Here Box:* This indicates the place to put the picture. (Further explanation will be given in Chapter 7.)

- *Name, Address, Home Phone, Email:* These are routine questions.

- *Birth date and Age:* At first, we just put birth date thinking some women might be reluctant to write down their age, but then we had to take time to figure the age. However, for the woman who is squeamish about writing her age in numbers, the birth date lets her give it to us in a different form.

- *Occupation:* This will help the **Prayer Day Team** know if the woman has a career outside the home or is a homemaker.

- *Business Phone:* For women working outside the home, make sure it is appropriate and convenient to call them at their place of work.

- *Marital Status:* It is helpful in matching women with commonalties in this area. Women should select all that apply. A woman may be married now, in a blended family, and have been divorced in the past. She would mark all three.

- *Spouse's Name, birth date, age:* This is information mentors and mentees are interested in knowing. Knowing the spouse's name is also helpful if you need to call the home. It is nice to be able to address the husband by name if he answers the phone.

- *Children's Names and Ages and Grandchildren's Names and Ages:* This information is good to have; the ages are considered in matching.

- *Stepchildren's Names and Ages and Living Status:* This information is also helpful in matching.

- *Have attended* **(your church name)** *since:* This is essential information to have, especially when selecting mentors. You want to make sure you can verify that the ladies serving as mentors are godly women with a strong Christian foundation and ties to your church family. Mentees do not have to be members of your church, but they should be attendees. These women may be new Christians or they may be finding their way back to the church and have not locked into a church family yet. If this is the case, your Mentoring Ministry can provide an excellent opportunity for outreach and ministry to these women.

Chapter 6: It's Coffee Time!

- *Accepted Christ and Rededicated Life:* These are extremely important answers. You need to know the woman's stage in her Christian walk. *Accepted Christ* is the date she knows she asked Jesus into her heart. She may only remember the year, and that is fine. The *Rededicated Life* question is for a woman who accepted Christ but slipped out of her walk and then later rededicated her life. If you saw "accepted Christ at age 10" on her card and she is now 40, you might think of her as a mentor unless she answered that she rededicated her life last month. Then you know she is one who needs a mentor. We NEVER match anyone until we have the answers to these two questions. They are key questions in being faithful to our Mission Statement.

- *The (your church name) Statement of Faith:* We have listed six key points of Saddleback Church's Statement of Faith. This helps in determining the spiritual understanding and beliefs of those women interested in being mentors. You can use ours if they are the same at your church or replace with the wording of your church's Statement of Faith or similar statement.

- *Mentor, Mentee, Either, Both:* These categories let you know how each woman sees herself and what role she wants in the mentoring relationship. *Either* and *both* categories give the **Prayer Day Team** flexibility if they have more mentees than mentors. They may ask a woman who marked *either* to be a mentor for this Coffee, and then try to find a mentor for her at the next Coffee. The woman who marks *both* would be in two relationships. In one relationship she would be a mentor, and in the other a mentee. She should be called to assure the **Prayer Day Team** she has time for both. You may not always be able to accommodate this request, but the category is helpful if you need her to be a mentor. You can also offer to try to find her a mentor at the next Coffee.

- *I would like to be matched with:* This gives the women an opportunity to put the name of someone they met at the Coffee with whom they would like to be matched. However, this does not guarantee they will automatically be matched with the person they requested.

- *Is there anything in your life that would interfere with you being a mentor?* A woman signing up to be a mentor needs to analyze her life and make sure she has thought through the expectations of a mentor. This question causes her to stop and consider what is currently happening in her life. If there is a personal crisis occurring, this is not a good time for her to be a mentor.

- *Hobbies, Interests, Gifts:* Filling in this section gives insight into each woman and helps identify commonalties.

- *What I desire in a mentoring relationship is:* The answer here is extremely useful in matching and praying that we fulfill her desire with someone who has a similar heart.

- *Please continue on the back of the card and share any personal or background information you feel would be helpful in making a mentoring match:* Hopefully this will encourage the women to continue writing on the back of the card any information they think would be helpful for the **Prayer Day Team**. Many women fill up the back of the card. The more information they write on the card, the more information available for praying and matching.

Our Profile Card went through several revisions, and the one you see as Form A has served us well. You want to take seriously the task of matching the women. The more information there is to pray about, the more insight there is available for matching. The Lord tells us to be specific in our prayers, and the Profile Card is one of the tools we use to do that. You will see the use of the Profile Cards in the matching process when you read Chapter 8, "The Coffee Is Over, Now You Pray."

WHAT IS THE SEQUENCE OF EVENTS AFTER A COFFEE?

The chapters in Section 3, "The Ministry," discuss these events in more detail.
- The day after the Coffee is Monday Matching Prayer Day.
- During the remainder of the week the women will receive a call telling them what time to attend Kickoff Night.
- Kickoff Night is the Monday night one week after the Coffee. Mentors attend a Mentor Halftime Refresher.
- Mentors and mentees attend a Six-Month Potluck Celebration.

WHAT ARE M&Ms?

Can you guess the answer to this question? M&Ms are what we fondly call the mentors and mentees. And if you turn the M&M upside-down, you have WW which abbreviates Woman to Woman, the title of the ministry. We get a lot of mileage out of this, and have M&M's® candies at every event. We fondly call the ladies in the ministry M&Ms. When I refer to M&Ms, you will know that I am talking about mentors and mentees!

CHAPTER 7

"Offer hospitality to one another"
(1 Peter 4:9).

The Orientation Coffee

LET'S GET READY!

It is important to be organized and good stewards of time on this important day. You want to be ready to start on time and stick to your agenda so you can finish on time. Therefore, advance planning and preparation make for a calm, stress-free day for you and all the ladies helping and attending.

Several weeks before the Coffee, the **Hospitality Shepherd Coach** sends all the helpers a Service Opportunity Description (Chapter 13, "Recruiting Help"). This description tells them the time to arrive and what they will do at the Coffee. Have all your helpers arrive at the host home promptly at 1:00 p.m. Each helper needs to start immediately setting up her area of service. The goal is to have everything ready by 1:30 p.m. If each woman understands that this is not a time for chatting or socializing but there is an express need to start working immediately, you will have plenty of time. For your first few Coffees you might want to ask everyone to come at 12:30 p.m. until they learn the process.

At 1:30 p.m., the **Prayer Day Shepherd Coach** (this might be you at first) asks the helpers to disperse themselves among the chairs set up for the guests. Someone should be sitting in or touching each chair. Then she asks the ladies to pray with her over the chairs. Take this time to pray for:

- all the ladies who will be attending and helping;
- the woman who will be sitting in each chair;
- the program;
- a hedge of protection around the host home;
- all aspects of the day.

Offer this as a time for each of the ladies to pray as they feel led. The **Prayer Day Shepherd Coach** will close the prayer time. The **Spiritual**

Shepherdess or the **Ministry Leader** may also use this quiet time to share a verse or an inspirational devotion appropriate for the day.

Next, pass out Form M, Orientation Coffee Helper's Pre-Coffee Review. This is a reminder for each lady to focus on why she is there and what it means to be a selfless servant. I actually read this with them before every Coffee even if I have the same helpers. You can feel free to modify it to include the specific needs of your situation.

Set an empty chair off to the side of the room with a Bible in it. Designate this as a chair for "Jesus" as a reminder of His presence, and that He is watching and blessing everything you say and do. It is amazing how this reduces the stress level of the helpers.

HERE THEY COME! WHAT DO WE DO NOW?

Cars are beginning to pull up and park in front of the house. You look at the clock, and it is 1:45 p.m. It is refreshing that some people still do arrive on time, not to mention a little early. The **Hospitality Shepherd Coach** takes a quick inventory to be sure everything is ready and each helper is at her assigned area. The Yes! We Are Ready checklist on the following page is helpful for the **Hospitality Shepherd Coach** to use as she checks to be sure everyone is in place and nothing has been forgotten.

If this is your Dress Rehearsal Orientation Coffee, remember that you will not have all the helper positions filled that I will be referring to in this chapter. As we have discussed, you should be starting small. Have the helpers at your first Coffee double up in some of the positions, and you can take on extra roles yourself. For example:

- The **Greeter/Hugger** can also be the **Name Tag Scribe** and the **Registrar**.
- The **Photographer** can take pictures and record the names herself without an assistant.
- The **Ministry Leader** (you) can open in song and prayer and do the biblical portion of the program.
- You, as the **Ministry Leader**, are the **Hostess** and **Hospitality Shepherd Coach**.
- One or two of these helpers can also form the **Prayer Day Team** the next day.

Note: All the forms referred to throughout this material are found in Section 5, starting on page 219. The Service Opportunity Descriptions are in Chapters 13 and 14.

Chapter 7: The Orientation Coffee

Yes! We Are Ready Checklist

- ❏ The coffee is brewed and on the serving table along with cream, sugar, sugar substitute, and spoons for stirring. Another pot of coffee is just starting to brew.
- ❏ Refreshments and punch are on the table.
- ❏ Cups for hot and cold drinks are out, along with plenty of napkins.
- ❏ Camera has batteries and film; the **Photographer** is ready to catch some candid shots.
- ❏ **Photographer's Assistant** has pen to mark on pictures.
- ❏ Smiling **Greeter/Hugger** is at the door.
- ❏ **Name Tag Scribe** has name tags and a black felt-tip pen.
- ❏ Registration table is set up with pens, Profile Cards, clipboards, donation basket, Programs, and handouts.
- ❏ Resource table is set up with samples of books available for sale, a price list, and cash to make change.
- ❏ Chairs are set up with a chair for Jesus, and the chairs have been prayed over.
- ❏ Music is playing on the CD or tape player, if live music is not available.
- ❏ **Prayer Day Team** has paper for taking notes.
- ❏ Tissue boxes are strategically positioned.
- ❏ There is an area designated for coats and umbrellas.
- ❏ A room is designated for the **Registrars** to check Profile Cards, **Photographers** to attach pictures to Profile Cards, and helpers to wait in during the Coffee.
- ❏ **Hostess**'s family is exiting out the back door, along with the dog and cat.
- ❏ The **Prayer Day Shepherd Coach** has prayed with all helpers.

LET THE COFFEE BEGIN!

There it is—the first ring of the doorbell. It's time to start the Greeting—Coffee—Music—Camera—Fun—and Fellowship.

THE IDEAL ORDER OF EVENTS

1. The **Greeter/Hugger** opens the door and in come the lovely women.
2. The **Greeter/Hugger** gives each woman a welcome hug, introduces herself, and directs them to the **Name Tag Scribe**.
3. The **Name Tag Scribe** asks for first and last names and prints them on a name tag using a black felt-tip pen. She then directs them to the **Registrars** at the registration table.

4. The **Registrars** give them: a Profile Card (form A), Opportunity to Serve Profile (form B), Program (form C) containing handouts—Recommended Book List (form D), Ways to Show Your M&M You Care (form E), Scripture Printout (form F), How to Get Involved in the Mentoring Ministry (form G), Areas of Opportunity for Service (form V)—a clipboard, and a pen. The **Registrars** instruct the women in filling out the Profile Card and Opportunity to Serve Profile and direct them to the **Photographer**.
5. The **Photographer** groups the women into twos and takes an instant picture.
6. The **Photographer's Assistant** writes a number on the border of the instant print below each woman's picture and the corresponding number in the upper right-hand box on their Profile Card. She then directs them to the refreshments and the area where they can sit down to fill out the Profile Cards.
7. The **Prayer Day Team**, **Prayer Day Shepherd Coach**, **Hospitality Floater**, and **Ministry Leader** mingle among the guests and check for any questions regarding the Profile Cards.

The completed Profile Cards and Opportunity to Serve Profiles are returned to well-marked boxes which contain alphabetical dividers. It is time for the guests to socialize, eat, and drink.

8. At 2:30 p.m., the **Spiritual Shepherdess** or **Prayer Day Shepherd Coach** announces it is time for the program to begin and the guests to take their seats. She says an opening prayer. The **Worship Director** (or you) opens the program with a group participation song.
9. The **Ministry Leader** makes the presentation with the help of those assigned on the agenda. During the program, the **Photographer** and **Assistant** go to another room, cut up the pictures, and use the assigned numbers to match and attach the pictures to the designated spot on the Profile Card and Opportunity to Serve Profile. They then give the Profile Cards to the **Registrars**.
10. The **Registrars** look for any areas not filled in on the Profile Cards and set those cards aside At the break the incomplete Profile Cards are returned to the women. They fill in the blanks that are missing and return the cards. The program reconvenes and finishes right on time.
11. Each woman receives a hug by the **Hugger/Greeter** as she leaves, and the **Photographer** takes candid shots of women talking together.
12. The last woman leaves.
13. The helpers stay and put the house back in order.

I can see you now. You are sitting in your chair laughing as you say to yourself, *Sure! You mean to tell me everything is that organized. Each woman does what she is supposed to do and follows directions before moving on to the next station. It kind of sounds like "just follow the yellow arrow on the floor to your next assignment."* You are

Chapter 7: The Orientation Coffee

right. In theory it goes as I described, and it sounds great on paper. In reality, the **Greete**r can have five or six women arriving at once, and what do we all head for first? The food, of course. Then with coffee cup and cookies in hand, they ask someone what to do next.

You do not care what they do, or in what order they do it. You want to have a very casual Coffee, not a regimented meeting. That's why you have it in a home. Where do most women end up? In the kitchen! We women love to gather in the kitchen and start chatting. I had not planned on this the first time the Coffee was at my house. I had set up my living and dining room, and for some crazy reason thought they would stay in there. The next thing I knew 10 women were standing in my less-than-clean kitchen and using the kitchen table to fill out their Profile Cards. I just moved the extra food that I was storing on the table and made room for more women to sit down. At the next Coffee I put a pretty tablecloth on the kitchen table and a vase of flowers. I was ready for them. What am I saying? Expect the unexpected and go with it. One of your helpers, or you, will gather in the strays and get them through the registration process.

Expect the unexpected and go with it.

When weather permits, as it often does in California, we set up the **Greeter/Hugger**, registration table, and **Photographer** in the front yard. The **Greeter/Hugger** literally meets the guests as they are coming down the sidewalk. Keeping the registration process outside frees up more space in the house. Then we have someone inside assigned to the front door to direct the guests once they enter the house. We have found it helpful to make signs that guide the guests through registration. The signs are numbered and have the name of the registration steps on them, and we put them in sequence at the designated area. For example: Sign #1 Greeter/Hugger, #2 Name Tag, #3 Registration Table, #4 Donation Basket, #5 Pictures, #6 Arrow to food table, #7 Completed Profile Card File, #8 Seating Area. Make the cards colorful and laminate them to reuse at each Coffee.

The initial socializing and filling out of Profile Cards should only last half an hour. If you go beyond that, you are going to run out of time, especially if you have over 40 women attending. At 2:20 p.m., the **Hospitality Shepherd Coach** and helpers need to start directing everyone to fill their coffee cups and find a seat. If they are still filling out Profile Cards that is OK. Collect them for picture attaching, and assure them they will have time later to finish.

All of your literature advertising the Coffee explains that you will not be able to match anyone who arrives after 2:30 p.m. and/or cannot stay until 6:00 p.m. Now comes the issue of how to enforce this policy. We have tried various methods. The one that works best is to have the **Greeter/Hugger** stand outside the door from 2:30 p.m. until 2:45 p.m. She explains to any late arrivals that the program has already begun, and they have missed too much of the orientation for placement into a mentoring relationship. Then she takes their names and phone numbers and assures them they will receive notification of the next Orientation Coffee.

At 2:45 p.m., the **Greeter/Hugger** comes inside. She puts a sign on the front door that states the Coffee has already begun (form H). It directs the late arrivals to call the voicemail and register for the next Coffee. Try to make the sign humorous and light, but still make the point that you cannot match anyone who arrives after 2:30 p.m. When we started putting this policy in all our advertisements and on our information line, we actually never had anyone arrive after 2:30. Quite the opposite—they started arriving at 1:30!

THE ORIENTATION COFFEE PROGRAM

As our Coffees grew in size, we found it helpful to have a microphone. Try to borrow one from your church, or a karaoke machine will work perfectly. The **Ministry Leader** is initially the program moderator and speaker, but you might want to have a separate position for a moderator as your ministry grows.

The **Program Moderator** (which is probably you) should position herself in an area visible from all parts of the room. It is good to have a small table or music stand to use as a podium to hold notes.

Following is an outline of your agenda. After the agenda, I will give you a complete discussion of each point and the amount of time you should allot.

Woman to Woman Mentoring Ministry
Orientation Coffee Agenda

1. Time Of Greeting as Women Arrive
2. Registration: Name Tags, Profile Cards, Pictures
3. Refreshments and Socializing
4. Time to Start the Program
5. Open in Prayer and Worship
6. Welcome and Introductions
7. Opening Remarks and Explanation of Profile Cards
8. Your Short Story
9. Discussion of "What Is Mentoring?"
10. Biblical References
11. Skit: "The Mentoring Game"
12. How to Get Involved in the WTW Mentoring Ministry
13. Stand-Up Break
14. Testimony from Mentor and Mentee
15. Help! We Need Help: How to Serve in the WTW Mentoring Ministry
16. Break
17. Time to Meet Everyone—Attendees Introduce Themselves
18. Closing Announcements, Song, and Prayer
19. Clean Up

Details of the Agenda

Let's take a look at what happens at each stage of this agenda and how much time to allot. I adhere as closely to this format as I can, and I do it the same way every time. This keeps me organized and consistent. The women will appreciate that it does not seem like something that was just thrown together at the last minute. They are considering entering into a very vulnerable relationship. You need to have their confidence in the process from the beginning.

You may want to write out what you are going to say in each section the first few times. After several Coffees, you will not need as much detail in front of you. I learn from each Coffee. I am always trying to improve and take into consideration suggestions from the women.

Following is a review of the flow of the Coffee, along with the time allotted for each activity. The presentation is for your use. The discussion and background information are to help you better understand the rationale behind the various sections of the program. The number for each section corresponds to the number on the preceding agenda.

As I mentioned, when weather permits, we set up all the registration activities in the front yard. The guests enter the house after they have had their picture taken. This, however, may not always be possible in your area or circumstance, so the following discussion will assume that everything is taking place in the home. Position all registration activities near the front door entrance.

1. *Time of Greeting as Women Arrive*—1:45-2:30 p.m. (**Greeter/Hugger**)
   The **Greeter/Hugger** hugs the women as they arrive at the front door. She asks their name, gives them her name, and expresses to them how happy she is they came to the Coffee. She then directs them to the **Name Tag Scribe**.

2. *Registration*—1:45-2:30 p.m. (**Name Tag Scribe**, **Registrars**, **Photographer**, and **Photographer's Assistant**)
   There should be a designated registration table containing all necessary supplies:
   - Name tags and black felt-tip pen
   - Clipboards
   - Pens either provided by **Hostess** or Mentoring Ministry
   - Programs (form C) containing handouts (forms D-G, and V),
   - Profile Cards (form A) and Opportunity to Serve Profiles (form B) stapled together for ease of filling out and to assure you receive both back.
   - Donation basket
   - A colorful, well-labeled box or hanging files with alphabetical dividers for completed Profile Cards. Having the Profile Cards alphabetized makes it convenient to access them if the ladies want to make additions or corrections during the afternoon.

The **Name Tag Scribe** is the first step in registration so she stands at the front of the registration table and in large, legible letters prints the first and last name of each lady on a name tag. She then directs the guests to continue the registration process.

The **Registrars** give each woman a Program, handouts, Profile Card stapled with the Opportunity to Serve Profile, clipboard, pen, and collect the donation or registration fee. They instruct each woman to fill out her Profile Card and Opportunity to Serve Profile before the program begins. This eliminates forgetting or not having enough time after the program. They point out the box for placement of completed Profile Cards.

The **Photographer** puts the women in groups of two and takes two pictures with an instant camera. The **Photographer's Assistant** writes a number on the picture border below each woman and the corresponding number in the appropriate box on her Profile Card. She then directs the guest to food and the area to sit and fill out the Profile Card.

The **Prayer Day Team, Prayer Day Shepherd Coach, Hospitality Floater,** and **Ministry Leader** should be mingling and answering questions. They show the guests where to put their completed Profile Cards.

3. *Refreshments and Socializing*—1:45-2:30 p.m.
   After the women finish their Profile Cards, they can socialize and enjoy the refreshments. This is a good time for you to mingle and introduce yourself. Look for anyone who is sitting by herself and might have come alone. She will really appreciate a smile and warm hello.

   As guests are arriving and socializing, the **Hospitality Shepherd Coach** (and **Floater** if you have one) look and listen for ladies to participate in "The Mentoring Game" skit (form N). Have the **Registrars** look for prospective participants, also. Ask the ladies selected if they would enjoy taking a role in the skit. When you have all the players, the **Hospitality Shepherd Coach** gives them each a sign to wear (see form N for details) and a copy of the skit with their role highlighted. She gives them a brief description of the part they will be playing. We usually have the parts of the host and mentee played by one of our ministry helpers, and the parts of the mentors played by guests.

4. *Time to Start the Program*—2:30 p.m.
   At 2:20 p.m., the Coffee helpers and the **Hospitality Shepherd Coach** should begin directing everyone into the meeting area. It will take a few minutes. This is a time when everyone is usually chatting and enjoying each other. Socializing is an important part of the women meeting each other, but you still want to be sure there is time to discuss the purpose of the ministry and meet each woman. If you are not keeping an eye on the clock, an hour can slip by. Rounding up 50 or 60 talking women can be a challenge. Have the helpers encourage the women to fill up their coffee cups and find a seat.

The **Greeter/Hugger** stays outside the front entrance from 2:30-2:45 for any late arrivals. She lovingly lets them know that it is too late to be admitted to this Orientation Coffee and then gives them information about the next Coffee date. At 2:45, she puts a sign (form H) with that information on the front door, and she is free to leave or stay and help with the rest of the Coffee.

The Coffee helpers now either take a seat with the guests or exit to another room in the house until the break. You will find that if you have the same helpers coming to the Coffee, they may not want to hear the first part of the program since they have heard it many times. You need them all available for introductions in the opening phase of the program and those with a part in the program need to stay, but the others can rest until the break. Our helpers like to go into another room and eat, read, pray, or just rest.

The **Photographer** and **Assistant** use this time to cut the pictures and attach one to the Profile Card and one to the Opportunity to Serve Profile, and then the **Registrars** review the cards for completeness. At the break, the **Registrars** give the Profile Cards back to guests who need to fill in blanks.

It is very important that the helpers remain quiet during this time, because any talking or noise can be distracting to the guests listening to the program. To help remind the helpers of this, we read the Orientation Coffee Helper's Pre-Coffee Review (form M) before each Coffee. Our helpers have even evolved to taking a vow of silence during this time and have found it a valuable spiritual discipline.

5. *Prayer and Worship*—2:30-2:35 p.m.
(**Spiritual Shepherdess** and **Worship Director**)
The **Spiritual Shepherdess** prays the opening prayer, and the **Worship Director** leads in a song. If you have not filled those positions, ask the **Prayer Day Shepherd Coach** or a **Prayer Day Team** member to open in prayer and worship. I encourage incorporating members of the ministry team into the program as much as possible. Have the women hold hands during the prayer. This introduces the feeling of unity and sisterhood between them. It also conveys a bonding together of Christian women in Christ. The prayer invites the Holy Spirit to come into the house and be among the women. Pray for a hedge of protection around the home and each woman's heart, mind, and spirit. Ask the Lord to speak to the women through those making presentations, and to let their words be His.

Worship was a new dimension we added in 1997. I have no musical gifts, but there are many who do at our church, and I am sure at your church, too. We have a woman from the church music ministry who plays guitar and sings as the guests arrive, and then she accompanies us in our first song. If you do not have someone like that available, a tape or CD works great. What a way to invite the Lord in with praise and worship music, and to break the ice as the ladies sing a song together!

If you do not have anyone musically gifted helping you with the ministry, I would suggest trying to find a woman in the church music ministry who would help. It does need to be a woman, because the Coffee is definitely not a place for men. If you cannot find someone right away, do not stress over it. Remember, it took us a year to add worship to our Coffees, and we did fine before we had it. Now, it definitely enhances our time together.

6. *Welcome and Introductions*—2:35-2:40 p.m. (**Ministry Leader**)
As the leader of the ministry you will probably be the person moderating this part of the program. Your goal, of course, is to raise up leaders from within the ministry who can help you lead the Coffees.

   Welcome the women to the _____ (fill in the number that represents the number of Coffees you have had) _____ (name of your ministry) Mentoring Ministry Orientation Coffee. Introduce yourself and the role you play in the ministry. Introduce the **Hostess** and convey appreciation for her willingness to open her home to you. It is nice to lead the women at this point in applauding the **Hostess**. Mention that hospitality is expensive, and point out the donation basket. Assure them that they shouldn't feel bad if they cannot make a donation. It is a blessing to have them there.

   Ask the helpers to introduce themselves and their role at the Coffee. (Cue the helpers in advance that at this part of the program you would like them to quickly line up ready to introduce themselves when you announce them.) Explain that the **Photographer** will be taking pictures throughout the Coffee for the ministry photo album. You can make them feel comfortable and joke by saying, "These are not blackmail pictures, so smile when the camera is aimed at you!" Tell them you will explain later the purpose of the pictures taken during registration.

7. *Opening Remarks and Explanation of Profile Cards*—2:40-2:50 p.m. (**Ministry Leader** or **Spiritual Shepherdess**)
Set the stage for what is going to happen next. Here is what I usually say:

   "I am sure many of you are wondering what you are doing here, or you might be questioning what mentoring means. First, let me say that while you may not know why you are here, you are not here by accident. God knows why you came, and if you let Him, He will reveal it to you. God wants to bless your life and someone else's through your being a part of this ministry. In these next few moments, we are going to discuss what mentoring is and how the Mentoring Ministry operates. However, we are not going to do all the talking. After the break, each of you will have an opportunity to introduce yourself."

   Next, go over the Profile Card (form A). Explain the various areas and ask if they had any questions filling it out? Stress that it is essential they fill in all blanks. Emphasize that putting extensive information on the Profile Card

Chapter 7: The Orientation Coffee **77**

helps in matching them with someone. Also, explain the Opportunity to Serve Profile (form B). Share with them that the ministry operates with those women willing to serve. If they have a gift or talent they would like to use in serving in the ministry, please indicate that and someone will call and talk to them about it.

Answer their questions and then ask anyone who might still have their Profile Card with them to turn it in. Ask one of the **Registrars** to collect them and explain that they will have plenty of time at the break or before the end of the Coffee to make any additions or changes.

8. *Your Short Story*—2:50-3:00 p.m. (**Ministry Leader**)
Here is a time when you will be using the short version of "Your Story" that you prepared in the early stages of starting the ministry. Now is a strategic time to tell it. This is the short version testimony of your journey and how the Lord gave you the vision of a Mentoring Ministry at your church. Soon they will be telling "Their Story." The more transparent and open you are with them, the more comfortable they are going to feel later. Someone once said to me, "You telling your story at the Coffee made it so easy for women to open up. I can't believe the things they say to a room full of strangers."

I cannot take all the credit for that. There are two factors present. (1) We invite the Holy Spirit into the room, and women are going to feel His comfort. (2) I do start the program by telling "My Story" so they can see that I am just an ordinary woman through whom God has chosen to do extraordinary things. So are you, and so are they! Close "Your Story" with reminding them this is God's ministry. You are just the facilitator. Ask them to help keep you accountable. The ministry is not yours, and you do not want to take control of it. Encourage their future suggestions and assistance.

9. *Discussion of "What Is Mentoring?"*—3:00-3:15 p.m. (**Ministry Leader**)
Now is the time to answer the question that has probably been on their minds. What does *mentoring* mean? What will I do as a mentor or mentee?

I like to start with this quotation from Lucibel Van Atta's book, *Women Encouraging Women*:

"Mentoring isn't just another activity to scrunch into our already over-crowded calendars. It is a relationship, a commitment, and a step of faith. A faith defined as giving God the opportunity to fulfill His promise through our lives. And this is indeed what pleases God, 'And without faith it is impossible to please God' (Hebrews 11:6)."

"I've discovered that a mentor is 'someone close and trusted and experienced.' Mentoring requires no special talent or God-given quality. All God asks is for us to take seriously the task of nurturing and building up other women. In her book, *Out of the*

Saltshaker, Rebecca Manley Pippert underscores this truth. She urges us to do what we can with who we are:

'We must not wait until we are healed first, loved first, and then reach out. We must serve no matter how little we have our act together. It may well be that one of the first steps toward our own healing will come when we reach out to someone else.' "[1]

Then I read a quotation from Vickie Kraft's book, *The Influential Woman*: "Just for the record, let's assure ourselves that women who reach out to women don't have to be graduates of colleges, universities, seminaries, or Bible schools. You may not have a degree from anywhere. But you do have something that is much more important. You have lived! You have experienced life. … No matter where life has taken you, you have gone through all kinds of joy and suffering and you have something to share."[2]

Mentoring is always a two-way relationship.

Read straight from these books and use this as a segue to talk about the Recommended Book List (form D). Mention that there are many excellent books on the list and give them the titles of those provided at the resource table. Hold up each book as you say the title. Recommend that they pick at least one to take home and begin reading immediately.

Reinforce that as Christian women we are to share with another Christian woman how Christ has helped us through the joys and pains of our lives. We are to remind our younger sisters in Christ to go to Christ and let Him walk beside us, comfort us, and guide us. Many new Christian women may feel lost and confused as to how to do this. Having someone who has had a "been there, done that and with God's help made it through" experience can teach, encourage, and disciple a younger sister in the Lord.

Define the concept of mentoring as being available and willing to share in another woman's life. Reinforce that women need women! Stress that mentoring happens at all ages. Someone in her 20s could be a mentor to someone in her teens. If they want to be *both* a mentor and a mentee, they can indicate it on their Profile Card. They may have marked *either* on their Profile Card, indicating that they would be willing to go wherever the Lord leads. *Praise* them for their flexibility, and stress that your goal will be to place every woman in a mentoring relationship.

This is a good time to address an issue that some of the women might be wondering about—should they be mentors or mentees? Reassure them that mentoring is always a two-way relationship. They will learn from each other and probably change roles often throughout the relationship. Above all, it is a friendship. Friends are there for each other throughout the changes and occurrences in each other's lives.

You can read them the following note one of the mentors wrote on her Profile Card after I addressed this point at her Coffee: "I must admit … my first

Chapter 7: The Orientation Coffee **79**

thought regarding this ministry was a somewhat selfish, 'Oooo, how neat to have a mentor/mother believer-type in my life.' My next thought was, 'Wait a minute here—I'm nearly 38 years old … shouldn't I be thinking about being the mentor?' Anyway, I think Janet has just 'solved' my dilemma. It's a two-way relationship—and so it should be, to be healthy and godly! (Thanks, Janet)."

Read what Paul wrote in Romans 1:12, "I want not only to share my faith with you but to be encouraged by yours: Each of us will be a blessing to the other" (TLB). Describe mentoring as:

- ***Sharing***: Your Christian walk and experiences are yours to share. Your "been there, done that, and with God's help made it through and so will you!" sharing will bless someone else, and you, too, in the process.
- ***Listening***: Many of us just need someone who will listen with love.
- ***Support***: Knowing that another sister in Christ is rooting for you to be victorious can be uplifting.
- ***Friendship***: We all need good friends. We are not to be "Lone Ranger Christians."
- ***Godly Perspective***: Friends who will give us God's perspective and not the world's can help us stay on the right path.
- ***Taking Time***: This will be the hardest to achieve. Our busy schedules keep us overbooked and frantic so much of our lives. Instruct them that they will have to give this issue over to the Lord in the very beginning of the relationship, and He will help them make the time for each other.

Remind them that they are there because God has spoken to their hearts about a need or call in their lives. This cannot be another activity to fit into an already overbooked calendar. It is a commitment to Christ and to another woman. They want to take it very seriously and be sure that they are willing to make the time in their lives for it. Assure them that the Lord will bless the time they spend with each other. They will find they have more energy after spending time with their mentor or mentee. The Lord truly will help them get everything accomplished.

Give some suggestions on how to schedule time together.
- Meet once a week or every other week.
- Agree on a length of time for meetings that is comfortable to you both.
- Try to find a consistent day and time that is convenient for both schedules.
- Always bring a calendar to each meeting to schedule the next get-together. This avoids playing phone tag and missed weeks of meeting.

Here are some ideas you can give them of things they can do together.
- Attend a Bible study.
- Meet for coffee, lunch, breakfast, or dinner at a restaurant or meet at someone's home.
- Go for walks.
- Talk and pray on the phone.

- Do a Bible study.
- Read a book and discuss it.
- Relax and enjoy each other's company.
- Go to special functions at church together or to the women's retreat.
- Attend weekend or Wednesday night church services together.
- Have a picnic at the park.
- Do a service project together.

Go over the handout Ways to Show Your M&M You Care (form E).

10. *Biblical References*—3:15-3:25 p.m. (**Spiritual Shepherdess**)

    The **Spiritual Shepherdess** discusses the biblical command of God in Psalm 145:4 that: "One generation will commend your works to another; they will tell of your mighty acts." She explains that God gave us the directions and the mandate of how to do this, and teaching the next generation is part of our heritage and responsibility as Christian women.

    Form F is the Scripture printout of Proverbs 31 and Titus 2:1-5. Having this as a handout allows the women without a Bible to follow along. Discuss the virtues of the Proverbs 31 woman and how overwhelming this can seem to us. Remind them that the Lord never meant for us to try to be Proverbs 31 women on our own. In Titus 2:2-5, He instructs us to teach and train each other. Explain that Paul was writing to Titus who was pastoring a new church they had started together in Crete. Paul was instructing Titus how to utilize the first generation of Christians to teach and model the Christian life to the next generation of new believers.

    This does not just mean older men and women teaching younger men and women. Chronological age is not as important as spiritual age. The first generation of believers in Crete were not all the same age, or all 50 and above. New believers were of all ages. Their instructions were to help teach, model, and disciple the next group or generation of converts to Christianity. That is why you stress that chronological age is not a determinate of whether you are a mentor or mentee. All ages are welcome. Your motto is: There is always going to be someone older than someone else. The Lord commands those of us who are spiritually older and mature in the Lord to help teach the new believers. Stress that even mature Christians want someone older in Christ to be there for them as they continue to grow spiritually. Assure them it is fine to want to receive, as long as they are still willing to give back to those they can help.

11. *Skit "The Mentoring Game"*—3:25-3:45 p.m. (**Ministry Leader**)

    This is a fun and interactive part of the program. Ask the ladies you have selected for the skit to come forward. Ask the audience if they remember "The Dating Game." Most will laugh and respond with a *yes*. I introduce the skit by saying something like, "Many of you may be wondering if you have what it

"One generation will commend your works to another; they will tell of your mighty acts" (Ps. 145:4).

takes to be a mentor. Let's take a look at what this mentee looks for when she selects a mentor." Then I turn my back to the audience, spin back around, and with great enthusiasm say, "Welcome to The Mentoring Game!"

When the skit is over solicit a round of applause, especially for the guests who participated. Then you can conclude with a brief summary of the point just made by the skit—you do not need to be a Bible scholar or a supermom with all the answers to be a successful mentor. You just need to be someone who loves the Lord and has a genuine interest in sharing your life experiences with another woman who may be younger in the Lord than you.

You do not need to be a Bible scholar or a supermom with all the answers to be a successful mentor. You just need to be someone who loves the Lord and has a genuine interest in sharing your life experiences with another woman who may be younger in the Lord than you.

12. **How to Get Involved in the Ministry**—3:45-4:00 p.m. (**Ministry Leader**) Direct the women to the handout (form G) that explains what will happen after the Coffee. Remind them that the reason this is called an Orientation Coffee is to orient them to the Woman to Woman Mentoring Ministry and help them decide whether or not they want to participate in a mentoring relationship. Announce: "If you choose to continue on with the process and be placed into a mentroing relationship, you will leave your Profile Card with us today. If you decide that you do not want to participate at this time, please let one of us know at the break or at the end of the Coffee and we will remove your Profile Card." Explain the process:

Tomorrow the **Prayer Day Team** will be praying over the Profile Cards and asking God to do the matching. The pictures the **Photographer** took are currently being attached to Profile Cards to help the team remember each woman and focus on her when they are praying for a match. Show an example of a Profile Card with a picture attached in the corner. Introduce the **Prayer Day Team**. Explain that while praying over the cards, the **Prayer Day Team** will be asking the Holy Spirit to let the team be the hands, minds, and hearts that He uses to match the women. In a few moments each woman will share what she would like in a mentoring relationship. The **Prayer Day Team** will be taking notes of that also. The **Prayer Day Team** tries to take themselves out of the matching as much as possible. They ask the Lord to put together the women that He knows will learn the most from each other.

Encourage them to feel free to match themselves today. Remind them that the opening prayer invited the Holy Spirit to join them at the Coffee. Therefore, He may be revealing to the guests today someone who would be a good match. Suggest that they talk to the woman, or at least put her name on their Profile Card. Explain that if they do match themselves at the Coffee, they need to be sure to indicate it on both of their Profile Cards.

Stress that God is doing the matching, and the **Prayer Day Team** would appreciate their prayers the next day while the matching is occurring. Ask them to pray for the **Prayer Day Team** when they come to mind during the day. The prayer request would be for the **Prayer Day Team** to be open to God; to be full of wisdom, energy, endurance, and stamina. Address again

Woman to Woman Mentoring: Ministry Coordinator's Guide

those who marked *either* or *both*. Let them know that you appreciate their flexibility, because the **Prayer Day Team** may need to use that option to come up with an exact match of mentors to mentees.

Remind them again that those who feel they would like to be in a mentoring relationship need to take it seriously and give the Lord the opportunity to use it to bless their lives. Point out that it may not seem like a perfect match by our human standards, but they should wait and see what blessings God has in store for them in the relationship.

Emphasize that Kickoff Night is very important in getting them off on the right foot with their new relationships. All of your advertising for the Coffee will have specified that they must attend the Kickoff Night as well as the Coffee in order to be matched. You will note that there is not a time on Form G, and this is for a specific reason. Due to the *either* and *both* categories on the Profile Cards, you will not know until matching day who will be mentors or mentees. If you give them times at the Coffee, someone will invariably become confused. Explain that they will be receiving a call the following week telling them what time they are to be at the meeting.

Let them know that the mentoring relationships receive constant prayer. A woman from the ministry will be a **Prayer Warrior**, praying for each of them and calling them once a month to see how they are doing and to hear any prayer requests. Explain that they will meet their **Prayer Warrior** on Kickoff Night.

It is important to stress at the Orientation Coffee that women who become part of the Woman to Woman Mentoring Ministry will be making a commitment to another woman. Keeping that commitment for the duration of the relationship is a must. Equate the mentoring relationship with the other valuable relationships in their lives. It will require a certain amount of time and energy. If they do not feel they can fulfill the commitment, they need to think about that now. Ask them to think about their motivation. Are they truly wanting to give or receive from another woman? Are they planning on "trying it out," or do they just like involvement in church ministries? "Trying it out," warn them, will not work here. They are actually going to enter into a covenant with another woman. The two of them will be committing to God and to each other that they will fulfill the commitment.

Do not pass the Mentoring Covenants (form I) out at the Coffee. The mentoring matches will go over the Covenant together at the Kickoff meeting. Read the Mentoring Covenant (form I) to them. This Covenant is not something you want to gloss over. It is important that they know from the beginning that it is not going to be OK to change their minds about being in a relationship three months into it, or to later decide they don't have enough time to give to another woman. Someone is always going to get hurt if that happens. It is best to establish the ground rules before they become involved.

Do not be afraid to use the word commitment.

At the first Coffee, I was so anxious for the ministry to be successful that I didn't want to scare anyone away by using the word *commitment*. One of the ladies attending, however, very wisely said, "Do not be afraid to use the word *commitment*. It is a word we are so in need of today. We are agreeing to commit to a mentoring relationship with another woman, and we should not be here if we are not willing to do that." I breathed a sigh of relief. One of the attendees had said exactly what I had wanted to say but feared would be intimidating.

Later I was to realize the wisdom of her comments. I found out how hard it really can be for people to commit. It can be devastating for a woman to decide she is too busy for her mentee halfway through the six months. I soon realized the need to stress the importance of a willingness to commit to the mentoring relationship, even if they did not feel they were matched with the right person. I cannot emphasize enough the importance of commitment to the success of the ministry. Be firm and serious at this point in your presentation. It is not a time to minimize the importance of the commitment. It is far better to have them drop out now then later. As a mentor to you, this is sound advice from someone who has "been there, done that."

Finish this section by going over the Code of Ethics (back of form C) printed on their Programs. The Code of Ethics came to me one day out of frustration over one of the relationships that was not going well. So many misunderstandings come from poor communication and lack of courtesy. Just as with the Covenant, I stress if they do not feel they can abide by the code of the ministry, they may need to consider if they want to join the ministry. I think that as you read it you will understand its significance.

I will discuss in a later chapter how to deal with someone who wants to get out of a relationship early. For now, tell them that the relationship will last for six months as part of the ministry. At the end of the six month commitment time, they will all get back together again for a Six-Month Potluck Celebration. At that time they can determine if they want to continue in the same relationship, move into another mentoring relationship, or not participate in the ministry any longer. Stress that they may not know why God has put them together with a specific woman, but He will be faithful to reveal it over the six months.

13. **Stand-Up Break**

    Have everyone stand up, face one direction, and rub the shoulders of the person in front of them. Then reverse. Let this be a laughing and fun time, but do not let it last too long or you will lose them and you still have a little more to go before the major break.

14. **Testimony from a Mentor, Mentee, or Both**—4:00-4:10 p.m.

    At the first Coffee you will not have any former mentors or mentees, so you can either skip this step or you may have experiences yourself you could describe. However, when you start hearing how the Lord is working in the mentoring relationships, ask the women if they would write down their testimonies for you. Then if they cannot attend the Coffee, you have "Their Story" to tell. Of course, if they can give it personally at the Coffee, it is much more effective. A true, live testimony helps the women see the potential for their new relationship.

15. *Help! We Need Help: How to Serve in the Mentoring Ministry*—4:10-4:15 p.m. (**Ministry Leader**)

    It is important to make it known that the ministry functions because of the women in the ministry who are willing to serve. Go over the Areas of Opportunity for Service handout (form V). Explain the various areas of service available and where you could use immediate help. Ask them to pray about it. If the Lord puts it on their hearts to serve, they can sign up today on the Opportunity to Serve Profile attached to their Profile Card, on the Areas of Opportunity for Service Sign-Up Sheet (form W), or call the phone numbers listed in the Program.

16. *Break*—4:15-4:30 p.m.

    You will want to keep this break short. The number of women you have to hear from during the sharing time will determine the length of your break. If you have 40 or more women, keep it as close to 15 minutes as possible. Let them take a stretch, get more food and drink, make a bathroom run, check out the resource table, and then settle back down again. Those women who have not completed their Profile Cards will receive them back to complete during this time.

    The rest of the agenda is extremely important. You do not want to cut too much into the sharing time. Ask your helpers to assist you in keeping the break short and getting everyone seated again. Here is where a bell or microphone comes in handy.

17. *Time to Meet Everyone*—4:30-5:45 p.m. (**Ministry Leader**)

    Now is the time that will truly be the most valuable in helping your **Prayer Day Team** the next day. Explain that you would love to meet everyone who is present and give them an opportunity to introduce themselves; if they are only comfortable saying their name and where they live, that is OK. However, you would appreciate hearing what drew them to the Mentoring Ministry, as well as what they are looking for in a mentoring relationship. Stress that since you want to hear from everyone, a minute or two is perfect.

    To break the ice, ask a couple of the mentors and mentees that are helping with the Coffee to start by sharing what originally brought them to the Orientation Coffee. Then pick a place to start and begin to move around the room. If someone tells you that she cannot speak at the moment, move to

Chapter 7: The Orientation Coffee **85**

the next person. I have had that happen at only two Coffees. Each time, the women looked at me with pleading eyes that said, *It is too painful. I cannot bring myself to say why I am here.* I smiled and said: "We are so happy that you came today, and I know this ministry will be a blessing to you." Then I moved on to the next woman. Both times, when we made it around the room, the woman who could not speak when it was her turn was waving her hand at me and saying, "I am ready now. Please, I want to talk and introduce myself." Everyone gave them encouragement as they expressed their pain. One of the women who could not speak when it was her turn later told us an incident in her childhood that even her best friend did not know. The other woman now gives her testimony at the Coffees.

What made them finally able to share? They had listened to a room full of women, many who did not know each other before that day, share their hurts, pains, and experiences. They now felt safe that they too could share their burdens, because they were not alone. When you invite the Holy Spirit into the room, miracles begin to happen. Women who have never met share things they have been unable to talk about before.

Have the tissue box handy because there will be emotion from the women sharing, as well as from those compassionately listening. So much ministry goes on at this time just from hearing that they are not alone in their life experiences. In some cases, they have been too ashamed to talk. It is comforting to watch the Lord work as they tell "Their Stories."

Every Coffee has what I call a theme. The Lord seems to place women with similar problems at the same Coffees. For example, at our second Coffee there were 4 women who had divorced and remarried at least 3 times. There were 32 women at that Coffee. What would be the odds that at a church where 14,000 people attend on a weekend, 4 women with this same experience would be at the same Coffee? One woman shared with me how freeing it was for her to hear these other women talk openly about something she had tried to keep secret. She thought people would not like her or would think badly of her because, in her words, "They would think I was a harlot." At that same Coffee, there were 6 women with unbelieving husbands. At our fourth Coffee there were 4 pregnant women. We only had one pregnant woman ever attend before. There were also 3 women with infertility problems. The Lord brought to the fifth Coffee women with deep wounds from abuse, molestation, abandonment, and loss. Many churches have called and told me similar stories about their Orientation Coffees. Chapter 16 has church testimonies and a common thread runs through them all. God has been faithful to bring incredible similarities and matches to all our Coffees. Can you see how just finding out there are other women who understand their circumstances can be so healing to these women? That is why I always say the Lord knows the Coffee each woman should attend.

When you invite the Holy Spirit into the room, miracles begin to happen. Women who have never met share things they have been unable to talk about before.

I could go on and on about the closeness that comes over the room during this time of sharing. I thought it would never be the same as the first test group of 20 women. However, healing, ministry, and miracles are easily observable each time the Lord brings His daughters together. I am sure this will happen at your Coffees, too. It never fails to surprise me that the women are so open. Some have come with so much need and loneliness, and others have come with such giving servant's hearts to help and lead. What an awesome God that gave us this concept of fellowship and sisterhood in Him. This time of sharing is a blessing to all. Many women comment to me after the Coffee that they had no idea there were so many lonely women in the world, not to mention at our church. Many women simply say, "I just want a Christian friend." Some have moved and have not met people, or they have non-Christian friends and miss the fellowship with believers.

The women who will be on the **Prayer Day Team** the next day need to be taking notes of what each woman is saying, because it may not all be down on her Profile Card. There will be invaluable information shared that will help in the matching. What usually happens is that as the women hear the hurts and pains of other women, they will stand up and say, "I thought I was coming here to be a mentee. But now that I have heard the needs in the room, I could be either. I have had a lot happen in my life, but I have been a Christian for many years. I think I could help another woman with the experiences God has given me."

It is important to give each woman sufficient time to speak, yet you do have to keep it moving so you do not run out of time. I have found that the last person usually talks the longest. They have waited so long that they either have thought of a lot to say or they know that no one will be going after them. Anyway, be ready for that to happen. You may need to tactfully bring the last person to closure.

As our Coffees grew in size, we needed to limit each woman to one to two minutes in order to give everyone time to share and still finish the Coffee on time. We tried various methods. What works best for us is to give them a format to follow. Print: *Your Name* and *What Brought You to the Coffee* on a large poster board placed where they can see it as they share. We also have one of our helpers wave a small flag if they go over a minute. Make a joke of it, but try to be consistent. They can begin to judge when they are taking too much time.

18. *Closing*—5:45-6:00 p.m. (**Ministry Leader** and **Worship Director**)
    The time of sharing may be emotional. As a transition into closing remarks, I like to thank everyone for being so open and honest. Then I usually say something like: "Don't you think a lot of ministry and mentoring went on during this time of sharing?" They always respond in the affirmative. Reinforce that if they felt a commonality or closeness with another woman, to

be sure to talk to her before they leave. Ask if there are any questions, and address them now. Tell them they can retrieve their Profile Cards if they have thoughts or comments to add, but be sure to return them before they leave, if they want to be matched in a mentoring relationship. Announce names of women who still have not returned their Profile Cards from the break. Remind them that the more they put on their cards, the more it will help you match them. Also remind then that they will receive a phone call from your team this week, and they need to return the call right away. Make any announcements of functions coming up at the church that they could attend together. Mention the donation basket again and point out where it is. Introduce the helpers who are available to pray with any woman who may feel she would like to pray with someone individually before leaving.

The **Worship Director** leads in a closing song followed by everyone standing and holding hands for a prayer. Important point: When the women stand up and walk around, they will migrate to those with whom they feel they had something in common. Have the **Photographer** taking candid pictures. You can look back later when you are praying over the Profile Cards and see which women were talking to each other. The **Greeter/Hugger** goes back to the front door to say good-bye to everyone and give them hugs as they leave. This brings a nice warm closure to the day, as opposed to women just quietly slipping out the door unnoticed.

We give each woman a keepsake gift as she is leaving which consists of:
- a laminated bookmark with her Coffee number on it;
- a favor consisting of a piece of colorful netting containing a large almond or peanut M&M® and a small M&M® tied together with a ribbon and a reminder note attached with the date and place of the Kickoff Night; and
- a copy of our last ministry newsletter.

19. *Clean Up*

When the last guest leaves, all the helpers need to work together to put the house back in order. This usually takes about 30 minutes. If the **Hostess** has moved furniture, be sure she receives help putting it back. Before the helpers leave, gather them together in a circle and thank them for their service. Then lead them in a time of prayer thanking the Lord for the awesome day, for each of the women who attended, and for their safe travel home. Ask the **Hostess** for receipts of her expenses and refund her from the donation money. Thank her for opening her home to you. Try to be out of her house by 7:00 p.m. so her family can have their home back for Sunday evening. Those of you who have Sunday evening services will have time to freshen up and get to church.

---

[1] Lucibel Van Atta, *Women Encouraging Women* (Multnomah Press, 1987), 23, 28. Used by permission of the author.
[2] *The Influential Woman*, Vickie Kraft, 1992, Word Publishing, Nashville, Tennessee, page 16. All rights reserved.

CHAPTER 8

"He answered their prayers, because they trusted in him"
(1 Chronicles 5:20).

The Coffee Is Over, Now You Pray

MONDAY IS PRAYER DAY

The first Dress Rehearsal Orientation Coffee is over. You and your helpers will probably collapse in a chair for a few moments and bask in the wonder of what the Lord has just done. It never fails to amaze me to see the mighty work that goes on during a Coffee. The unbelievable sharing and vulnerability expressed by the women at the Coffee is indescribable. Until you have experienced it yourself, it is difficult to appreciate the magnitude of the ministry that takes place. It is a revelation of the number of lonely women in our churches who do not know how to reach out for friendship. Even more devastating is that the means for them to do that is not available in many of our churches today.

After you have caught your breath, there still may be work to do. If you were not able to use an instant camera at the Coffee, the **Photographer** needs to take the pictures to a store with one-hour developing. The **Prayer Day Shepherd Coach** (which initially might be you) will pick up the pictures later that night and attach them to the Profile Cards. Hopefully, you were able to use an instant camera and this step took place at the Coffee.

Expect to be tired. It has been a full day and you have been "on" all day. The Lord has filled you with His energy and Spirit, but it is not unusual to feel slightly drained or even exhausted after this day. Relax and take a bubble bath before you go to bed. Do not plan any big activities for Sunday night. You will be up bright and early the next day with a full day of praying ahead of you. Allow the Lord to refresh you and fill you back up Sunday night.

THE PRAYER DAY TEAM

When to Pray?

We have found the sooner we pray over the Profile Cards the better. The memory of each woman who attended the Orientation Coffee and what she said is still fresh in our minds. The designated Prayer Day for the **Prayer Day Team** is Monday, the day after the Coffee. This will probably take the entire day, so members of the **Prayer Day Team** usually do not work or are able to take the day off.

I have talked to churches that were not able to pray on Monday and still had a successful Prayer Day later in the week. Others have started in the afternoon and gone into the evening, and even others have divided it over two days. Be flexible, but also remember you still have to call the M&Ms and tell them what time to come and the **Prayer Warriors** need to be assigned—there is still work to do. My recommendation is to pray on Monday after the Coffee, if at all possible.

How Many Should Pray?

"Again, I tell you that if two of you on earth agree about anything you ask for, it will be done for you by my Father in heaven. For where two or three come together in my name, there am I with them" (Matt. 18:19-20). We have prayed with as few as two and as many as four. Three is ideal because two may agree just because they are tired. A third opinion adds a check and balance. If there are more than four on the team, it is difficult for everyone to pray for each match, and it could become cumbersome with too many opinions.

All members of the **Prayer Day Team** must attend the Orientation Coffee and stay the entire time. They should have experience being either a mentor or mentee. Obviously, this will not be possible for your first test Coffee, but try soon to recruit the **Prayer Day Team** from within the ministry. I was the **Prayer Day Shepherd Coach** for the first four Coffees. At one time, we also successfully combined this position with that of **Spiritual Shepherdess**. As I have stressed all along, do not wait until you have every position filled before you start.

The environment you pray in needs to be free of distractions. Babies or children should not be present on Prayer Day. If a woman cannot attend the Coffee or is not available on Monday and wants to serve on the **Prayer Day Team**, suggest that she serve as a **Prayer Warrior**. The **Prayer Warriors** pray for an assigned group of mentoring relationships for the six months and attend Kickoff Night. Another option would be the **Prayer Chain**.

Where to Pray?

Pray in the home of one of the **Prayer Day Team** members. It is important that the location is quiet and free of interruptions. The **Prayer Day Team** also needs to be able to stay as long as it takes to finish the matching. The answering machine picks up all phone calls. The family living in the home needs to know that this is a very important process, and it is a blessing that they are contributing

"Again, I tell you that if two of you on earth agree about anything you ask for, it will be done for you by my Father in heaven. For where two or three come together in my name, there am I with them" (Matt. 18:19-20).

their home. We have found the best spot in the house is a living room or family room that has good lighting. It helps to have soft praise music playing in the background. Do not forget to think ahead about food, because you will get hungry and need nourishment for strength and energy.

Be Prepared for Delays

This is a very full day. You will see the value of having the pictures already attached to the Profile Cards. If you are not using an instant camera, the **Prayer Day Shepherd Coach** is responsible for this task. She uses the numbers on the cards and the film sequence number to identify each woman. Be prepared for attacks from Satan in this area. It seems that with every Coffee, he has tried his best to delay our praying. One time before we used instant film, the one-hour developing service turned out to be three-hour, next-day developing! We were not able to pick up our film until 11:00 a.m. on Monday. We had 46 women to match that day! The next Prayer Day got off to the same precarious start. I had to have repair work done in my home Monday morning, and one of our **Prayer Day Team** members woke up with a headache. The next time—yes, there was another attack—when our **Photographer** arrived at the photo shop we always use, the film developing machine had just broken, and they did not know how long repair would take. It had just mangled the last role of film it was developing, so we knew the Lord had spared us from that disaster. We had to wait for the pictures until noon on Monday, so we just started praying without them. We matched the first two Coffees without pictures, and we could do it again, if necessary.

We soon realized that we had to use an instant camera to prevent this potential frustration and hassle. For one year we borrowed an instant camera from a lady in the ministry, and then we had one donated. If your church does not have an instant camera, ask your Coffee helpers, and try to find one to borrow. We have found that many stores are even willing to donate the film for a church function. Later, you can use the donations you collect at the Coffee to pay for the film.

Satan does not take lightly a day devoted to prayer that will result in the furthering of God's kingdom among Christian women. Expect that he is going to try with all his might to discourage you with delays, emergencies, headaches, backaches, cramps, broken air conditioning—whatever he can think of to prevent this from happening. How can you fight back? By instructing each woman to put on the armor of God the minute she wakes up Monday morning. If she is not in the habit of doing that, have her read and personalize Ephesians 6:13-18:

> "Therefore, I put on the full armor of God, so that when the day of evil comes, I may be able to stand my ground, and after I have done everything, to stand. Stand firm then, with the belt of truth buckled around my waist, with the breastplate of righteousness in place, and with my feet fitted with the readiness that comes from the gospel of peace. In addition to all this, I take up the shield of faith, with which

I can extinguish all the flaming arrows of the evil one. I take the helmet of salvation and the sword of the Spirit which is the word of God. And pray in this Spirit on all occasions with all kinds of prayers and requests. With this in mind, be alert and always keep on praying for all the saints."

The morning that the **Prayer Day Team** member called with the headache, I encouraged her to spend some time putting on the armor of God. When the delays start happening, put on your armor quickly.

Let the Matching Begin!

Arriving at the prayer house protected with the armor of God, the **Prayer Day Team** begins the most crucial part of the entire ministry. Without mentoring matches there would be no Woman to Woman Mentoring Ministry. What you do on this day affects many lives, as you will read later in some of the testimonies I have received. I should stop here and clarify the last sentence—*you* are not doing the work, *He* is doing the work. You and I are only the hands, eyes, mouths, and brains the Lord is using to perform His heavenly work here on earth.

Let me share with the **Prayer Day Team** some guidelines for this very important task the Lord has set before them. I know that until they experience this process for themselves, it can seem a little foreboding. However, once they have seen the Lord at work on this intercessory Prayer Day, they will be in awe of how the Lord truly does do the matching. I receive so many calls of churches overflowing with stories and amazement of what they saw the Lord do through them. I particularly remember one woman who said, "It was just like you said it would be. I couldn't believe it! At first we did not see how the matches would ever work out and then after praying and changing a few we had matched previously, we suddenly realized they were all matched!" Just yesterday I received a call from Kristi Hambrice at Southside Community Church in Paragould, Arkansas. She was rejoicing that Prayer Day was a day her team "enjoyed as much as the Coffee." She said as they read the Profile Cards, they noticed that two women wrote the same identical sentence on their cards! Do you think they were a match?

First-time pray-ers on the **Prayer Day Team** should read this chapter the week before Prayer Day. (You do have permission to duplicate this chapter for that purpose.) If you have a **Prayer Chain**, ask them to be in prayer for the team. "They all joined together constantly in prayer, along with the women" (Acts 1:14).

1. Pray

To get yourselves in the proper frame of mind after greeting each other and getting your coffee or glass of water, take off your shoes, get comfortable on the floor, and start to pray. You are going to be entering into a day of intercessory prayer. You need to prepare your hearts and minds to be emptied of self and refilled and renewed by the Holy Spirit.

Put on the armor of God the minute you wake up Monday morning.

- Each of you verbally turn the day over to the Lord.
- Ask the Lord to bring to mind any ways you have sinned against Him or others in your actions or thoughts and ask forgiveness.
- Put all distracting thoughts out of your minds.
- Open yourselves up completely to the Lord to use you as He so desires.
- Empty yourselves and let Him fill you with the Holy Spirit.
- Ask the Lord to take all your humanness out of the matching and reveal to you the matches He wants made.
- Acknowledge that you know He brought each woman to the Orientation Coffee for a purpose. Only He knows who He wants matched together.
- Pray for His wisdom, strength, energy, and endurance.

As each of you prays whatever the Lord brings to your minds, you will feel a calmness coming over you mixed with an excitement and anticipation of what He is going to do. Advise the **Prayer Day Team** not to come to this day with any preconceived ideas of which woman is going to match well with another. Wait totally on the Lord to see who He thinks will go well together. Until you have experienced this for yourself, it is difficult to describe the feeling of completely turning yourself over to the Lord. He fills you with His magnificent power—the enabling power to do His work. Power that you could never have on your own.

"They all joined together constantly in prayer, along with the women" (Acts 1:14).

"In the same way, the Spirit helps us in our weakness. We do not know what we ought to pray for, but the Spirit himself intercedes for us with groans that words cannot express. And he who searches our hearts knows the mind of the Spirit, because the Spirit intercedes for the saints in accordance with God's will" (Romans 8:26-27).

After you have each prayed these opening, cleansing, filling prayers, spread the Profile Cards out on the floor and have everyone put their hands on the cards. Pray again. This time focus your prayers on the women represented on the cards. Look at their pictures as you pray.
- Pray for the Lord's will in each of their lives.
- Pray that He will bless each of them and their families.
- Acknowledge that only He knows which women to match together.
- Ask Him to take your willing hands and help you do His will.
- Pray for the hurts and problems these women shared yesterday.
- Praise Him for the joys and praises they spoke.
- Thank Him for those willing hearts who are open to take His direction in being both mentees and mentors.
- Pray whatever the Lord puts on each of your hearts.

2. Separate the Profile Cards

When you have finished laying hands on the cards, put the cards into four piles according to how they are marked—*mentor, mentee, either* and *both*. We have had to use the flexibility of the *either* and *both* categories each time. Most of those women become mentors if we feel they have the spiritual maturity, because there is usually a predominance of woman wanting to be mentored.

Many women come to the Coffee wanting to be mentees, even though they have been Christians many years. After hearing everyone share, they realize they really should be filling the God-given role of mentoring the next generation of believers. They will mark the *either* or *both* spot on their Profile Cards.

3. Read the Profile Cards

After separating the Profile Cards into the four piles, take turns reading out loud what each woman wrote on her card, as well as what you each wrote down as they shared at the Coffee. If you come across any cards where the women indicated the name of the woman they would like to be matched with, put those cards aside and continue with the rest. As you read a card, or share what you wrote when the woman spoke, one of you might think of someone who would be good with her. Temporarily put them together and continue reading until you have gone through all the cards once.

4. Take a Break

Get up and stretch. Get a drink of water. Step outside for a breath of fresh air.

5. Pray Some More

- Continue reading and rereading all the cards, praying for the Lord to tell you who He would like to be together.
- Set aside those that seem like a natural match.
- When you feel you have exhausted the matches that initially come to your minds, take the mentee Profile Cards one at a time and go through the mentor Profile Cards praying for a match.
- Proceed with the rest one-by-one.

I wish I could give you a formula for how we know that the Lord is directing us, or what it is that makes us know two women will be good together. Each situation is so unique and special that there is not a set format or criteria we use. As a rule, we first look at life circumstances and challenges or special requests on the Profile Cards before looking at logistical things, such as where they live or their occupations. We go for the *heart issues* before we take into account the *statistical facts*. You might guess though that the two usually fall into line.

For example, as you look at the Profile Card of a mentee:

- First, look at the woman's marital status, whether she has children, and how long she has been a Christian. Then skip down to how she answered the questions: *What I desire in a mentoring relationship* and *Please share on the back any personal or background information you feel would be helpful in making a mentoring match*.
- Second, look at your notes of what she shared at the Orientation Coffee.

We go for the heart issues before we take into account the statistical facts.

- Third, begin to look for a match for the mentee by reading those same areas on the mentor cards.

Usually when you find a *heart* match, you find that the other areas like age, hobbies, interests, activities, gifts, and city where they live will match, also. Let me give you a true example of what I mean. The mentee was a 30-year-old newlywed of 3 weeks. She was struggling with giving up her independence after doing things her own way for many years. What she desired in a mentoring relationship was, "Some Christian advice on being a wife. I just got married, and at 30 years of age it's a challenge not to live just for myself. But also I'm looking to encourage others with new changes in their lives." After reading this, we matched her with a mentor married one year and expecting her first baby in two months. What she desired in a mentoring relationship was, "The ability to share knowledge and experience as well as to learn from someone else; exploration of women's issues in business and family and spiritualism; new friendships." The mentor at 40 had the experience of marrying even later in life than the mentee. She was also going through a life change of having a baby, which the mentee would probably someday experience, also. The mentor was a step ahead of the mentee in similar life experiences, so they had a lot in common. The mentor could share God's perspective on these changes in both their lives. The mentee wanted to be able to encourage someone with new changes in her life, which certainly the mentor was having. They both also wanted new friendships. Then we went to the logistical areas of the Profile Card and found out they both lived in the same area and had careers. For *Hobbies, Interests, Activities, Gifts,* the mentor had put golf, running, swimming, cooking, and youth ministry volunteer. The mentee answered tennis, outrigger canoeing, swimming, youth ministry volunteer! Both were active in sports, even down to liking to swim, and both had served in youth ministry. We all three agreed that this was a match!

Do you get the idea of how this works? Continue through the cards in this same way until you have most of the cards temporarily matched. I say temporarily because you never consider the matches locked in until the process is complete.

6. Take Another Break

During this process you may begin to feel a little tired or stumped when there seems to be no natural match for someone. This is the time to take another break. You need to refresh yourselves and get a new perspective.
- Get up and stretch again.
- Get something to drink.
- Take a trip to the bathroom.
- If it is lunch time, stop and have something to eat.

7. Pray More

When you come back to the Profile Cards, begin to pray again.
- Pray for the specific cards that are still unmatched.

- Pray for wisdom and the Lord's will accomplished in these women's lives.
- Pray that He will reveal if you need to change any you have already matched.
- Pray for energy, enthusiasm, courage to continue, and a new way of looking at the women represented on the cards.

Immediately after you do this, you should have new insight. You realize that someone you already matched goes better with one of the remaining unmatched cards. You find yourselves doing some reshuffling. Other times, when you do not need a break but reach a roadblock, immediately begin to pray again and turn the matching over to the Lord. Ask for His will to be done. Sometimes singing a praise song helps. Most recently we broke out into praise and worship, singing three different times during the day. How awesome it is to feel the presence of the Holy Spirit. When you have finally matched everyone into a mentoring relationship, stop and pray. It is not over. This is just the first round.

8. Pray Until You Feel Peace

- After you have each prayed for wisdom and for the Lord to achieve His will through you, go through each paired set of Profile Cards again and reread each card you matched together.
- Ask the Lord if there is any reason that the two women in each match should not be together and to give the entire team a peace about each match.
- Go through every match this way.
- If one of you does not feel right about it, set the card aside and begin to pray for direction in rematching those women.

Your job is not over until you are in complete harmony and each member of the team has no hesitation about any of the matches. This has resulted in some major reshuffling at the end. Then we usually see something we did not see before and feel the new matches are even better than the first.

Pray until you feel peace.

QUESTIONS AND ANSWERS

Following are some questions you may be asking yourself.

Question: What do you do if you have an odd number of Profile Cards that will not go into even matches? For example, 35 cards instead of an even 36?

Answer: That has actually happened to us on several occasions. What you do then is establish some three-way relationships. This gets a little more complicated, but we have done it with quite a bit of success. Take a woman who has checked *both* on her Profile Card, in other words she would like to be both a mentor and a mentee, and match her with two other women. To one she is a mentor and to the other she is a mentee. Always call the person to make sure she will have the time to be in two relationships.

As your ministry progresses, you can call some of your former mentors in advance of the Coffee and ask them if they would be a back-up if you need more mentors on Prayer Day. They have already attended an Orientation Coffee and are experienced mentors, so this is the exception you can make to the rule of everyone attending a Coffee. However, they do need to attend Kickoff Night. It is good for them to review the training, and they need to be there to meet their mentee. Of course, when you make that call, you can encourage them to come to the Coffee. You can also tell any woman you were not able to match that you will match her first at your next Coffee. This is the beauty of having Coffees frequently. Sue Brockett at River of Life Fellowship Church used this solution when they had 31 attend a Coffee in September. She wrote, "We prayed from 9:30 a.m. to 1:30 p.m. on Monday and came up with 14 good matches. A couple of ladies are disappointed, but God will cover them and match them in January if they are ready." Another option would be if one of the **Prayer Day Team** is not mentoring someone, she may agree to be a mentor since that is usually the greatest area of need.

Question: What if you have more mentees than mentors or vice versa?

Answer: You can use the solutions to the above question. Another option is to look at some of the women who marked *either*. You stressed at the Orientation Coffee that this would be a two-way relationship. Each woman will at different times be mentoring the other. However, if a woman has been an active Christian for a number of years, it is her God-given responsibility to help newer Christians learn about a Christ-centered life. Take the position that you all are going through challenges in your life, and that is life. To wait until everything is right in your own life before you become a mentor is futile. That day is probably never going to come.

The Christian is continuously in the process of learning how to take the challenges that are going to always be there and give them over to God to handle. Putting difficulties at the feet of Jesus is what a mentee needs to see modeled. It is actually good if a mentor has things going on in her life, because then she is real. The mentee can see that we all have problems and bad days, but it is how we handle it that sets a Christian apart from the world. Of course, you would not encourage anyone to be a mentor who is going through a draining crisis or is not feeling emotionally stable. That is why the Profile Card asks if there is anything that would prevent the women from being mentors at this time. At the Orientation Coffee you announced that if the women were not new Christians and put *either* or *both* on their Profile Cards, they may need to serve as a mentor. Announcing in advance the need for flexibility, and then using it, helps us in matching everyone.

Several weeks before a Coffee, pray continuously that the Lord will bring the women He wants to attend. Ask Him to provide you with a sufficient number of women who are capable of mentoring, even though they may not know it. This may be the stretching that the Lord wants to do in their lives. Only He knows for sure.

Question: How long does the matching take?

Answer: Matching has been as quick as 3 hours and as long as 14 hours. The **Prayer Day Team** frees their calendar for the entire day and evening. That way there are no time commitment pressures. Our minds are open and willing to take as long as we need. We arrive at the prayer home at 8:00 a.m. for coffee, bagels, and reflection of the Orientation Coffee the previous day. Admittedly there is some tiredness, but also tremendous energy from what we observed and took part in the previous day. We are eager to see how the Lord will use us this day. Matching prayers begin by 9:00 a.m. and end when the Lord finishes.

Question: Do you ever worry or have second thoughts about the matches?

Answer: Not really, and let me tell you why. First of all, I know that this is a ministry the Lord wants and has tremendously blessed. We bathe the entire day of matching in prayer, as we repeatedly ask Him to do the matching and give us the wisdom to hear His direction. He knows exactly who will be at each Coffee and the mentoring relationships that will result. Our job is only to listen to His directions and guidance. We also do not settle on a match until all those who are praying over the Profile Cards have a complete peace about it. If one of us feels that something is not right, that is good enough for all of us. We keep praying and looking for a better match. When we have gone through all the final matches and feel comfortable with them, there is a sense of inner peace that comes over each of us. It is the sense of goodwill you feel when you complete a job correctly.

There is a feeling of calm in your soul when you finish Prayer Day. It would be bringing our humanness back into the picture again if we were to start worrying and doubting the matches the Lord made. If I feel myself falling into that worrying and wondering mode, I again give it to the Lord, and then I call one of the **Prayer Day Team**. They remind me of the reasons we saw for making the match, and they assure me that they are still comfortable with it. If they should call me with concerns, I do the same for them.

I have had many excited calls from Woman to Woman Mentoring Ministry leaders after their Prayer Day, and unanimously they say the same thing, "We could not imagine how this would work, but it was a miracle to watch the Lord do the matching! Even situations where we could not at first see how it could possibly happen, by the end of Prayer Day everyone was matched. We could truly see the work of the Lord as He matched the women He wanted to be together!"

A Woman to Woman Mentoring Ministry leader in Oregon who had just experienced her first Prayer Day was in awe of how the Lord worked in making the matches. She called to tell me that one lady said the only reason she joined the ministry was because she knew the matching was done through prayer. The **Ministry Leader** went on to say, "This whole process has been a matter of lots of prayer, and I am convinced that's why it works so well. I kept having questions about how God would match these ladies, but He did it perfectly! We had one lady that the Prayer Team matched who had "family health concern" written on her card. She ended up matched with a lady whose husband went through a near-death experience a few years back. In another match, one young mother said she wanted someone to be a prayer partner. Another woman said she wanted to support someone through prayer! A single mother asked to be discipled and a mentor signed up asking to disciple a single mother! And the stories go on."

Soon you will have your own stories to tell of the Lord's awesome presence on your Prayer Day.

There is a feeling of calm in your soul when you finish Prayer Day.

CHAPTER 9

"Love and faithfulness meet together"
(Psalm 85:10).

The Kickoff Night

The Moment of Truth

The unveiling of the mentors and mentees is always an anticipated event. It is what the whole ministry is all about—the one-on-one relationships that are going to form as a result of each Orientation Coffee and Prayer Day. The entire ministry has been working toward the purpose of women enjoying mentoring relationships together. The announcements, the fliers, the Orientation Coffee, the Prayer Day all have been leading up to the two women meeting each other and starting a new friendship. The high point of the process is when they meet their mentor or mentee and begin to discover what God has in mind for their relationship. It is so exciting when you are finally ready to move to this next step.

As exciting as this moment should be, it took us three Coffees to figure out the best way to do it. Let me share with you how we started and then evolved to today's method. In our newness, we probably created more sheer terror than excitement. I am giving you the old and the new in case you were thinking of doing it the way we started out. The old way is much simpler for you, but it places much more responsibility on the new relationship than it is ready to take.

The Old Way

For the first three Coffees, we prayed and did the matching on the Monday following the Coffee. Then a **Phone Communicator** would call all the women we had designated as mentors and invite them to a training at my house. Since everyone was so eager to find out their match, I held this training on the Sunday afternoon or Monday evening of the week following the Coffee.

I started with a mentor training session and then the unveiling of their mentees. I gave them the Profile Cards of their mentees so they could get all the information. Then part of their training was instructing them to call their mentees

The unveiling of the mentors and mentees is what the whole ministry is all about.

as soon as possible and set up a time to meet. Everyone seemed satisfied with this method, and I really did not see any reason to change until I began to have the Halftime Refresher sessions with the mentors. At these sessions I would hear how they played telephone tag for the first month and had just now started meeting—three months after the Coffee! Others would share how scared they were or how awkward it felt at the first meeting to walk into a restaurant to meet someone they didn't know. To some of them it didn't feel natural until they had met several times. The longer between the Orientation Coffee and the first meeting, the more awkward it became. When I first heard these comments, I thought that I just needed to stress more the importance of the first meeting and making time in their schedules. I soon began to realize this was not going to change. Some women were still going to be apprehensive about making the first phone call and going to their first meeting.

The **Prayer Day Team** and I began to brainstorm ideas of how we could make this easier for them and get the first meeting to occur in a more timely, comfortable fashion. One of them said, "I wish there was some way that we could get them together to meet on that first training night." I began to think through the logistics of this and at first could not see how we could do it. I needed to meet with the mentors by themselves to train them, and I could no longer fit these larger groups of mentors and mentees into my home. However, with more thought and prayer, the light went off in my head, and I saw the answer clearly. I came up with an idea that has worked incredibly well. *Thank You, Lord, for friends that help, and answered prayer.* Not only has the new way proven great for the women, but it also became a wonderful blessing for the **Prayer Day Team**. Let me tell you the change and the amazing difference it made in the immediate success of the relationships.

The New Way

Coffee #4 marked the initiation of the change in how the women received their training and initial meeting. It turned out to be an unexpected blessing for the **Prayer Day Team**, also, as we were actually able to see the end product of all our prayer and hard work. Here is what we currently do with an explanation for you to follow.

At the Coffee you will pass out the handout How to Get Involved in the Mentoring Ministry (form G). The handout explains to the women that they will be receiving a phone call the next week telling them what time they should come to a meeting being held at the church. The handout gives the room numbers and the date, but no time. It also instructs them to bring their calendars to this meeting, and explains that Kickoff Night attendance is required for being matched in a mentoring relationship. You will not put times in the handout because at the Coffee you won't know who will be mentors and who will be mentees. You want to eliminate confusion as to which time they should attend. After Prayer Day, they will receive a call to give them their time to arrive.

Hold Kickoff Night in a controlled environment so they quickly take ownership of their relationships. I suggest having it at church to emphasize the sanctity and seriousness of this step. The Orientation Coffee in a home creates a comfortable atmosphere to meet and share their hearts for the first time. On the other hand, a church setting offers just the right degree of formality to the soon-to-be committed relationships. Request a room at church that will accommodate 8 to 10 round tables with 4 to 6 chairs around each table, depending on how many women are going to attend. If possible, use a microphone and podium. You may need to adjust this step to whatever is available at your facility.

WHO ATTENDS KICKOFF NIGHT?

For the first four years, I was responsible for this night and all the training, and then the Lord blessed us with a wonderful, gifted **Training Leader**. You can expect to lead this night until a **Training Leader** surfaces in your ministry. The **Prayer Day Team** usually wants to be present so they can see the fruits of their labor. You will also need a **Photographer** and a **Resource Guide**. **Prayer Warriors** should arrive by 8:00. (See Chapter 12, "Ways to Enhance the Ministry," for details.) The mentors arrive at 7:00 p.m. and mentees at 8:30 p.m.

STEPS IN NOTIFYING THE MENTORS AND MENTEES

1. The day after praying over the Profile Cards, have a **Phone Communicator** call all the mentors and tell them to come to Kickoff Night at 7:00 p.m.
2. The **Phone Communicator** waits to get an affirmative from the mentor that she will be able to attend, before calling her mentee and inviting her to come. This prevents a mentee showing up with no mentor present to meet her. That would not be a good way to start their relationship.

    The mentor who says she cannot come is reminded she will not be matched into a relationship this time. If you have the time, you can make special arrangements to meet with her individually to give the training. However, you would also want the mentee to come so you can introduce them. This is very time consuming. As we grew, I had to set a policy that everyone must attend the regular Kickoff Night or we could not match them. They would have to wait until the next scheduled Orientation Coffee and Kickoff Night.
3. When the **Phone Communicator** gets an affirmative from the mentor, she calls the corresponding mentee and instruct her to come at 8:30 p.m.
4. At the Orientation Coffee and in all your pre-Coffee advertising, you will have made it clear that this is a very important night. It is instrumental to getting them off to a good start. Therefore, everyone must know they can attend before you match them into a relationship.

    I find that most women really appreciate the effort we put into making their first meeting comfortable. It is definitely easier for them to meet this way than

Imagine in your mind what takes place as these women meet.

the old way. This way the relationships get off to a speedy and pleasant start. Taking the time to make the personal phone calls really expedites the process.

5. We have learned that it is not advisable to disclose the matches before Kickoff Night. The policy is that every woman finds her match at the same time on Kickoff Night. If told in advance, some ladies become concerned or want to know the reasons for being matched with a certain person. They may try to remember who she is, and perhaps involve the **Phone Communicator** in long conversations asking for explanations. At the Coffee, let the ladies know that this information is confidential until Kickoff Night. It would not be fair for some to know and others not to know. They will receive answers to all their questions on Kickoff Night. Most importantly, they will be reminded that their matching was a result of prayer.

Following is a Kickoff Night Agenda with corresponding explanations. A detailed discussion of each area, as well as the lessons marked with an *, are found in the *Training Leader's Guide*, *Mentor Handbook*, and *Mentee Handbook*.

Agenda for Kickoff Night

7:00 p.m.
1. Welcome to mentors
2. Opening prayer
3. Distribute *Mentor* and *Mentee Handbooks*
4. *"With God's Help You Can Be a Mentor"
5. *Mentor Training: "Thoughts for the Mentor"
6. Announce date for Mentor Halftime Refresher _____
7. Question and answer time
8. Pass out Profile Cards

8:30-8:45 p.m.
9. Break: Mentees arrive and are greeted by their mentors

8:45-9:00 p.m.
10. Welcome mentees and pray
11. *Mentee Training: "Ways to Get the Most Out of Your Mentoring Relationship as a Mentee"
12. Discuss Mentoring Convenants and commitments
13. Review Areas of Opportunity for Service
14. Announce date of Six-Month Potluck Celebration _____
15. Introduce Prayer Warriors who will be praying and calling once a month

9:00-10:00 p.m.
16. Mentors and mentees sign Covenants; Prayer Warriors witness and pray
17. M&Ms get acquainted
18. At 9:45 Prayer Warriors meet and pray with assigned M&Ms as a group
19. Hugs as ladies leave; collect Profile Cards

KICKING OFF THE MENTORING RELATIONSHIPS

Let's take a closer look at this night. I hope you will be able to imagine in your mind what takes place as these women meet. I will discuss each part of the agenda for the evening by number, and you can follow as you did for the Orientation Coffee Agenda. More in-depth coverage of Kickoff Night is located in the *Training Leader's Guide*. The following will be an overview, but you can read the *Training Leader's Guide* for specific details.

1. Start promptly at 7:00 p.m. with the women who are there. If you delay starting for late mentors, you will not be finished when the anxious mentees arrive. It is good to get in the habit of starting everything on time. The women in the ministry will learn that you start at the specified times. If they are late, they will definitely miss something.

2. Open in prayer and pray for all the women still on their way. When they walk in you can say: "Welcome! We just prayed for you." What a nice thing to hear when you have been running around all day and arrive late.

3. Give each mentor a *Mentor Handbook* and a *Mentee Handbook*. The mentor will use the *Mentor Handbook* during her training, and when her mentee arrives she will present her with a *Mentee Handbook*.

4. Reassure them: "With God's Help You Can Be a Mentor." This discussion is located in the *Training Leader's Guide* and *Mentor Handbook*.

5. Begin the formal mentor training: "Thoughts for the Mentor." Lesson plans and training materials are in the *Training Leader's Guide* and *Mentor Handbook*.

6. You instructed them to bring their calendars to this meeting. It is good to have a date for a Mentor Halftime Refresher already scheduled. They can put it on their calendars tonight and in the spot indicated on #6 of the Kickoff Night Agenda in their *Mentor Handbook*. Stress the importance of attending this training and encouragement session.

7. It is always good to address any questions that come up in response to what you have covered. It also gives them a chance to talk, since you have probably been doing most of the talking up to this point.

8. Next is the anticipated unveiling of the mentees. Pass out the Profile Cards and instruct each mentor to look for her mentee as she comes in at 8:30. The mentors can identify their mentees by the pictureon the their Profile Cards. They can also use the Profile Cards to get information such as phone numbers, addresses, and review with each other what they put on their cards. Be sure to remind them to return the Profile Cards to you before they leave.

9. The eager and excited mentees usually start arriving at 8:15, but there is always that last one that keeps you looking at the door. You watch the mentor anxiously scanning the room for her, and then at 8:45 the door swings open and in she comes. This is when the fun really begins, as you watch the matches you have diligently prayed over actually take place right before you. The smiles and hugs and laughs as they introduce themselves to each other

This is when the fun really begins, as you watch the matches you have diligently prayed over actually take place right before you.

are thrilling. Have the **Photographer** take pictures at this point, because this is a memory-making moment that everyone will want to remember. Use this as a break time, but stop the break at 8:45, even if the last mentee has not arrived. You want everyone who is there to have as much time together as possible. At 8:45, ask everyone to find a seat. Encourage them to spread out at all the tables, so they will have privacy as they get to know each other.

10. Welcome the mentees who have now joined you and let them know you prayed for their arrival. Pray again for any mentees who are still on their way and for the new relationships that are being formed that night. Ask that the Lord bless these new friendships and open up each woman's heart, mind, and spirit as she takes into her life a new sister in Christ. Ask that the time they spend together tonight will be enjoyable and exciting, and that they will each begin to see what God had in mind when He put them together.

11. This is a training time for the mentees: "Ways to Get the Most Out of Your Mentoring Relationship as a Mentee." Lesson plans and training materials are located in the *Training Leader's Guide* and *Mentee Handbook*.

12. Now is the time to go over the Mentoring Covenant (form I) located on the inside front cover of their handbooks. Ask them to read along silently as you read it aloud to them. Explain that the Covenant is what they are going to commit to each other. Stress that they are making the Covenant to each other. Suggest they take their handbooks to all their meetings together for a reference. The Covenant will be a reminder of the commitment they made to each other.

13. Explain that the ministry operates with women who want to give a blessing back to the ministry by offering their time and energy. Have available the Areas of Opportunity for Service fliers (form V) with the various areas of service they can sign up for, and encourage them to do it at this time. Pass around the Areas of Opportunity for Service Sign-Up Sheet (form W).

14. Announce the date when they will get together again at their Six-Month Potluck Celebration to share testimonies, blessings, and stories. At that time, they will have the option of continuing in the same relationship or just staying friends and perhaps moving on to a new mentoring experience. Advise them to put this date on their calendars and the spot indicated on #14 on the Kickoff Night Agenda in their handbooks.

15. "How special it made me feel when you told me there would be someone who did not even know me praying just for me!" That was the response of a mentor after I explained that **Prayer Warriors** would be praying for the six-month mentoring relationships. Introduce the **Prayer Warriors**.

16 and 17. The remaining time in the evening is for the M&Ms to sign each other's Covenants, spend time getting to know each other, exchange information off the Profile Cards and transfer it to the Profile Card on the inside back cover of their handbooks, and plan their first meeting. Each mentor and mentee will sign her own Covenant and then sign her partner's Covenant. Their assigned **Prayer Warrior** will then witness and initial the Covenants

and pray over them. The **Photographer** will take pictures as the women meet and begin to chat. It is always fun to walk around and hear things like:

"You sew? So do I. You take Tae Kwon Do? No way—so do I!" These were not interests these two matched women put on their Profile Cards. One of the mentors had brought a bouquet of flowers picked from her home garden to give to her new mentee. When the mentor looked at the Profile Card, she saw the new mentee was a florist! One matched couple came up to the **Prayer Day Team** and said they had talked together outside the Orientation Coffee home as they were leaving that day. The **Prayer Day Team** did not know that. Another woman had already gone to the doctor with one of the women who had shared at the Coffee that she was going to the doctor to have a lump under her arm diagnosed. The woman going along for support had had a radical mastectomy and wanted to give comfort and experienced advice. You guessed it—not knowing this story, the **Prayer Day Team** matched them. The woman who had already had the surgery was the mentor. The lump under the arm was benign, but a mentoring bond took place even before they knew they were a match. Then there were the two women matched together who found out the first night that they each had a rare breed of dog never found in California. That was not on their Profile Cards.

Many of the mentoring relationships will come up after this time together to share with you what a wonderful match the Lord made. Again, if they try to thank you, accept their gratitude as the Lord's vessel. Remind them you prayed for Him to do the work of matching.

18. **Prayer Warriors** close in prayer. Have each **Prayer Warrior** call out the names of her assigned M&Ms, gather them together in one area of the room, and take a few minutes to introduce herself and meet them. She will again review the role she will be playing in their relationship and then close the evening in prayer with them as a group. (For further details see Chapter 12, "Ways to Enhance the Ministry.")

19. Kickoff Night ends at 10:00 p.m. Try not to let any of the women sneak out without a hug, smile, and words of encouragement. This is the time they often share with you some of the amazing God-incidences (not coincidences) that they have discovered about each other. It is a very nice closure to the evening. Be sure and collect their Profile Cards before they leave.

This quote from Eveline Davis from The Church at Rocky Peak in Chatsworth, California captures the excitement and essence of Kickoff Night: "Thank you for the opportunity to observe your Kickoff Night last Monday evening. It was a magical experience to see a room with nervous mentors wondering what they had gotten themselves into being transformed into a room filled with women laughing, embracing, and making joyful noises unto the Lord. The love and intervention of the Holy Spirit was very evident. The Prayer Warriors prevailed and the matches were truly made in heaven! I would probably have never matched them that way had I not observed the perfect results."

> "It was a magical experience to see a room with nervous mentors wondering what they had gotten themselves into being transformed into a room filled with women laughing, embracing, and making joyful noises unto the Lord."

CHAPTER 10

"A friend loves at all times"
(Proverbs 17:17).

Six-Month Potluck Celebration

DO WE HAVE TO SAY GOODBYE?
What do you do at the end of the six-month covenant? Have a party! This gathering will be a real celebration to the Lord. I can guarantee you will hear of changed lives, mended marriages, and stronger faith.

After the Orientation Coffee many of the women ask, "When are we all going to get together again?" Assure them that you will all gather again at the end of the six-month commitment. Explain that they will be able to determine whether they want to continue in this relationship and/or start another one. This lets those who may be nervous about mentoring know that this is not necessarily a lifetime commitment. In case there are some relationships that never quite gel, they can learn and grow but still have the opportunity to move on in six months. Some of the mentees may have grown to a point where they are ready to now mentor. As you will read in the testimonies in Chapter 15, most of the women want to remain friends for life! Let's talk a little bit about this party.

WHERE DO WE HAVE THE PARTY?
If possible, have the Six-Month Potluck Celebration at the home of the original Orientation Coffee. It is nice to do this for several reasons. The obvious is that everyone knows how to get there. More importantly, at the Coffee there were many lonely, seeking, hurting, and lost women. The mentees will have memories of where they sat when they shared and the feelings they were having in the room that day, compared to where they are today after six months of being mentored. The mentors will have similar memories of how excited, or maybe how nervous, they were at the prospect of mentoring. They too will have grown and matured in their faith and relationships after spending six months mentoring another woman. There will be a sense of a journey they have traveled together, and now they are

bringing closure to this part of the trip. Returning to the place where they took the initial step of faith and reached out to another woman in their church greatly emphasizes the value of the past six months. This is similar to a husband and wife who return on their anniversary to the place where they met.

It may not always be possible to go back to the same house. Don't worry if that does not work out. I usually ask the **Orientation Coffee Hostess** if it would be all right to announce that we will all come back in six months and share our experiences. If her home is not available, perhaps one of the mentors or mentees would be willing to open her home. Someone will always offer to have everyone over to her house. Another option is to actually have a **Potluck Hostess** position and have all the Potlucks at her home. She develops a team to help her and takes responsibility for coordinating the Potlucks.

The **Publicity Shepherd Coach** or the **Potluck Hostess** (if you have one) sends out the Potluck Celebration Letters (form R) and organizes what everyone brings so you do not just eat brownies and chocolate cake and have a sugar high. The hostess can provide the eating utensils and drinks, and the ladies bring the rest. This usually makes the hostess much more willing to have you all back! One thought about the best time to have your Potluck—we find that 1:00 p.m. on Sunday afternoon works out great. Everyone is hungry for lunch, and they enjoy bringing a favorite dish.

This gathering will be a real celebration to the Lord.

WHO ATTENDS THE PARTY?

Of course, the M&Ms! Definitely you, the **Ministry Leader,** because this is the time you see the work the Lord has done in the lives of the mentoring relationships. I always come away from a Potluck with a renewed commitment to the ministry. The testimonies, some of which you will read in Chapter 15, are reminders from the Lord of the purpose of the Woman to Woman Mentoring Ministry. If ever I am feeling tired or discouraged, attending a Potluck restores my energy and determination to keep on feeding sheep. For that same reason, the **Prayer Day Team** should also be there to hear the results of their matching prayers. The **Prayer Warriors** have been a vital part of the mentoring relationships as they prayed for and met with the M&Ms, so this is a party for them, too. The **Photographer** is essential for pictures of this memorable event. She will also bring the instant camera to take pictures for the Keepsake Photo Card described later in this chapter.

WHAT DO WE DO AT THE PARTY?

Eat, talk, and laugh! Everyone will be eager to share what has been happening in their lives. During coffee and dessert, give a short presentation. The presentation should be informal, because you want to keep the atmosphere light. Start by showing the brief video message from me (available in the *Woman to Woman Mentoring: Leader Kit*). This message is designed to affirm, encourage, and inspire both mentors and mentees. Make sure you have a video-cassette player and television set up for this part of the presentation. Continue your time together by thanking all the women present who have agreed to help with the ministry. Remind the others of the service opportunities available and encourage everyone to participate. Mention areas where you specifically need assistance and pass around the Areas of Opportunity for Service Sign-Up Sheet (form W).

Remind them that this is only the end of the formal covenant relationship they agreed to six months ago. Encourage them to stay in the mentoring relationship for as long as they choose. Suggest that many M&Ms want to continue for a full year; others want to continue the friendship but the mentor is ready for another mentee. Many mentees will have matured and will be ready to be mentors. That is the fruit of the ministry. Your hope is that the ministry is growing and maturing the next generation of mentors. Other women may feel they need a break from mentoring, and this lets them make a graceful exit. Do not feel like a failure if this happens with some of them. Perhaps their plates are too full right now; or maybe they just never really hit it off with their partner. Do not take this personally. Remember this is God's ministry, and you are the facilitator. God may have something else planned for them, and they have learned what they needed through this mentoring relationship—whether it was successful in their eyes or not. He may still be refining them and is going to now use a different method. Whatever the reason they choose to not continue, that is why we have the covenant relationships for six months.

After you present the options, ask them to get together the next week. If they have not already done so, advise them to decide the future of their relationship and then let you know. It is good to be aware of the relationships that are continuing so you can keep praying for them. Also encourage those who are ready to have another mentoring relationship to come to the next Coffee. Announce the date and place and have fliers to hand out if possible. Conclude your presentation by commending each of them for completing their covenant with each other. A nice touch is to give them a momento of their time together. There are several things you can do.

Make an M&M Keepsake Photo Card

Purchase blank greeting cards or design a card using a greeting card computer program. Customize it with: the name of your church, the name of your Mentoring Ministry, Coffee number, date, and a Scripture such as Titus 2:3-5, Proverbs 17:17, or Psalm 145:4. Leave a space on the front of the card blank and under it put the names of the M&M couples. Make two cards per M&M couple.

As the M&Ms arrive, the **Photographer** will take two instant pictures of each mentoring couple together. While everyone is eating, she will attach the pictures to the blank area on the front of the card. You should have two cards per M&M couple so they each have one to keep.

The fruit of the ministry— that the ministry is growing and maturing the next generation of mentors.

Make a Certificate of Completion

Purchase certificate forms at a stationery or office supply store. Customize the certificate with:

- the Mentoring Ministry or church logo, if you have one;
- the beginning and ending dates of the mentoring relationship;
- your church name;
- the name of your Mentoring Ministry;
- the name of the mentor or mentee; and
- a congratulatory message, such as: "For Successful Completion of a Six-Month Mentoring Relationship."
- the signature of the **Ministry Leader** and perhaps your pastor.

Present the Keepsake Photo Card and Certificate of Completion as a ceremony with applause. Completing the Mentoring Covenant is a special achievement that furthers the work of the Lord in their lives. Be sure the **Photographer** takes pictures of you presenting these remembrances from the Mentoring Ministry.

Charms for Mentors

Pass out charms to those mentors who have a Mentor Life Investment Pen. They receive the charm appropriate for the number of times they have mentored. (For details about this pen, see chapter 12, p. 129.) Commend these women for being so willing to pour their lives into other women and thank them for their repeated service to the ministry.

Testimonies

Then open the time up to them to share any blessings or testimonies they have from the last six months. You might want to take a few notes. What you hear is the encouragement you need when you feel overburdened or wonder if this really is where the Lord wants you to serve Him. As the women share, there will be no question in your mind that you have been doing the Lord's work. He has been very busy working in these women's lives the past six months. His presence will begin to fill the room again, much as it did at the Orientation Coffee, but this time in a way that enhances the tales of new found hope, renewed faith, and friendly encouragement.

THE M&M QUESTIONNAIRE

Conclude your presentation before handing out the M&M Questionnaire. Ask them to fill out the M&M Questionnaire (form J). You can learn from the ladies ways to improve the ministry and receive insight into how mentoring actually worked in their lives. Tell them they do not need to put their names on it unless they choose to. Encourage them to go off by themselves to fill it out. They can write freely without someone looking over their shoulder. If they are sitting next to their mentor or mentee, they might feel uncomfortable filling out answers that are not expressing satisfaction with their mentoring relationship. You would like to get as honest an answer as you can to help with the future of the ministry.

The use of this M&M Questionnaire after the first Dress Rehearsal Coffee helped me to know that six months seemed like an appropriate time for the women to be in a committed relationship. The majority of them answered *six months* to the question regarding what they would recommend for the length of the commitment, and six months it has been.

Pray

Pray for all the women before dismissing them to continue having fun and filling out the M&M Questionnaires. The prayer I pray is for:
- those who are continuing in their relationships;
- those who are going to enter into new relationships; and
- those who are going to take what they learned in the past six months and move into other areas of ministry.

I pray a blessing of peace and fulfillment on them and their families, and I pray that the Lord will continue the work He has begun in each of them during the past six months. Then I am quiet. I ask if any of them would like to offer up a prayer, and many do. There is usually not a dry eye in the room, and I know the Lord's smile fills the room with sunshine and glory as He hears the praises of His daughters.

This is such a precious time. My heart always swells with love for each of them as I hear and see the work the Lord is doing in all their lives, and how He has used another sister in Christ to be the instrument that chisels and fine tunes His lovely daughters. It really is such a special moment. Once you experience it, you will know what I mean.

I know the Lord's smile fills the room with sunshine and glory as He hears the praises of His daughters.

CHAPTER 11

"They will proclaim the works of God and ponder what he has done" (Psalm 64:9).

Advertising the Ministry

Before you take the ministry to all the nations, or at least to your church, let's do a quick review.

1. You have developed "Your Story" and can put into words the source of your passion and enthusiasm for a Women's Mentoring Ministry.
2. You have developed a plan and taken the steps to have the new Mentoring Ministry approved at your church.
3. You have recruited some friends and family to help, networked to find guests, and gone through the steps of a Dress Rehearsal Orientation Coffee. → p 52
4. You have prayed over the Profile Cards, made mentoring matches, and had a Kickoff Night.
5. Your test group went for three months. At the end of three months you brought them back together again to evaluate the process and determine what changes you might need to make.
6. You have taken your findings back to the church, and you all agree it is time to go public and announce the new Women's Mentoring Ministry to the congregation.

If you have done your homework in the previous chapters, you now are ready to have some fun announcing the Women's Mentoring Ministry at your church.

ANNOUNCING YOUR WOMEN'S MENTORING MINISTRY
Fliers

Fliers are a good start (forms K and L). There is an exciting new ministry for women at your church, and you want everyone to know about it. Fliers are one of the best communication tools churches use. Put fliers around the church office and everywhere women are meeting. If you have a Women's Ministry Information Table at your church, be sure you always have some type of flier on it. Have your fliers ready to disperse at women's retreats, Bible studies, and fellowship functions; wherever women gather you want Mentoring Ministry fliers there, too.

Church Bulletin

Run a weekly advertisement in the church bulletin under the Women's Ministry section. The weeks you are not advertising an Orientation Coffee it could read *Woman to Woman Mentoring Ministry* (or the name you have given your ministry)—*information at Women's Fellowship Table or call information line* (ministry phone number). Starting one month before an Orientation Coffee it might read: "*Woman to Woman Mentoring Ministry Orientation Coffee* (date and time) *information available at the Women's Fellowship Table or call the ministry information line* (ministry phone number). Our church has a trifold bulletin with ministry information and colorful inserts announcing special events in the ministries. If you have something similar at your church, the following is a sample announcement for an insert in the bulletin. Run it one month before an Orientation Coffee. To draw attention to it, use clip art of two women talking, or a coffeepot and two cups, or border it in a tapestry design. You can use your creativity to make it stand out among the other advertisements in the bulletin.

The bulletin will be the most visible and widely read document in your church.

Woman to Woman Mentoring Ministry
Orientation Coffee
Women of all ages welcome
Sunday, October 20
2:00-6:00 p.m.
Please join us if you are interested in a one-on-one
mentoring friendship with another woman in our church.
Register at the Women's Fellowship Table or call (insert phone number).

If you sense you might need mentors, use the following script for the description.
Titus 2 instructs Christian women to help each other in our walk with God.
If you would like to experience the joy of using your life experiences to encourage
and mentor another woman, or if you are seeking the support and friendship
of a Christian mentor, please join us.

I have not been to a church yet that does not use some type of bulletin at weekend services. Therefore, I am going to assume this is a resource for you. If you don't know who is in charge of assimilating information for your church bulletin, you will want to find out immediately. The bulletin will be the most visible, widely read document in your church. When you are ready to announce your new ministry to the entire church, this will be an important vehicle to use. Here are some questions to ask the person in charge of the bulletin.
- What is the deadline for putting announcements in the weekly bulletin?
- Does the deadline change for holidays?

- Is there a limit to how many weeks I can advertise prior to an event?
- Do I have to get anyone's approval before I turn in an announcement?
- Do you need a disk with graphics, or do you have graphics you use?
- Are there guidelines as to the size of the announcement?

Phone Number

What contact phone number should you use? If you are on the church staff, use of a phone number is probably not a problem. You will use the church phone and your extension. However, since I was not on staff, I initially used my home phone number. At first, I really enjoyed receiving all the phone calls personally. If I happened to be going through a tough time, the women's enthusiasm about being a part of the Woman to Woman Mentoring Ministry always uplifted me. The Lord really used these calls to brighten some particularly tough times in my personal life when the ministry was first getting started.

As the ministry began to grow, so did the phone calls. The phone rang continuously night and day. At times my husband laughingly referred to himself as my secretary. It was difficult for me to do anything at home right before a Coffee because the phone would many times start ringing before I even got out of bed! Don't get me wrong—I met some wonderful women that way, and I love to talk on the phone as much as any woman. However, talking on the phone took away from the other ministry tasks, as well as time with my family. After a while, I become weary of saying the same things over and over, especially when it was just giving directions to the next Coffee. As the ministry was starting to grow, and I began to write this material for you, it was evident that I needed help. There are several things you can do at this point.

1. *Recruit a* **Phone Communicator**. If you have others helping you in the ministry, ask one of them if they will be responsible for registration for the Coffee and taking the phone calls. Ask her (or another helper if you have one) if she would be the information source. If you do not have a voicemail box at church, use her phone number between Coffees when women just want to get information about the ministry and find out the date of the next Orientation Coffee. If you do not have helpers yet, you will have to take the calls, but recruit help at the first Coffee. Do not think you can do it all by yourself. You and your family have needs, too. Do not let the ministry become all-consuming. Christian women love to help. What a wonderful revelation this was to me!

2. *Make use of voicemail.* Another solution that is a real time-saver for me is voicemail. If that option is available at your church, ask for a voicemail box and extension number. You can leave an outgoing message with a brief description of the Woman to Woman Mentoring Ministry. If you are having a Coffee, actually leave all the details and directions on the message and ask the caller to leave her name and phone number to register.

On the outgoing message, ask callers to leave a phone number if they have any questions or want more information, and you will call them back. Voicemail allows you to leave directions one time instead of repeating them over and over to every caller. The callers can get all the information they need from your message.

Following is a message that is clear and concise and gives the caller the information necessary to decide if she would like to join the ministry. Most women feel this is sufficient, and they can wait to learn more at the Orientation Coffee. Later, when you have help, assign someone to return calls to those women who request to talk to someone before the Coffee. Until then, you will need to return these phone calls yourself. However, voicemail dramatically reduces the number of calls you need to make.

Sample Voicemail Message When You Are Between Coffees

Hello. You have reached (your name) *with the* (name of your ministry) *Mentoring Ministry. The Mentoring Ministry places women of* (your church name) *into one-on-one supportive, encouraging, mentoring relationships. Women of all ages are welcome. If you would like to learn more about the Mentoring Ministry, you are invited to attend an Orientation Coffee* (fill in the month of your next Coffee if you know it). *Please leave your name and phone number at the end of this message. We will contact you with details one month before the Orientation Coffee. Also, look in the bulletin for announcements regarding the next Coffee. Bless you and thank you for your interest in the* (name of your ministry) *Mentoring Ministry.*

Through trial and error, I learned a great deal about what to say in this message. The purpose of the message is to give the caller enough information to decide if she wants to attend an Orientation Coffee. It lets her know that she will find out the details at the Coffee. You also may not yet have the help to immediately return all the women's calls. There is no need for that if you do not have another Coffee planned soon. Telling them that they will receive a call one month before the Coffee removes the expectation that you will be able to get back to them that day or even the next. Be sure you remember to record the names and phone numbers of the women who leave messages, so you can call them back when you schedule the date for the next Orientation Coffee.

Sample Voicemail Message When You Are Taking Registrations for Your Next Orientation Coffee

Hello, you have reached (your name) *with the* (name of your ministry) *Mentoring Ministry. The Mentoring Ministry places women of* (your church name) *into one-on-one supporting, encouraging, mentoring relationships. Women of all ages are welcome. You can learn more about this ministry by attending our next Orientation Coffee on* (day and date). *The Coffee will start promptly at 2:00 and end at 6:00. In order to be matched into a mentoring relationship, you will need to be at the Coffee for the entire time. You also need to attend a follow-up Kickoff meeting on* (give the date of your Kickoff Night) *from 7:00 p.m. to 10:00 p.m.,*

so please plan accordingly. We will not be able to admit anyone to the Coffee after 2:30 p.m. Everyone must attend an Orientation Coffee and Kickoff Night for placement into a mentoring relationship. If you are not able to schedule time for this Coffee, we will be having another one in (name the month). *The Coffee is at the home of* (state the name of the **Hostess**, then give her address and phone number followed by detailed directions to her house). *Child care will not be available. All of this information is also on a* (state the color of the flier) *at the Women's Fellowship Table. If you would like to register for the Orientation Coffee, please spell your first and last name and leave your phone number at the end of this message. God bless you, and thanks for calling.*

This message gives callers the information they need to attend the Coffee. We have actually had women call the day of the Coffee and use the directions on the message to find the house. Also, if there is bad weather, our information tables are not on the church patio on the weekends, so the information fliers are not available. If the voicemail number is printed in the bulletin, women can still call and register and receive the information they need to attend.

You want to answer as many questions on the message as possible to prevent making a return phone call. Questions like:
- "What if I have to leave early?"
- "I cannot come until 3:00. Is that OK?"
- "I am baby-sitting my niece that weekend. Will there be child care?"
- "I cannot make it to this Coffee; can I still get a mentor?"

Voicemail may seem impersonal to you, but for our first Orientation Coffee we had close to 200 phone calls. It would have taken a full-time staff to answer all those questions for every caller. Remember, you still have a Coffee to get ready for, and you do have a life of your own outside this ministry. You are going to answer all their questions and more at the Orientation Coffee, and you would not go into all that information on each call anyway. What they need to know before the Coffee is:
- Location
- Start and end time
- Directions
- How to register

All fliers and messages should clearly communicate that you start on time, and that everyone must attend a Coffee and Kickoff Night to participate.

Sample Voicemail Message the Week Following a Coffee

Hello, you have reached (your name) *with the* (name of your ministry) *Mentoring Ministry. The Mentoring Ministry places women into one-one-one supporting, encouraging, mentoring relationships. Women of all ages are welcome. If you missed the Orientation Coffee on* (give date), *please leave your name and number. We will call you for our next Coffee scheduled in* (give date or month if you have already scheduled it). *You do need to attend an Orientation Coffee for placement into a mentoring relationship, and I am sure God knows just the Coffee you should attend. Thank you for calling, and God bless you.*

You want to put this message on your voicemail when you come home from the Coffee. The morning following a Coffee, you will have messages from women who missed it and want to know what to do. They will all finish their message with, "Please give me a call, and let me know what I should do." The next day is Prayer Day. You have a very full week ahead. You are not going to have the time or energy to return all the calls, and that will hurt their feelings. Better that you tell the women on your message exactly what they should do, and give them the comfort that there will be another Coffee scheduled soon.

You might be thinking to yourself that this is overkill on the topic of voicemail. I guarantee that once your ministry starts to grow, you will fully appreciate this section and the scripts I have given you. When I first received my voicemail extension at church, they gave me a quick rundown on how to use it and recommended I write out my message before I recorded it. That was very good advice. When I did not write it out first, I wasted a lot of time making mistakes as I was recording. Other times I could tell from the messages women were leaving that I had not given them all the information they needed, because they still had questions and asked for a return call.

There is one last (I promise) important point about voicemail. You have to remember to pick up your messages several times a day. Coming from the business world where I always had voicemail, it was an ingrained habit for me. When I first quit my job, I kept reaching for the phone all day to check messages. If you have not used voicemail before, it might take you awhile to become accustomed to picking up your messages. Until it becomes familiar to you, try designating certain times of the day on your calendar. Start with once in the morning, afternoon, and evening. You will soon see how voicemail allows you to budget your time and pick up messages at your convenience rather than having your schedule continually interrupted by a ringing phone. It will become part of your daily routine until you can get someone to help you receive and return calls. As I said before, that will be one of the first positions of service you fill.

If you do not have voicemail available at your church, perhaps there is someone on staff who can give out the information for the Coffee and take messages for you. If that is not an option, most phone companies have voicemail capabilities for your home phone. That would definitely be worth looking into. Then apply all the previous tips to your home voicemail box. Regardless of whether or not you have voicemail, the first helpers you recruit will need to take phone duty. Sharing the load refreshes you for the work the Lord has planned.

NETWORKING YOUR MINISTRY

1. Carry fliers with you when you are at church or church functions. If someone

asks you about the ministry, you can have information readily available. Take the fliers to your small group if you are in one. Give some to any ministry that has women in it, and ask them to distribute the fliers to their members. If there are areas in the church office or church facilities for advertising, be sure you always have a fresh flier on display.

2. Offer your services to speak on topics such as mentoring, women encouraging women, friendships of women, shepherding, discipling—almost any topic involving women would be appropriate. It is surprising how many groups will take you up on that offer. They are always looking for guest speakers.

   "I am not a speaker," you say. Neither was I until I just did it. I heard myself offering my services to speak to women's groups, and I noticed that there was no hesitancy in my mind. Afterward I panicked! What had I been thinking? Then the Lord reminded me I would not be speaking. The Lord would be speaking through me. All I needed to do was ask for His help, and He would be sure I spoke the right words. It worked. I am now a public speaker and spend a great deal of my time in front of audiences! However, if this thought terrifies you, then try to recruit someone who likes to speak and would be willing to represent the ministry in that way.

3. Involve ministry members. Initially, you will be the primary source of knowledge about the ministry. However, as others become involved in the ministry, encourage them to also network. Give fliers to ministry members. Do not just rely on your ministry **Administrative Team**. The involved women receiving the blessings of a mentoring relationship will be your best advertisement. Soon you should be hearing, "Mary told me all about the ministry—she is a mentor *(or mentee)* and said I should call you to find out when your next Coffee is being held. Can I come?"

4. Hand out a business card if you do not have a flier with you. If your church has business cards, ask if they will make a generic card for the ministry with the ministry name and phone number. If that is not available, use a computer program and buy business card forms at a stationary store. Members of the **Administrative Team** can carry these cards to hand out when women approach them at church and ask questions about the ministry. They are also great to use if you see a woman you would like to invite to the next Coffee. Maybe you spot the perfect mentor sitting in front of you at church, and you want to share the Woman to Woman Mentoring Ministry with her. A business card is very unobtrusive and well accepted during an introduction.

5. Our **Administrative Team** wears name tags at church to identify themselves as part of the ministry. Print out a name tag on a computer and put it in one of the plastic name tag holders that has a pin on the back for attaching to your clothes. Mine says:

Janet Thompson
Ministry Visionary
Woman to Woman Mentoring Ministry

Information Table

Is there an information table on Sundays at your church? Is there a patio area or foyer at your church where various ministries can set up information tables? Six weeks to one month before a Coffee, put out fliers that contain all the information about the Coffee and a phone number to call for registration (form L). Between Coffees, put out an Announcement Flier (form K) containing general information about the Woman to Woman Mentoring Ministry and a phone number to call for details. Try to have an **Information Table Representative** (see the Service Opportunity Description on page 159) standing at the table to answer questions when women stop to pick up a flier. Staffing the table is a great way to involve M&Ms in the ministry. The month before a Coffee, put out a display board with the ministry name in large letters and tape on pictures from various Coffees. Decorate the table with a colorful tablecloth, a coffeepot with two cups and saucers, and a vase of silk flowers. Put out a registration sign-up sheet and the Orientation Coffee Flier with directions (form L). A colorful display always attracts women to come over and inquire about the ministry, so be sure to have someone there to answer questions.

Other Information Channels

How does your church disseminate information? Take note of any publications your church uses to transmit information to the congregation. Provide those responsible for the publications with information about the Woman to Woman Mentoring Ministry. Here are some examples of communication tool possibilities.

1. Is there a church information brochure? Does it contain ministries to join? Be sure to put the Women's Woman to Woman Mentoring Ministry material in it.
2. Does your church have a lay counseling or biblical counseling ministry? Many women seeking this counseling also need a woman friend and someone to help them grow spiritually. We receive referrals from the lay counselors who have the Woman to Woman Mentoring Ministry information and phone number.
3. Is there a church newsletter that features articles about what is happening in various ministries? Have one of your M&Ms serve as a liaison to the newsletter staff. She can send the editors Orientation Coffee dates and give them information for articles on the growth, latest happenings, and blessings of your Woman to Woman Mentoring Ministry.
4. Is there a church class that focuses on helping members discover their spiritual gifts and areas of ministry in which they can participate? When they complete the class, do they receive a list of ministry opportunities? The Woman to Woman Mentoring Ministry should be on that list!
5. Do you have an internet ministry that provides 24-hour information about the church and a web page for ministries? This is a great place to announce Orientation Coffees and give general information about the ministry and a link for them to register.

A colorful display always attracts women.

6. Many churches have video screens in the sanctuary to display the church service. Often, before the services, they scroll through events happening in the church. Ask for an announcement on the screen that reads: *(name of your Mentoring Ministry)* Mentoring Ministry welcomes *(your church)* women of all ages to grow in their spiritual walk with the Lord through one-on-one encouraging, supporting, friendships. For information call *(ministry phone line)*.

Does that give you some ideas? While your church may not have the exact same publications and means of communication I suggested, I am sure you can identify similar opportunities in your church. For example, do you have a welcome package for new members? This is a great place to include a flier about the Woman to Woman Mentoring Ministry. How do people at your church find out what is happening at the church and areas where they can become involved? Whatever methods are used at your church, be sure you have information about the Woman to Woman Mentoring Ministry included.

Names and Numbers

Take down names and phone numbers. Be prepared. When the word gets out that there is an exciting new ministry for women, the phone is going to start ringing. This is what you have worked and waited for, so you do need to have a system ready to record their names and phone numbers. This may seem obvious to you, but I found myself writing names down on scraps of paper wherever I was when the phone rang. Later when I had voicemail at the church, I might pick up the phone and check messages while I was standing in the kitchen. I would panic when the voice on the other end said I had 12 messages. I picked up an envelope or magazine and started writing. Then I was always worrying that I would lose whatever I wrote on, or forget to transfer it to a list. If you are on staff at the church office, you will probably have a secretary keep this information for you. If you are a layperson like me (and your future helpers will be), you need a system.

I have learned to use a phone message book that has duplicate copy pages that are spiral bound. I keep one of these books by all my phones. That way I have a running record of all my messages. Just remember to check all of your message books if you have more than one phone. I seldom find a reason to tear off the first copy of the message, but if I do, the duplicate feature keeps the message safe. After I have taken care of the message or transferred the name and number into the computer, I put a line through the message indicating I have taken care of it. I shared this system with one of my helpers who was lamenting that she had pink notes and Post-its® everywhere. She was having trouble remembering who said what and the sequence of the calls. The other nice thing about having the messages bound is that they remain in sequence. The ministry helper thanked me profusely for this system that helped her eliminate the stress she was encountering.

Form T is a roster format that allows you to keep a running list of all the women participating in the ministry, according to the Coffee they attended. This system allows you to use only one form for a number of functions. After a Coffee,

Chapter 11: Advertising the Ministry **119**

record the matched names on the roster as mentors and mentees. In the first column, the *M* is for mentor and *E* for mentee. There is a number beside each. (1M next to the mentor's name and 1E next to the mentee's name indicates a matched M&M pair. See form T for an example.)

Letters Versus Phone Calls

Should we send out invitation letters to those women on a waiting list for the next Coffee? In my experience, the answer to that question is *no*. Let me qualify that. Letters by themselves will not be sufficient. If you are going to send out invitation letters, mail them one month to three weeks before the Coffee. A week before the Coffee, you are going to have to call everyone anyway—even those who did RSVP—because people forget to put it on their calendars and they lose directions. After the first two Coffees, I determined that mailing out the letters was a waste of postage. Everyone was going to need a reminder phone call anyway, so why not just eliminate one step that did not seem very effective.

Let me share with you the system that I found works for us. Give your **Phone Communicators** the following lists of women to call.

1. Three weeks before the Coffee, call:
   - all women on the waiting list who called right after the last Coffee.
   - all women who RSVPed to the last Coffee but did not actually come. Do not ask why they did not attend. Just tell them you know they wanted to come but could not make it, and you wanted to invite them to the next Coffee. This is not a guilt call. It is a grace call. They probably did not call you on their own initiative because they never called and canceled for the last Coffee. Ignore that. You just want to let them know you would love to have them attend this one.
2. The week before the Coffee, call:
   - those women who have registered. This includes all women who have called from announcements, fliers, bulletin notices, word of mouth, and women you called three weeks ago! They are grateful for the reminder, and you will get a better idea of who is actually coming. Notice I said *idea*. You never really know for certain. At this point, you and your helpers have done your best. Now relax and let God do His best.

You may have noticed that I used the word *register* above. When I first started making fliers and sending out letters, I asked for RSVPs, and I have told you how ineffective that was. Then one day I noticed a flier for a women's Bible study group. They had used the words *registration is a must*. Then it hit me—RSVP is an appreciated courtesy, whereas the word *register* sounds like something you must do if you want to participate. The other thought is to charge a registration fee. Women might be more accountable if they have already paid. Many women expect to pay at the door, so that may or may not help with advance planning.

120 *Woman to Woman Mentoring: Ministry Coordinator's Guide*

CHAPTER 12

"For this very reason, make every effort to add to your faith goodness; and to goodness, knowledge; and to knowledge, self-control; and to self-control, perseverance; and to perseverance, godliness; and to godliness, brotherly kindness; and to brotherly kindness, love. For if you possess these qualities in increasing measure, they will keep you from being ineffective and unproductive in your knowledge of our Lord Jesus Christ" (2 Peter 1:5-8).

Ways to Enhance the Ministry

THROUGH PRAYER
Prayer Warriors

As the women leave the Kickoff Night, sometimes arm-in-arm, sometimes with big hugs for each other, I say a special prayer of thanks to the Lord. I thank the Lord for using me to start this ministry, for matching these women so beautifully, and for the women and their special uniqueness. I thank the Lord for giving these women an opportunity to share in each other's lives. Then I pray a prayer of blessing for their relationships. A blessing of time for each other, spiritual growth, energy, love, friendship, openness, and healing for the brokenness. I continuously pray for the ministry and all the mentoring relationships.

However, as the ministry began to grow, I quickly realized that I would not be able to personally pray for each relationship on a daily basis. By the fourth Coffee, we had 135 women in the ministry and that number doubled by the seventh Coffee. I could pray for all of them as a group, but I wanted them each bathed in individual prayer. **Prayer Warriors** were the answer. **Prayer Warriors** evolved after the second Coffee. I asked 4 women whom I knew had strong prayer lives, if they would each pray for 4 mentoring relationships and call the 8 assigned women once a month. All 4 women agreed, and we were off and running with our first **Prayer Warriors**.

The **Prayer Warriors** are your communication link. As the ministry grows, it will be impossible for you to stay in touch personally with all the women in the ministry. The **Prayer Warriors** do that for you. If they run into a problem or question they cannot answer, they call and talk with the **Prayer Warrior**

Shepherd Coach. This is also the avenue you have for knowing if a particular relationship is struggling, or if there is a situation in which your **Ministry Relations Shepherdess**, or you, need to become involved.

Prayer Warriors must be former mentors or mentees. They need to have experienced the ups and downs of a mentoring relationship, so they can relate to the women they are praying for and be equipped to give them constructive input. This will not be possible at your first Coffee, so select women whom you know have a fervent prayer life and an understanding of mentoring and ask them to pray for your dress rehearsal M&Ms. A good place to recruit **Prayer Warriors** is at the Six-Month Potluck Celebration. These M&Ms have just experienced a relationship and the blessings of their **Prayer Warriors**, and many of them want to serve in this way themselves.

The Prayer Warrior Shepherd Coach performs the following steps after each Coffee:

- updates the Mentoring Roster (form T). This form allows her to keep an updated roster of all the M&Ms in the ministry. In the first column, the M stands for mentor and the E for mentee. Each mentoring relationship will have the same number by it. For example, 11M and 11E are in the same relationship. If you have a three-way relationship use an EM by the name of the woman in the middle. She is a mentee of the woman above her name and a mentor to the woman below. All three women will have the same number by their names—48M mentors 48EM and 48EM is mentoring 48E.

- assigns the **Prayer Warriors** a group of mentoring relationships and puts the number of the M&M relationship from the roster onto the Prayer Warrior Journal (form U). She tries not to assign more than 6 mentoring relationships to a **Prayer Warrior**. Calling 12 women once a month and praying for them daily is probably a maximum comfortable number for someone. The Prayer Warrior Journal allows the **Prayer Warriors** to note each time they pray for the women and check off when they call them each month. There is a section to write the prayer requests and praises they receive when making the phone calls.

- compiles the Mentoring Roster (form T), Prayer Warrior Guidelines (form S), Prayer Warrior Journal (form U), and the Prayer Warrior Service Opportunity Description (chapter 13, p. 157) into a Prayer Warrior Handbook given to each **Prayer Warrior** on Kickoff Night. She staples the forms together or put them in a nice folder.

The **Prayer Warriors** attend Kickoff Night, arriving at 8:00 p.m. They meet in a separate room with the **Prayer Warrior Shepherd Coach** who gives them their **Prayer Warrior Handbooks** and reviews it with them. The **Prayer Warrior Shepherd Coach** may prefer to meet with the **Prayer Warriors** at a coffee shop at 8:00 p.m., and then come to the Kickoff Night meeting together at 9:00. Either way works well.

At Kickoff Night, the **Prayer Warriors** meet their assigned mentoring relationships. They initial the M&Ms signed Mentoring Covenants (form I) and

Thank the Lord for giving these women an opportunity to share in each other's lives.

pray for each M&M pair. At 9:45 the **Prayer Warriors** gather in a group all those they will be praying for and take a few minutes to meet the ladies. They all pray together before they leave. This first meeting establishes a relationship between the mentors, mentees, and **Prayer Warriors.**

Prayer Warriors make a phone call to their assigned mentors and mentees the first week of each month and ask for prayer requests. They commit to pray for these requests throughout the coming month. They also meet with their assigned mentors as a group during the second month of the relationships, and meet with all their assigned mentors and mentees as a group during the fifth month. These meetings do not have a formal agenda. They are an opportunity for the **Prayer Warrior** to have personal interaction with the women they have been praying for, and to allow the group to share and learn from each other. At the first of each month, the **Prayer Warrior Shepherd Coach** calls all the **Prayer Warriors** to be sure they have made their monthly phone calls and to see if they need any assistance. The **Prayer Warriors** prayer assignment is for the six-month duration of the mentoring relationship commitment. When that group has finished their six months, the **Prayer Warriors** take another group.

Prayer Chain

As the Woman to Woman Mentoring Ministry approached the fall of its first year, the Lord put on my heart to start a Prayer Chain. I had just read Evelyn Christenson's book, *What Happens When Women Pray.* Hundreds of women were joining the ministry, and I knew there were probably many prayer requests. "What if we began to pray for each other?" I asked the Lord. "What would God do in these women's lives and in our ministry?"

In a newsletter to the Woman to Woman ladies, I expressed that thought as well as my dream to provide a Prayer Chain for our ministry. I asked them to pray about it and call me if the Lord put it on someone's heart to research how to start one. Several weeks later, a mentor who was recuperating at home from an accident called and said she had lots of telephone time and would be happy to do the research and actually start and lead the Prayer Chain! That was my confirmation that, indeed, the Lord did want us to see what would happen when Woman to Woman women prayed for each other.

This may not be something you can start right away in your ministry and, of course, you need women in the ministry to form the Prayer Chain. Plan for it, and when you have a **Prayer Chain Shepherd Coach**, start one. As always, my advice is to start small. The other advice I would give you is to keep it simple. You do not want this to be so complicated or time consuming that it becomes more of an effort than a privilege to pray.

Organizationally, a **Prayer Chain Shepherd Coach** leads the Prayer Chain. Under her are **Prayer Chain Shepherds**, and each **Shepherd** has 12 **Prayer Chain Lights** in her chain. Chapter 13 discusses how to recruit help, and contains the Service Opportunity Descriptions for each of these positions. We called the

What if we began to pray for each other? What would God do in these women's lives and in our ministry?

Prayer Chain pray-ers, **Lights**, because we envisioned the Prayer Chain lighting up as they received and prayed for the prayer requests. I will give you the format for the Woman to Woman Prayer Chain, and you can adapt it to your church.

> *Woman to Woman Mentoring Prayer Chain*
> 1. Instruct M&Ms to call the ministry phone line and leave prayer requests on the voicemail box. This is a private line accessed only by several **Administrative Team** members.
> 2. The **Prayer Chain Shepherds**, on a rotating schedule, pick up those prayer requests and pray them onto a second voicemail box exclusive to the Prayer Chain.
> 3. Then the **Prayer Chain Lights** can call the second voicemail box 24-hours-a-day at their convenience, pick up the prayer requests, and pray for them.
> 4. The **Prayer Chain Shepherds** monitor when to remove prayer requests from the voicemail boxes.
> 5. The **Prayer Chain Shepherd Coach** interviews all **Shepherds** and **Lights** and instructs them in the Prayer Chain procedure and the importance of confidentiality and privacy.
> 6. Never give the ministry and Prayer Chain voicemail passwords for retrieving prayer requests to anyone outside the Prayer Chain.
> 7. Never discuss prayer requests outside of praying for them on the Prayer Chain! That also means no discussion with the person who left the prayer request. The prayer requests are left privately, and that is how they stay. Prayers lifted only to the Lord.
> 8. When you have a Prayer Chain up and running, include a Prayer Chain information sheet in your Coffee handouts and always have an article about it in your newsletters. We also encourage the ladies to call back with praises.
> 9. The Prayer Chain prays for all of the ministry events and any special needs we might have for those events.
> 10. The **Prayer Chain Shepherd Coach** is on the **Administrative Team**, so she is aware of the events and needs of the ministry and can put these requests on the Prayer Chain. You might ask your **Prayer Day Shepherd Coach** if she would also oversee the Prayer Chain. Prayer Day only occurs several times a year, so this is a good combination of efforts.

THROUGH TRAINING

Kickoff Night is the night for the mentors and mentees to meet their matches, but it is also a night of training. We do not match any woman who cannot attend this night because the information they learn is essential for both of them to hear and understand. They also are making a formal commitment to each other, and we feel it is vital that they have this time together to meet and determine if they are willing to make and honor that commitment.

Midway through each six-month commitment, gather the mentors back for the Mentor Halftime Refresher session. This is also a time for them to share any stories, testimonies, and blessings from their relationships. Encourage the mentors at these sessions to share any struggles they are having, perhaps with meeting regularly or praying together. Usually someone else in the group has a suggestion of how they worked through a similar situation in their relationship. It seems that there will always be those who meet regularly at the same time every week, and there will be others who have only met twice in two months. It is encouraging for them to hear from each other that regular meetings are achievable. The *Training Leader's Guide* and the *Mentor* and *Mentee Handbooks* contain the agenda, lesson plans, and training materials for both training nights.

Through Chance Meetings

I hope you have a good memory for names because you will soon find yourself surrounded by women from the Mentoring Ministry whenever you are at church or at a church function. It is exciting to have them come up to you and share how their relationships are going. My husband teases that he is afraid to leave me alone or even let me leave his side to go to the bathroom, because I may not be back for an hour. I cannot go to church without running into mentors and mentees, and I always ask them how their mentoring relationships are going. In the beginning, I used to ask this question hesitantly because I was not sure I wanted to hear the answer. However, as their faces lit up in big smiles and they began telling me the wonderful things happening as a result of their mentoring friendships, I realized what a mighty work the Lord was doing in these women's lives.

An added blessing of this type of ministry in a large church is that the other women have the same experience you do. They suddenly find they know at least 30 or 40 more women from the Coffee they attended or the mentor's training. New Christians or new attendees will realize that they have found a home at your church. On Sunday morning, chances are pretty good that they will know someone to say hello to on the church patio. Better yet, they may be attending church with their mentor who can introduce them to people.

I am so grateful that the Lord has given me a new gift of name recollection. I was never good at this before, but now I am able to remember almost every woman's name. This is important to the women. I know they appreciate that I call them by name. Now that we have hundreds of women in the Woman to Woman Mentoring Ministry, I often feel that I could be reaching my limit. I hope not. I would be grateful if the Lord would continue to help me know His sheep by name.

As their faces lit up in big smiles and they began telling me the wonderful things happening as a result of their mentoring friendships, I realized what a mighty work the Lord was doing in these women's lives.

Through Communication

In a large church, communication can be a challenge. If there are multiple weekend church services, you might only regularly see the women who attend the same service you do. Also, the design of the Woman to Woman Mentoring Ministry is one-on-one relationships. Once the matched women start having their own weekly meetings, you may not see them on a regular basis. This makes it difficult to disseminate information. As the ministry begins to grow, you are going to have a wealth of information to pass on to them. In the beginning, I needed a way to let them know the areas where I needed help.

I personally have no artistic or graphic ability and can do little more on a computer than word processing. However, I decided I was going to write them all a letter. We had about 70 women at that time in the ministry, and I had many ideas to share with them. The single-spaced, double-sided letter I sent them was jam packed with information. I addressed the envelopes by hand. It felt so good to be able to communicate with all of the women at once. Several weeks later I received the following letter in the mail.

September 28, 1996

Dear Janet,

Thank you for the update on our Woman to Woman Mentoring Ministry. I was mesmerized by your letter. It was full of interesting items about the ministry. I have benefited greatly by having a mentor. That night after I read your letter, Janet, I woke up at 3:00 a.m. wide awake thinking about it. I found it odd that I would wake up so suddenly and think and think and think about your letter. Then it came to me, actually I think God was talking to me. "Hey, put that great letter into one of your desktop publishing programs."

So first thing after I got my two kids off to school, I recreated your letter. There are a few words misspelled and a paragraph or two missing. But I really enjoyed playing with the fonts and different layouts. I would love to help the Mentoring Ministry with some desktop publishing work. If you have a need for it, I'm volunteering my services. I would love to do it. It would really fulfill me!

Have a wonderful week and God bless!
Jane

Jane is now our **Publicity Shepherd Coach,** and she designs all the graphics on our forms and publicity items. Thanks to Jane, and all the ministry team who contribute articles and proofreading skills, we are able to send out the newsletter, *Beyond Coffee ... Encouraging Words for M&Ms* (Form X). We send the newsletter to all the women and keep them on the mailing list even after their six-month commitment. This keeps them involved in the ministry, and they know they are always welcome to participate again.

There is a Jane in your church, also. Pray about the need and let the Lord find her. I never even knew what I was missing until I received Jane's letter and saw the potential of her offering her creative gifts and talents to the ministry. However, do not get me wrong. While the publications enhance the ministry, they do not make the ministry. We started and grew without them.

The first Coffee was in January 1996, and Jane sent her letter on September 28, 1996. Even though we keep Jane very busy today, and I do not know what we would do without her, do not wait until you find a Jane before you start the ministry. Many mentoring relationships blessed lives when all I had for publicity was what my husband and I could produce from our home computer. Every computer has some basic capabilities, and that is all I had in the beginning. The Lord honored those meager efforts with a blossoming ministry. So work with what you have and use our ministry forms to get started, but continually ask if anyone has a gift for computer graphics. Our next computer servant was a woman who put the Ministry Roster (form T) in her computer, and she now updates our roster after every Coffee and prints labels for mailings.

THROUGH MEMENTOS

Remember that this is the *enhancement* chapter and you will not be able to do all these things in the beginning. You will have a full plate just getting your ministry started and growing. As you settle into a routine, become more organized, receive funds from donations or church budget, and recruit gifted helpers, you can begin adding some of the extra special touches that women so enjoy. I would recommend that you not try to do any of these the first year. Put them on the Opportunity to Serve Profile (form B) and wait on the Lord to bring you women who are willing to develop the areas for you. Here are some suggestions of things we have developed. If you like these ideas, use them, and then let the creativity and imagination flow in your Woman to Woman Mentoring Ministry.

Laminated Bookmarks

We actually have a helper position called **Bookmark Maker**, and she works with the **Publicity Shepherd Coach**. On her computer, she designs a different bookmark for each Coffee with a Scripture verse, the Coffee number, and our ministry logo. The ladies attending an Orientation Coffee receive the bookmarks as they leave the Coffee, along with the last issue of our ministry newsletter, an M&M favor, and a hug!

M&M Favors

In keeping with the theme of M&Ms, we take a peanut or almond M&M® and a plain M&M® (to represent the mentor and mentee) and wrap them in colored tulle or netting and tie with a ribbon. Attached to the ribbon is a card thanking them for attending the Coffee and reminding them of the room number and date of the Kickoff Night.

Pens

Promotional catalogs have different styles of pens to customize for marketing purposes at very reasonable rates. We chose a feminine pen design and had our ministry name and phone/Prayer Chain number printed on them. M&Ms receive a pen at the Coffee Registration Table and at all Woman to Woman events. I love it when I am sitting in church and look down the aisle and there is an M&M taking notes with her Woman to Woman Mentoring pen.

Refrigerator Magnets

We were brainstorming at one **Administrative Team** meeting about ways to help the ladies remember important dates during their six-month mentoring relationships. We wanted a system that would keep the dates in front of them and not just a piece of paper that would be stuck away in a drawer. Refrigerator magnets were our solution. Use your computer to design a colorful card that contains:
- The Coffee number;
- Mentor Halftime Refresher date, room number, and time;
- Six-Month Potluck Celebration date and time;
- Ministry phone/Prayer Chain number; and
- A spot to write the Prayer Warrior's name and phone number.

Attach a magnet to the back and pass these out at Kickoff Night. Give them a second one without a magnet to put in their purses or calendars.

T-Shirts And Sweatshirts

Do not undertake this project until you have a willing servant to orchestrate it! She works under the **Financial Shepherd Coach**. We designed t-shirts and sweatshirts with our ministry name and logo, the church name, and *Titus 2 Women*. You can have fun and be creative designing something that the ladies of your ministry would be proud to wear. This is definitely not a one-woman project, so, again, do not attempt it until there is a team or committee organized.

The t-shirts and sweatshirts are a great way to market the Woman to Woman Mentoring Ministry and to evangelize. As the ladies wear their t-shirts and sweatshirts, people will ask them: "What is Woman to Woman?" "What is mentoring?" "What church is that?" It is a great way to start a conversation with another woman at the gym, at the park, in the grocery line, at the bank. Of course, it also adds some community to the ladies of the ministry. Sell the t-shirts and sweatshirts at the resource table at the Coffee and at Kickoff Night and at your ministry table on the church patio or foyer on weekends. All funds go back into buying more t-shirts and sweatshirts.

Mentor Life Investment Pins

As we completed the fourth year of the ministry, I had a real desire to honor mentors who had mentored more than once—those women who had chosen to invest in the spiritual growth and maturity of other women. When we looked at our roster, we found that 35 women had invested their lives in more than one mentee. They were choosing to take the time to pour themselves into other lives.

I had an idea along the lines of the mother's or grandmother's pin or necklace where you add a charm for each child or grandchild. Keeping our limited budget in mind, we found our Mentor Life Investment Pin at a bead store. It looks much like a very large silver-plated safety pin, and hanging from the lower portion of the pin are five posts for adding charms. It was perfect and the price was right. The first charm we give for one mentee is a coffee cup and saucer, the second charm is a cross, the third an angel, the fourth a heart, and the fifth praying hands. When a mentor has mentored twice, she receives her pin with the first two charms, and then we give her a charm to add to it each time she mentors.

At our annual Christmas party, we award the pins. Those mentors who now qualify for a pin receive an elegant invitation to the party, as do the mentees they have mentored. During the party, we have an awards ceremony with a special presentation of the pins with the appropriate number of charms, and their mentees give them a rose. These mentors receive additional charms to add to the pin at the Six-Month Potluck Celebration of their future mentoring relationships. Often, the exciting part for us is passing out Mentor Life Investment Pins to mentees of mentors who are also receiving a pin. We see the continuation of generational life investment.

This is not something you need to think about right away until you have had several Coffees and mentors repeatedly mentoring. Keep your eyes open now for ideas. Our entire pin with all five charms was only $5.00, and the bead store gave us a discount because we were a church organization. The ladies wear their Mentor Life Investment Pins proudly. Frequently we hear mentors who have only mentored once saying they want to do it again because they want a pin, too!

You will have multiple benefits of honoring those women who have mentored repeatedly, but it will also serve as an incentive for them to mentor again to fill their pin with all the charms. It is also a great witnessing tool when they wear it, and others ask them about it. As they explain its significance, they will often have the opportunity to share Jesus as well as further the message of the Woman to Woman Mentoring Ministry.

Six-Month Potluck Celebration

Look in Chapter 10 (p. 108) for a discussion of the M&M Keepsake Photo Card and Certificate of Completion.

Through Shepherdesses

As the ministry progresses and women complete their six-month commitments, keep your eye open for a mentor who has had a good mentoring experience and wants to share it with others. Ask her if she would be the **Ministry Relations Shepherdess**. Refer her to women struggling in their relationships, and she can give them encouragement and suggestions. The women of our ministry have appreciated having this resource available to them. There are some suggested answers to common problems in Chapter 17, and in the Appendix of the *Mentor* and *Mentee Handbooks*. Give a copy of those to the **Ministry Relations Shepherdess**. Be sure that she is a woman who is loving and compassionate but also understands the value of staying in the mentoring relationship and keeping the commitment.

Another very helpful position is the **Spiritual Shepherdess**. This would be a woman well versed in the Bible with a gift of sharing God's Word with others. She also should understand the meanings of the Scriptures. She will be of great value to the mentors in finding answers for their mentees or perhaps in their own studies.

Both of these positions again are enhancement and not necessary especially in the beginning. However, be in prayer and watch to see when the Lord brings the right women into the ministry. Both Service Opportunity Descriptions are in Chapter 14.

Through Letting the Lord Do His Mighty Work

Once the women meet each other and establish their relationships, it is time to let the Lord take over and orchestrate how each one progresses. After you have given the women ideas of things to do and ways to keep their relationships growing, turn the responsibility for the relationships over to the mentors and God. This will probably be the hardest part if you are like me and really want to be in charge of everything. It may take awhile, but when you hear a few testimonies of changed lives you will realize they did just fine without you. Besides, you have another Coffee to organize and another training to plan. Your job is to keep the ministry growing and continue to offer the opportunity for more women to enjoy the benefits and blessings of mentoring relationships. And believe me, that can be a full time job, so be glad the mentors and God are doing the daily operational and maintenance work.

Turn the responsibility for the relationships over to the mentors and God.

CHAPTER 13

"In my distress I called to the Lord; I cried to my God for help. From his temple he heard my voice; my cry came before him, into his ears" (Psalm 18:6).

Recruiting Help

OPPORTUNITIES FOR SERVICE

I hear you taking a deep breath of relief and saying, "Finally! She is finally going to tell us how to recruit the help we will need to grow a ministry of this magnitude." Never fear, I promised you we would get to this part. The reason I waited was really not to keep you in suspense. That was not my purpose, but when I started to talk about recruiting, I wanted to be able to discuss the various areas in which you will need help. If I had not first taken you through the steps of the ministry, these position titles would not have much meaning to you. Now, as I mention the various job titles, you will have background as to how they interface in the workings of the ministry.

To be honest with you, my first recruiting was very informal and completely orchestrated by the Lord. Every time I was ready to expand into a new area, someone would call or come up to me at church and ask how she could help give back to the ministry. If I needed phone calls made, I would no more than think about the upcoming need and someone was there to fill it. I was continually thanking the Lord for blessing me with new ideas and new helpers.

The first women I asked to help were two friends of mine who were attending the first Dress Rehearsal Coffee. I asked them if they would help me pray over the Profile Cards the next day, and they gladly agreed. I also asked one of them if she would bring some cookies and folding chairs. Other than that, I really did not know yet where I needed help. As I mentioned earlier, if you do not already have a group of women to help you start the ministry, do not despair. If the Lord has given you the call, start the ball rolling, and He will bring those women to you who will keep the ball in motion.

As the second Coffee approached, I realized this could not be a one-woman ministry for long. I needed to start recruiting help right away. One woman expressed an interest in the Woman to Woman Mentoring Ministry when I called to see if she was going to attend the first Coffee. We must have talked an hour, and we had never met. She shared with me how she had long felt the Saddleback Church women needed this type of ministry, and she would be willing to help in

If the Lord has given you the call, start the ball rolling, and He will bring those women to you who will keep the ball in motion.

any way I needed her. When you have someone mention that she has been praying about a Mentoring Ministry and offer to help, make a note of it for future use. Most women are not just idly saying this. They are serious and may actually feel offended if you do not contact them. I figured if a woman said she wanted to help, she was serious, and I did not hesitate to call her when the time came that I needed help.

At the second Coffee, I announced that the Woman to Woman Mentoring Ministry was out of its "in-the-making stages." We were going to need help, and I listed specific areas. From that moment on, whenever I had any of the women together for a Coffee, a training, or a Six-Month Potluck Celebration, I always announced the areas in which we could use service.

One of the mentors suggested I design a job description for each task. I wrote the job descriptions and then summarized them into the Areas of Opportunity for Service (form V). Form V is continually updated as our needs change and is a handout at every Coffee, training, and meeting. At each Coffee women fill out an Opportunity to Serve Profile (form B), and let us know the areas where they are gifted and willing to serve.

Other women will call later to offer their service. Many mentees, blessed by their mentors and the ministry, feel a desire to give back to the ministry by offering assistance. These willing hearts come to me continuously—a message on my voicemail at church or my answering machine at home, a word at church, or a note in the mail. My heart swells with the beauty of the Lord's work in this ministry. He has blessed these women's lives with spiritual growth and maturity.

I still cannot believe how different it is in the Christian and secular worlds. Christians help because they believe in servant leadership, not ego leadership, and they are so willing to give of their time and energy. This is especially true if they are receiving the benefits of the ministry. Trust me—if you say you need help, the workers for the harvest will report for duty.

You may have been in church work for a long time and are used to this type of servant attitude, but it was new to me and so humbling. I actually almost hesitated to make a formal request for help, because the Lord had been so gracious to bring workers for the harvest to my door. However, as the ministry began to grow, it was obvious that we could offer better service to the mentoring relationships if we had help.

You will notice in all *Woman to Woman Mentoring* resources that unless I am quoting someone, I do not use the word *volunteer* or *volunteering*. Instead, you will see the terms *helper, servant, opportunity to serve, service opportunities, offer,* or *want to serve*. When we choose to volunteer, we are often still in control. When we offer to be a servant or a helper, God is in control. Richard Foster wrote in his book, *Celebration of Discipline:* "True service comes from a relationship with the divine Other deep inside. We serve out of whispered prompting, divine urgings. Energy is expended, but it is not the frantic energy of the flesh ... True service finds it almost impossible to distinguish the small from the large service."[1]

This is the type of help you truly want in your ministry—women who serve because God has put it on their hearts to give where they have received. Serving selflessly and for no other reason than that it pleases God.

At your first Coffee and every one thereafter, hand out the Areas of Opportunity for Service (form V) and ask if anyone wants to have the next Coffee at their house. Always have an Opportunity for Service Sign-Up Sheet (form W) in a prominent place and encourage them to sign up that day. Christian women want to serve and give back. The blessings, life changes, and growth happening in the women's lives as a result of their mentoring relationships will lead them to help the ministry that has offered them so much.

PRACTICAL IDEAS

Every time women from the ministry gather together, have the Areas of Opportunity for Service (form V) and Areas of Opportunity for Service Sign-Up Sheet (form W) on display. Announce the areas where you need immediate help. For example:

- A **Hostess** and a home
- Helpers for the next Coffee
- **Prayer Warriors** for the mentoring relationships for the next Coffee
- A **Training Leader**
- Administrative help
- A computer knowledgeable person

When a woman comes up to you at church and offers to help, write her name down so you will not forget, and call her as soon as possible. She is not just being nice. She has sought you out and genuinely wants to help, so it would be an insult if you did not give her an area of service. If you have messages on your answering machine or voicemail from women offering to help, call them back right away. Even if you do not have an immediate job for them, let them know that you received their message and you will call them as needs arise.

At the Coffees, staple the Opportunity to Serve Profiles (form B) to the back of the Profile Cards. Then, as the ladies are filling out their Profile Cards, they will automatically fill out the attached form and return the two together. One of the two pictures you took of them at the Coffee is attached to the Opportunity to Serve Profile. The **Publicity Shepherd Coach** makes copies of the filled out Opportunity to Serve Profiles (form B) and distributes them to the **Administration Team** and **Coordinators** to contact. The picture helps them recall the M&M they are calling and makes it a more personal conversation. The women who fill out Opportunity to Serve Profiles should receive a call within a month after the Coffee. If there is not an immediate need in an area they circled, let them know their offer of service is appreciated, and they will receive a call when a need arises.

If you say you need help, the workers for the harvest will report for duty.

Chapter 13: Recruiting Help

Send thank-you notes to your helpers. We all love to receive a thoughtful note in the mail. It can really pick us up on a down day. Never take your helpers for granted. They are giving from their hearts and certainly do not expect a pat on the back, so that is all the more reason to do it. It is tough for most of us to be like Jesus and serve selflessly. We like to feel appreciated and needed. Thank you's and thank you notes of appreciation are a sure way of preventing burn out and keeping your waiting list full of women wanting to serve. Sending out thank you notes is on the **Ministry Relations Shepherdess's** Service Opportunity Description. A **Servant Coordinator** is also helpful in the future. She can take the responsibility of following up on those who offer to serve and assigning them to the various areas of service

SERVICE OPPORTUNITY DESCRIPTIONS (JOB DESCRIPTIONS)

Job descriptions is a term that many of us relate to from our work and career experience. Whenever someone assumes a new position, whether in the secular or Christian world, they receive a job description. This is valuable for the person assuming the new role because they know the expectations. They can also determine if the job is one that fits their skills, desires, talents, and gifts.

In the Woman to Woman Mentoring Ministry we call the job descriptions, Service Opportunity Descriptions. Print each Service Opportunity Description on a separate sheet of paper, ready to hand to the servant who says, "What do I do?" The description should answer most of her questions. She can take it home with her to have on hand in case she forgets when or what she is to do. You can adapt the Service Opportunity Descriptions to your specific situation and church. (If you have access to a computer, the CD-ROM included in the *Woman to Woman Mentoring: Leader Kit* will make the descriptions easier to customize for your ministry. Or you have permission to make copies of the descriptions as they appear in this book. You will also find a Service Opportunity Description index on page 4 for your future reference.)

This may seem like extra work. You may be thinking you can just tell everyone what they need to do. Let me assure you that you will wish you had given a Service Opportunity Description to your **Greeter/Hugger** who shows up at 2:30 p.m. instead of 1:00 p.m., and says to you, "I couldn't remember what time you said to be here." Or you arrive at the Coffee and the **Hostess** asks you where the food is, since she understood *you* were bringing the refreshments! Or your **Photographer** announces halfway through the Coffee that she has to leave to go to a birthday party.

Do you get my point? I had the late arriving **Greeter** and **Registrar** at a Coffee once, and it was very hectic. That was my first clue that we needed to clarify the importance of arriving early and staying until the end. I also had a **Hostess** who told me when I arrived at her house for the Coffee, that she would have to leave before the Coffee was over and I could lock up! So you will notice that the Service Opportunity Descriptions are very complete and thorough, but you still need to be prepared for the unexpected.

You will really need the person who said they would do the job to be there on time and stay a certain length of time. That is why each description has a service duration time. This indicates how long they perform the service as well as the time frame for which they are signing up to serve. The expectations are clear, and the woman serving can easily determine if she will be able to meet them or not. There will be fewer misunderstandings and disputes if everyone knows what you expect.

When one of the women agrees to serve in an area, give her the appropriate Service Opportunity Description. Ask her to let you know if she has questions or if there is anything on the description that she cannot do. If she says everything is fine, then the job is hers! However, if she cannot do part of the requirement, try to find another area of service that will suit her schedule better.

As you develop an **Administrative Team** and **Coordinators**, they take responsibility for sending the descriptions for the areas of service for which they are responsible. For example, the **Phone Coordinator** gives the **Phone Communicators** their descriptions; the **Hospitality Shepherd Coach** sends out the descriptions for the Coffee positions.

Never question, as I have said before, that you are going to need help. Your ministry should begin growing very rapidly, especially when some of the women start talking to others in the church about how much they are enjoying their mentoring relationships. Soon you will not even need to advertise. Your Coffees will all be filled by word of mouth.

We began to reach that point by our fifth Coffee. Don't be caught off guard. There is no doubt that women are hungry for female companionship and friendship. When they find out that their church is providing this opportunity and they begin to hear success stories, you will have a waiting list for every Coffee. What a great problem to have when your goal is serving the Lord and doing what He wants you to do among His people!

Following are the Service Opportunity Descriptions we currently use. You can use them just as they appear or customize them for your own situation and needs. You may also want to add others of your own. All of the descriptions of positions for the Orientation Coffee have an added explanation preceding them.

---

[1] Richard J. Foster, *Celebration of Discipline* (New York: HarperCollins, 1988), 128.

There will be fewer misunderstandings and disputes if everyone knows what you expect.

Orientation Coffee Hostess

The **Orientation Coffee Hostess** will usually be a woman who has attended a Coffee and is a mentor or mentee herself. Therefore, she will have a good idea how to prepare for a Coffee. However, being a guest and putting a Coffee on yourself are two different things. I found the Hostess Checklist (form P, p. 240) to be very helpful, and the **Hostesses** are very appreciative. Whatever you can do to keep your **Hostess** calm, cool, and relaxed is important. You want this to be an enjoyable experience for her as well as the ladies attending.

After a year of organizing the Coffees myself, I was able to recruit a **Hospitality Shepherd Coach** who corresponds with the **Hostess** in the weeks before the Coffee. The **Hospitality Shepherd Coach** calls the **Hostess** once a week the month before the Coffee to see if she has any questions. She also lets the **Hostess** know that she is being prayed for and prays with her on the phone. The **Hospitality Shepherd Coach** sends the Hostess Letter (form O), Hostess Checklist (form P) with the helpers' names, and the **Hostess** Service Opportunity Description to the **Hostess** at least one month before the scheduled Orientation Coffee. The **Hostesses** always thank us for this and tell us how reassuring it is for them to know exactly what they need to do to get ready for the big day.

I learned to not alarm the **Hostess** with large numbers of registrants because that only gets the **Hostess** crazy. In a large church, 40 to 50 is going to be an average number of attendees at a Coffee. I would imagine 20 to 30 would probably be average in a mid-size church, and 10 or 12 in a small church.

"Offer hospitality to one another" (1 Peter 4:9).

"Do not forget to entertain strangers, for by so doing some people have entertained angels without knowing it" (Hebrews 13:2).

SERVICE OPPORTUNITY DESCRIPTION FOR
Orientation Coffee Hostess

Service Requirements:
- Willing to open your home to 40-50 women
- Enjoy entertaining and hospitality
- Desire to have your home blessed with the presence of godly women
- Attended a previous Coffee as mentor or mentee

Service Responsibilities:
1. Make your home available from 1:00-7:00 p.m. on a designated Sunday afternoon.
2. Provide seating for approximately 40 women in a centralized area of your home.
3. Provide:
   - coffee
   - punch or cold drinks
   - light refreshments
   - napkins, cups, and paper plates

   (A donation basket will be used to help defray costs.)
4. Communicate with the **Hospitality Shepherd Coach** in finalizing last minute details.
5. Provide a table for registration and resources.
6. Be present at the Coffee to welcome women into your home.
7. If possible, make your home available for the women to return for the Six-Month Potluck Celebration.
9. Relax and enjoy what the Lord is about to do in your home.

Service Duration:
We only expect that you **Hostess** one Coffee. However, experience has shown that **Hostesses** feel so blessed by having the gracious and grateful women in their homes, that they often want to do it again. It is nice if the Six-Month Potluck Celebration is at the same house. There is a sense of a journey traveled when the women come back together again at the place where their journey launched. It is also helpful because everyone knows how to get there. All dates for Orientation Coffees and Potluck celebrations accommodate the **Hostess's** schedule and availability.

Woman to Woman Mentoring

Greeter/Hugger

The **Greeter/Hugger** is a key person. After a few women arrive at the Coffee, you will find yourself starting to talk with them. Then the doorbell rings again—what do you do? Leave the conversation and run for the door, or let the person at the door finally come in by herself? Neither one is a good option. The solution is to have someone stationed at the front door to continuously greet the new arrivals with a hug and a welcoming smile. This is a great way to help the women feel at ease and glad to be there.

The **Greeter/Hugger** is this person. Some women might be taken aback by a hug. Most women appreciate a hug and in many cases need a hug. The women know they are welcome, and you are glad they are there. It sets the pace for the comfortable and relaxed atmosphere you want them to experience. At 2:30 p.m., the **Greeter/Hugger** closes the front door and puts a friendly Coffee Closed Sign (form H) on the door which explains that you will not be able to match anyone arriving after this time. The sign also suggests the late arrivals register for the next Coffee. The **Greeter/Hugger** stays outside to lovingly explain the sign to anyone who arrives after 2:30 p.m. At the end of the Coffee, she again positions herself at the front door and gives each woman a hug good-bye with blessings for a safe trip home. You do not want anyone slipping out the front door without knowing you are glad she came.

Your church may not be a hugging church, and this may seem uncomfortable for you at first. I would challenge you to try it. If hugging is just too much for you at first, start with handshakes. I guarantee by your second Coffee you will be greeting everyone with a hug!

"Greet one another with a kiss of love" (1 Peter 5:14).

Service Opportunity Description for
Greeter/Hugger

Service Requirements:
- Available to attend the Orientation Coffee
- Able to arrive at 1:00 p.m. to help set up and stay until the last attendee leaves
- Not required, but helpful if you can stay with others to clean up afterwards
- Enjoy smiling and giving hugs

Service Responsibilities:
1. Between 1:30 and 2:30 p.m., stay positioned at the front door (or at the street if registration is outside) to greet all new arrivals with a big smile, friendly hug, and a word of welcome to the Coffee.
2. Direct the new arrivals to the registration table.
3. Stand outside until 2:45 p.m. to greet any latecomers. At 2:30, put out the Coffee Closed sign and lovingly ask them to attend the next Coffee, since the program has already started.
4. When the Coffee is over, again position yourself at the front door to give every woman a good-bye hug and thank her for coming to the Coffee. Be sure to ask the women if they completed their Profile Cards and left them in the appropriate box.
5. Ask the **Hostess** what you can do to help clean up.

Service Duration:
Women will start arriving around 1:30 p.m. It is important to arrive at 1:00 p.m. so you can help with any last minute preparation and be at the front door for the first arrivals. The last person may not leave until around 6:30 p.m., and then there is cleanup. It is good to plan on being at the Coffee from 1:00 p.m. until 7:00 p.m. You serve at one Coffee; however, if you enjoy sharing your welcoming spirit and would like to do it again—every Coffee needs a **Greeter/Hugger**. We would love to have your smiling face at the front door of the next Coffee.

Name Tag Scribe

The **Name Tag Scribe** positions herself in front of the registration table. Her sole function is to make name tags for the women as they arrive. Why don't we let them make out their own? Experience. In the beginning, we just handed the women a name tag and asked them to fill it out. As you might expect, some wrote small and flowery, and others put only their first names. Legible names are very important, especially later in the Coffee when the women are introducing themselves and the **Prayer Day Team** is trying to see their name tags. One person printing first and last names keeps it consistent and readable. This also helps the registration line move quicker. If the line gets long, the **Name Tag Scribe** can move down the line asking the ladies their names and making out the name tags in advance.

It is not good to have the **Greeter/Hugger** double as the **Name Tag Scribe** unless you must in the beginning for lack of helpers. The **Greeter/Hugger** needs to stay at the front door from 1:30 p.m. until 2:45 p.m. to accommodate the early and late arrivals. If she is also writing name tags there could be a bottleneck at the front door, or someone could slip in without a hug.

The **Name Tag Scribe** uses a black felt-tip pen and prints first and last names on a name tags as the women arrive. She directs them to the registration table but stays at the front door. During the Coffee, she helps where needed or can leave after the Coffee begins.

"He calls his own sheep by name and leads them out" (John 10:3).

SERVICE OPPORTUNITY DESCRIPTION FOR
Name Tag Scribe

Service Requirements:
- Able to stay calm when the line gets long and things are hectic
- Able to print legibly
- Able to arrive at 1:00 p.m.

Service Responsibilities:
1. After getting her hug, each woman comes to the registration table. Ask her first and last name and print it on a name tag in large, legible letters with a black felt-tip marker. This keeps the name tags uniform and legible. If the registration line is long, walk along and make out the name tags. This will help the registration process move quickly.
2. Use only the provided name tags and black felt-tip pen.
3. Once everyone in line has a name tag, help the **Registrars**.
4. If you stay for the Coffee, please help clean up afterwards.

Service Duration:
You need to arrive at 1:00 p.m. to set up and be ready for the early arrivals. You are free to leave at 2:30 once the Coffee begins and registration is completed, but if you do stay, please assist others and help clean up.

You serve at one Coffee; however, if you enjoy this area of service, we always appreciate your experienced name tag talents.

Woman to Woman Mentoring

Registrar

A **Registrar** or two is needed to set up the registration table and direct registration. The registration table will need the following items:

- Name tags and black felt-tip pen
- Profile Cards with Opportunity to Serve Profiles stapled to the back
- Writing pens
- Orientation Coffee Programs with handouts inserted
- Clipboards—if you have them. This makes it easier for the guests to fill out their Profile Cards legibly.
- Donation basket with a sign indicating suggested donation or registration fee

Registration can be a bottleneck if you have a large turnout, so I recommend having two **Registrars**. Their job is to set up the registration area and then:

1. Give each woman a clipboard, Profile Card (form A), and Opportunity to Serve Profile (form B).
2. Explain how to fill out the cards and where to return the completed cards.
3. Provide pens to those who need them.
4. Give each woman a Program (form C) that contains any handouts.
5. Collect donation or registration fee.
6. Direct the women to get their pictures taken and then to move on to the area where they can sit down, fill out their cards, and enjoy refreshments.
7. Help with the Profile Card process during the Coffee.
8. Be available after the Coffee to pray with any woman who might like to have individual prayer before she leaves.
9. At the completion of the Coffee, return to the front door and hand out any take-home favors or newsletters.
10. Assist women in signing up to help with the ministry and answer any questions they may have.

"My heart is stirred by a noble theme ... my tongue is the pen of a skillful writer" (Psalm 45:1).

SERVICE OPPORTUNITY DESCRIPTION FOR

Registrar

Service Requirements:
- Able to stay calm when the line gets long and things are hectic
- Willing to answer questions about Profile Cards
- Able to get all women through the registration process by 2:30 p.m.
- Arrive at 1:00 p.m. and stay until 7:00 p.m.

Service Responsibilities:
1. Set up the registration table with: Profile Cards, clipboards, pens, Programs, handouts, donation basket, name tags, and a black felt-tip pen.
2. After receiving hugs from the **Greeter/Hugger** and obtaining name tags, the women move to the registration table. Give each woman a clipboard, pen, and Profile Card with an Opportunity to Serve Profile attached. Instruct that the more thorough she is on the card, the easier it will be to match her with another woman. Answer any questions she may have regarding filling out her forms.
4. Show the women where to put their completed Profile Cards.
5. Give each woman a Program with a set of handouts.
6. Collect donation or registration fee.
7. Direct the guests to the **Photographer**.
8. Keep the process moving so that they will all be ready to start by 2:30 p.m.
9. Between 2:30 and 4:00 p.m., once the program has begun and before the break, you will perform the following tasks in a designated area:

- After the **Photographer** has attached the pictures to the Profile Cards, check the cards for omissions or areas not filled out completely. You are only checking the data information. Please do not read the private information written on the Profile Cards, and do not give the cards to anyone else to read. Please do this quietly.
- Flag each omission on the Profile Card with a Post-it® note and set aside.
- Put remaining Profile Cards back in the alphabetized hanging file box.
- At the break, return the incomplete Profile Cards to the women for completion.
- Answer any questions about the Profile Cards.
- At the end of the break, collect corrected Profile Cards, check to be sure all areas are completed, and file in the alphabetized hanging file box.

10. Be available to pray for anyone who would like to stay after the Coffee and pray.
11. At the completion of the Coffee, position yourself at the door and give a newsletter and favor to each departing woman.
12. Stay and help clean up after the Coffee.

Service Duration:
You need to arrive at 1:00 p.m. to set up the registration table and be ready for the first arrivals. After the Coffee, some women will want to add information to their Profile Cards, and you can help them with this. You serve at one Coffee; however, if you want to do it again, we always appreciate your experienced registration talents.

Photographer

A **Photographer** will be taking candid pictures of a number of activities at all your events. At the Coffees she will take candid shots of women arriving and becoming acquainted. Other important pictures are of women who talk to each other at the end of the official program. During Coffee registration, the **Photographer**, with the help of a **Photographer's Assistant**, will take two pictures of every woman.

At the Coffees, the **Photographer** positions herself near the registration table, puts women in groups of two or three, and takes two head shots. If you have a small church where everyone knows each other, this might not be as necessary. However, at a large church quite often the **Prayer Day Team** will not know all the women at the Coffee. Picture taking is vital. Even if you do know the women, it is still helpful to have their pictures in front of you while you are praying for them.

Make this a fun part of the Coffee. There is an explanation during the program of the significance of the pictures to the matching and praying process. The women will be grateful and appreciative that you take the matching of relationships so seriously.

The **Photographer** also takes pictures at breaks and after the formal part of the Coffee as women begin to mingle and chat. You can see a tremendous amount from these pictures. Quite often a woman will feel that she has something in common with another woman who shared her story. She will approach that woman to offer comfort or to share her own experience. Much ministering takes place right at the Coffee, and the **Photographer** can capture this on film. Natural matching might be taking place and without the pictures, you could miss it.

You will find that many **Photographers** prefer to use their own camera for the candid shots, or you can loan them one. Reimburse the **Photographer** for the film and developing from the donation basket at the Coffee. If you are not using instant film, the **Photographer** will be responsible for dropping regular film off at a one-hour developing store on her way home from the Coffee. The **Prayer Day Shepherd Coach** picks up the pictures later that night and attaches them to the Profile Cards so that they will be ready for the **Prayer Day Team** in the morning.

At the Six-Month Potluck Celebration, the **Photographer** takes two instant pictures of each M&M relationship and attaches them to Keepsake Photo Cards (see chapter 10, p. 108). She also takes candid shots during the Potluck. Ask one of your **Photographers** if she will maintain a Ministry Photo Album and have it on display at all your Mentoring Ministry events.

"The things revealed belong to us and to our children forever" (Deuteronomy 29:29).

Service Opportunity Description for
Photographer

Service Requirements:
- Enjoy taking pictures
- Familiar with the operation of a camera—especially how to change the film
- Not necessary that you have your own camera, although you will probably prefer using your own if you have one
- Able to arrive at 1:00 p.m. and stay until 7:00 p.m.

Service Responsibilities:
1. Arrive at 1:00 p.m. to familiarize yourself with the camera, if you are not using your own. Take pictures of women during registration and social time.
2. Position yourself with the **Photographer's Assistant** near the registration table.
3. After the women have received their registration packets, group two women together and take two head shots with an instant camera. Be sure to take each woman's picture.
4. Give the pictures to the **Photographer's Assistant**.
5. At 2:30, when registration is over, go to the designated work area in the house.
6. With the help of the **Photographer's Assistant,** coordinate the pictures by the numbers on the picture and the numbers on the Profile Cards.
    - Cut the faces out of each picture.
    - Tape the cut photos to the corresponding Profile Cards in the designated area and on the Opportunity to Serve Profile.
    - When completed, give the Profile Cards to the **Registrar**. Please do not read the cards.
    - Work as quietly as possible so as not to disturb the Coffee.
7. At the break and after the closing prayer, begin taking candid pictures of the women talking to each other. This is a crucial picture-taking time, as some women will go up to those to whom they relate after hearing their stories. Seeing these photos will help the **Prayer Day Team** as they pray over the Profile Cards.
8. Be sure that you finish the roll of film in the camera during the candid shots.
9. Take all the rolls of film to the designated one-hour film developer. Film and developing are reimbursed.

Service Duration:
Arrive at 1:00 p.m. You will probably finish around 6:30 p.m., but you may still need to drop the film off on your way home. It is fabulous if you would like to be the **Ministry Photographer**, since you have the experience. It is not mandatory, however. We appreciate whatever help you can give us.

Photographer's Assistant

A **Photographer's Assistant** is a position we decided to add after the sixth Coffee in which 86 women attended. We were trying to match pictures with cards until midnight! The system we use now works well.

If you do not have an instant camera and film, use this format.

- After the **Photographer** takes the women's pictures, the **Photographer's Assistant** writes the picture number (as displayed on the camera) on the top of the Profile Card.
- As an extra security measure, the **Photographer's Assistant** also prints the women's names on a numbered form, again to correspond with the picture number shown on the camera as the film advances. For example, if you are using 36 shot film, number 1 to 36 down the left side of a sheet of paper and leave space next to each number to write 2 names. This second step is important because you put 2 women in each picture so there will be 2 names for each picture. The **Photographer's Assistant** writes their names down in the same order as positioned in the picture.

My recommendation is to use an instant camera, even if you have to borrow one each time. The Service Opportunity Description is written using this system.

- The **Photographer's Assistant** will write a number in the white border under each woman's picture. Then she will note the corresponding number on each woman's Profile Card in the designated box in the upper right-hand corner.
- During the Coffee, she will help cut the pictures and attach them to the Profile Cards, matching names and numbers.

"If one falls down, his friend can help him up. But pity the man who falls and has no one to help him up!" (Ecclesiastes 4:10).

Service Opportunity Description for
Photographer's Assistant

Service Requirements:
- Able to attend Orientation Coffee and arrive at 1:00 p.m.
- Enjoy assisting and facilitating to keep the process flowing
- Provide a roll of adhesive tape for the Coffee

Service Responsibilities:
1. After the **Photographer** has taken pictures of groups of two women with an instant camera:
   - Write a number on each Profile Card in the designated box.
   - Place the corresponding number on the picture border below each woman's picture.
   - Let the pictures dry.
2. Continue the above process until all the women's pictures have been taken.
3. Finish by 2:30 p.m., when the program begins.
4. Assist the **Photographer** with obtaining new rolls of film, changing film, and any other needs that arise.
5. Between 2:30 and 4:00 p.m., once the program has begun and before the break, you will assist the **Photographer** in the following tasks:
   - Coordinate the pictures to the Profile Cards by number.
   - Cut the faces out of each picture.
   - Tape the cut photos to the corresponding Profile Cards in the upper right-hand corner and the Opportunity to Serve Profiles.
   - When completed, give the Profile Cards to the **Registrar**. Please do not read cards.
   - Work as quietly as possible so as not to disturb the Coffee.
6. Assist as needed with taking candid pictures.

Service Duration:
The individual picture process finishes by 2:30 p.m. Ask the **Photographer** where she needs help. You do not need to stay for the whole Coffee if you need to leave; however, if you can stay to assist where needed, we would appreciate it. Once you know the process and get used to working with the **Photographer**, it is always helpful if you can assist at future Coffees. Let us know if we can count on you. We appreciate your help.

Resource Guide

The **Resource Guide** serves at the Orientation Coffees and Kickoff nights. She obtains the books from the Recommended Book List (form D) you would like to offer for sale and puts them on display for purchase. Ask her to read all the resources, so she can help answer questions and guide the ladies to the books that might be the most applicable for them. The **Resource Guide** needs to be comfortable handling money and making change. She needs to familiarize herself with your church's procedure for purchasing books from your local Christian bookstore on consignment. She needs to communicate with the **Administration Team** to see what books they would like made available. She also needs to keep an inventory of the books sold and reorder when necessary. It is good if she is comfortable talking to people and answering their questions. Someone with a sales background is often very good at this position.

It is highly recommended during the Orientation Coffee presentation that the women begin immediately learning as much as possible about mentoring. Having the books available for purchase encourages them to start right away rather than having to make time to go to the bookstore. The **Resource Guide** should share this same philosophy so she understands that she is doing the women a service and not just selling books.

We have found it helpful for the **Resouce Guide** to transport the books to the events in an upright suitcase on wheels. This prevents injury and backache from carrying boxes of books.

"She sets about her work vigorously; her arms are strong for her task" (Proverbs 31:17).

SERVICE OPPORTUNITY DESCRIPTION FOR

Resource Guide

Service Requirements:
- Arrive at Coffee at 1:00 p.m. and stay until 7:00 p.m.
- Comfortable taking money and making change
- Able to work at Kickoff Night from 6:30 p.m. until 10:00 p.m.

Service Responsibilities:
1. Set up the resource table and arrange the books with appropriate signs to detail the price of the books.
2. Stay at the table during registration, all breaks, and at the end of the Coffee.
3. Replenish the resource table as needed.
4. Familiarize yourself with the books so you can answer questions.
5. Encourage women to stop and look at the resources and be ready to give suggestions as to which might best apply to them.
6. After the Coffee, break down the set up and put everything away.
7. Inventory the remaining books.
8. Give the record of sales and money to the **Financial Shepherd Coach.**
9. Follow the same procedure for Kickoff Night.

Service Duration:
You do need to arrive at 1:00 p.m. and be able to stay until the Coffee is over. You will also serve at Kickoff Night. We would appreciate your service for a minimum of one year, since there is extensive training and research on your part for this position.

Hospitality Floater

(Optional Position)

A **Hospitality Floater** is an optional position when you have more helpers at the Coffees. She can serve as a backup to fill in for another position that has an emergency and cannot make it to the Coffee. She can be the person who does all those last minute things that everyone forgot about, or who goes to the store if you run out of something. The **Hospitality Floater** is a backup, "please-could-you-do-this-or-get-that," position.

The **Hospitality Floater** can be the **Greeter** at the front door, if registration is outside and your official **Greeter/Hugger** is out on the sidewalk. She can make the coffee when it gets low and fill the punch bowl. She can help set up extra chairs if needed. She can perform the vital task of mingling with the guests to see if they have any questions or seem not to have anyone with whom to talk. She can be the one to tactfully remind any helpers who might be huddled together talking that they too need to be working or mingling with the guests. While this is a very vital role, your other helpers can be **Hospitality Floaters** if you do not have enough women initially for the luxury of this position. Keep your eyes open though for that outgoing, gregarious, yet gentle and caring, woman, who is humble enough to be a joyful gofer.

"If your gift is that of serving others, serve them well"
(Romans 12:7).

Service Opportunity Description for
Hospitality Floater

Service Requirements:
- Arrive at 1:00 p.m. and stay until 7 p.m.
- Enjoy mingling and talking with people
- Sensitive to when someone needs help or is looking lost or uncomfortable

Service Responsibilities:
1. As guests arrive, direct them to the food and areas to sit while they fill out their Profile Cards.
2. Walk around and talk to the ladies as they fill out their cards. Ask if they have any questions. Be sure and remind them to fill out everything on their cards.
3. Direct your attention to the guests and their needs.
4. If someone is sitting alone or looking uncomfortable, go up to her and chat for awhile. Let her know how glad you are that she is with us.
5. Keep an eye open for any helpers who might be huddling and kindly ask them to help you mingle.
6. Show the ministry hospitality to all the ladies present.
7. Be on the alert for any areas where your help might be needed, such as making more coffee, setting up more chairs, running an errand, filling in for a missing helper.
8. Inform the helpers to put their purses and belongings in a designated area.
9. Familiarize yourself with the inside operations of the Coffee so that you can help everyone be set up and ready by 1:30.
10. If registration is outside, position yourself to be the **Greeter** as the ladies enter the home.

Service Duration:
Your position is key to helping the guests feel warm and welcome and assisting your fellow Coffee helpers in the overall smooth operation of the day. You will need to plan on staying from 1 p.m. to 7 p.m. to help anyone who may need your assistance. Thank you for giving your heart and time.

Prayer Day Team

The **Prayer Day Team** makes all the work of the Orientation Coffee become a reality. They are essential to the heart of the Woman to Woman Mentoring Ministry. The women who serve on this team should be devoted to prayer and truly believe with conviction in the awesome power of intercessory prayer. Select women whom you know have a strong daily prayer life and have faith that God answers prayer. I recommend that you, or the **Prayer Day Shepherd Coach**, interview each woman who would like to serve on the **Prayer Day Team** to ensure she understands the important role of praying for the Lord to do the matching.

It is also essential that every woman on this team understand and commit to the confidentiality that must be part of the work they do for the Lord on this day. Nothing they read on the women's Profile Cards or discuss during the praying and matching process goes beyond the **Prayer Day Team**. They must understand that means even their husbands! You have assured the women being matched that everything they wrote on their Profile Cards would be kept in strictest confidence and only read by those who are praying over the cards. It is essential to the success of the Mentoring Ministry that this promise be honored, and that your **Prayer Day Team** operates with strict guidelines of trust.

I feel that praying for the mentoring matches is one of the most rewarding jobs in the Woman to Woman Mentoring Ministry. The Lord using a person in this way is incredible. The feeling of closeness to Him is truly divine!

"Then you will call upon me and come and pray to me, and I will listen to you. You will seek me and find me when you seek me with all your heart" (Jeremiah 29:12-13).

SERVICE OPPORTUNITY DESCRIPTION FOR

Prayer Day Team Member

Service Requirements:
- Able to attend the Orientation Coffee being prayed for
- Available for the entire day following the Orientation Coffee
- Love to pray and commune with God
- Willing to pray as long as it takes to get everyone matched
- Willing to keep everything read on the Profile Cards in strictest confidence and not discuss anything with anyone outside of the **Prayer Day Team**

Service Responsibilities:
1. Arrive at the Coffee at 1:00 p.m. to help with last minute preparation.
2. Act as a floater during registration time and breaks, and talk to the guests. Answer questions about Profile Cards. This will help you get to know the guests better.
3. After the break, position yourself in a place where you can see and hear all the women sharing.
4. Take notes as each woman shares what she is looking for in a mentoring relationship, as well as anything that might be helpful in matching her.
5. On Prayer Day, the Monday following the Coffee, arrive at the designated house on time and ready to put in a full day of prayer.
6. Participate in praying and interceding over the Profile Cards and letting the Lord speak through you as to whom He wants matched together.
7. Pray and interact with the other members of the **Prayer Day Team**.
8. Share the notes you took at the Coffee to refresh everyone's memories about the person's Profile Card being prayed over.
9. Continue the praying process until all Profile Cards are matched.
10. Attend and assist at Kickoff Night. You will see the fruition of your prayers and intercession in matching the M&Ms.
11. Attend the Six-Month Potluck Celebration and hear the testimonies of what God has done in the relationships. You won't want to miss this!

Service Duration:
You pray until you match everyone. Depending on the number of women praying and the number of Profile Cards, it can take as little as 4 hours and as long as 14. This job is so rewarding as you watch the women the Lord has used you to match get together and impact each other's lives. It is humbling to see how the Lord worked through you to perform miracles. There is no way you could have made such perfect matches on your own. Once you do it, you will probably be a regular on the team. It is great to have the continuity of women who have previously served on Prayer Day. Stay on as long as you feel used and at peace with it, whether that is one time or every time.

Woman to Woman Mentoring

Phone Communicator

Phone Communicators are essential to the operation of the ministry and should be enlisted as soon as possible. They should be women who enjoy communicating the blessings of the ministry and who are willing to receive phone calls in their homes. It is important that the **Phone Communicators** have a good understanding of the operation of the ministry and a good attitude about it. This might seem obvious, but beware of overlooking it in your enthusiasm to get help in this area. It is best if they have participated in a mentoring relationship and had a positive experience. They need to be organized women who will keep good records of the phone calls they made and the results of those calls.

You can never have too many **Phone Communicators**. As the ministry establishes itself and begins growing, there are many phone calls to make and receive, and follow-ups requiring a personal touch. The **Ministry Leader** should never try to do this all herself or she will soon be overwhelmed. There are many women who cannot serve outside their homes for various reasons but would be delighted to make phone calls.

"Let her work bring her praise" (Proverbs 31:31).

SERVICE OPPORTUNITY DESCRIPTION FOR

Phone Communicator

Service Requirements:
- Have a phone
- Enjoy talking on the phone
- Have opportunities during the day when you can make phone calls

Service Responsibilities:
1. Periodically there is a need to communicate with members of the ministry by phone. These are often unscheduled and may occur at various times throughout the year. A **Phone Communicator** is an "on-call" position, notified when there is a need. Some usual times are:
   - the week before a Coffee—those who have registered get a reminder call.
   - three weeks before a Coffee—call the waiting list.
   - information call to announce an upcoming training or event.
   - call to arrange food for a meeting or party.
   - take a shift retreiving and returning calls from the ministry voicemail box.
2. Communicate back to the **Phone Coordinator** the results of the calls.
3. Need to be flexible about the times you will serve.

Service Duration:
When you offer to be a **Phone Communicator**, we assume you are willing to be "on-call" until you request removal from the communication list. If there is a change in your life and you can no longer be a **Phone Communicator**, just call and ask to have your name removed from the list. Phone call assignments usually do not last longer than a week.

Prayer Warriors

Prayer Warriors are the eyes and ears of the ministry. These are the women who will communicate regularly with the M&M relationships. They also will be covering them with a hedge of protection as they pray daily for the Lord to bless the relationships and for His will to be done in the six months they will be meeting. The **Prayer Warriors** are essential to the ministry. As we continually changed the role of the **Prayer Warriors** to have a more interactive role with the M&M relationships, we saw a corresponding growth in the success rate of the relationships. Many women attributed the miracles and blessings they saw in their M&M relationships to the consistent praying and communication of their **Prayer Warriors**.

Prayer Warriors are by definition women who love to pray and are committed to a daily prayer time with God. They are willing to make the monthly phone calls to their assigned M&Ms and meet with them during the six-month commitment period. We have had women who said they could commit to pray but were not good at phone calling. We thanked them for their offer but kindly explained that it was essential for the M&Ms to talk to their **Prayer Warriors** regularly. The M&Ms need to have an opportunity to give the **Prayer Warriors** their prayer requests and know they are receiving prayer. They are willing to be the first line of communication if the M&M relationships have questions or run into problems. The **Prayer Warriors** need to have been in mentoring relationships and had positive experiences or worked through any problems. They are encouragers to their M&Ms and will give constructive advice. If a relationship is seriously having a problem, the **Prayer Warrior** should report this to the **Prayer Warrior Shepherd Coach** immediately. Because the M&Ms may be sharing some personal information about their relationships, there is a need for confidentiality with the **Prayer Warrior, Prayer Warrior Shepherd Coach**, and **Ministry Relationship Shepherdess**.

"Be joyful always; pray continually"
(1 Thessalonians 5:16-17).

Service Opportunity Description for

Prayer Warrior

Service Requirements:
- Enjoy prayer and have a daily prayer life
- Have a phone
- Be a prayer intercessor
- Be available to attend the Kickoff Night for the Coffee for which you pray
- Be willing to arrange for two M&M meetings during the six months
- Attend the Six-Month Potluck Celebration of your assigned M&Ms

Service Responsibilities:
1. On Kickoff Night, you will receive a Prayer Warrior Handbook with the names and phone numbers of four or five mentoring relationships. You can use the Prayer Warrior Journal to record for yourself each time you call and pray for them.
2. On Kickoff Night, meet each of the M&M relationships you are praying for, initial their signed Mentoring Covenants, and pray for them.
3. Pray for your assigned M&M relationships in your daily prayer time.
4. Call each woman the first week of each month to let her know both that you are praying for her, and to see if she has any questions or prayer requests.
5. If you run across someone who is having trouble in her relationship or has a question you cannot answer, you are to report this to the **Prayer Warrior Shepherd Coach**. She may have you call them back with a suggestion for the problem, she may take care of it herself, or she may have you call the **Ministry Relations Shepherdess**.
6. During the second month of their M&M relationships, coordinate a date when all the mentors you are praying for meet to pray together as a group and ask any questions they may have. Ask the **Ministry Relations Shepherdess** and **Prayer Warrior Shepherd Coach** to attend also, if possible. Again, report any problems or concerns to the **Prayer Warrior Shepherd Coach**.
7. One time during the fifth month of the M&M relationships, coordinate a time for all the mentors and mentees you are praying for to meet together to pray and discuss their relationships. Ask the **Ministry Relations Shepherdess** or **Prayer Warrior Shepherd Coach** to attend, and report any problems to the **Prayer Warrior Shepherd Coach**.
8. Attend the Six-Month Potluck Celebration of your assigned M&M relationships.

Service Duration:
The mentoring relationships you are praying for last six months. You will pray for them beginning the first week and call them once a month for six months. That will complete one prayer assignment. Each Coffee needs **Prayer Warriors**. If you would like another assignment, please tell the **Prayer Warrior Shepherd Coach**.

Information Table Representative

You may call this position something different in your church. I am referring to a spot at church to advertise the Woman to Woman Mentoring Ministry, a place for ministries to display information about their ministry during weekend services. Hopefully this is available in your church. You want a representative from the Mentoring Ministry to be at the table to answer questions and hand out fliers explaining the ministry. This is especially important in the weeks prior to an Orientation Coffee. If you have multiple services, it is good to share the load and have an **Information Table Representative** work a shift at the service she attends. It is ideal if you can find women who will take a shift of duty on a regular basis and are willing to work at the table every weekend. That helps with consistency and may even become their permanent position in the ministry.

It is imperative that the **Information Table Representative** has been in an M&M relationship and had a good experience. She is essentially your public relations representative for the ministry. You want her to encourage the women who come to the table with apprehension and questions. We have many testimonies where an M&M shares that she was nervous about attending the Orientation Coffee, but the smiling face and kindness of the **Information Table Representative** at the table assured her and gave her confidence to attend. You want everyone to have that kind of response.

"Now you are the body of Christ, and each one of you is a part of it. ... God has appointed ... those able to help others" (1 Corinthians 12:27,28).

SERVICE OPPORTUNITY DESCRIPTION FOR

Information Table Representative

Service Requirements:
- Work the same church service for one month
- Like to meet people and enjoy talking
- Enjoy giving information and encouraging women to participate in the ministry
- Have been a mentor or mentee and had a positive experience

Service Responsibilities:
1. You will need to arrive a half hour before the service and stay at least 30-35 minutes after the service.
2. If your shift is the first service of the day, please set out the materials. If your shift is the last service of the day, please put all the materials away.
3. As women come up to the table and ask questions, answer their questions and give them information about the ministry and the next Coffee.
4. If there is a sign-up sheet for the next Coffee, register their names on it or advise them to call the ministry phone number.
5. Hand out fliers describing the Woman to Woman Mentoring Ministry or announcing the next Coffee.

Service Duration:
You sign up to serve at the table for one month. If you are willing to take more than one month, please let us know. It is a great way to become acquainted with women of the church and share blessings you receive from the Woman to Woman Mentoring Ministry. Your enthusiasm will go a long way in encouraging another woman to participate. Thank you for your servant's heart.

The church service you signed up for is _____ for the month of _____.

Prayer Chain Shepherd & Lights

The **Prayer Chain Shepherd** retrieves the prayer requests from the general ministry voicemail box at the church. She notes the prayer requests in a succinct sentence, using the person's name and the same words of the requester. She then erases the prayer requests from the message center. Next she calls the Prayer Chain voicemail and leaves the prayer requests in the form of a prayer. She also records the praises. **Prayer Chain Shepherds** are put on a "**Shepherd** of the Day" rotating cycle of picking up prayer requests and transferring the prayers. The **Prayer Chain Shepherd** keeps the prayer requests on the Prayer Chain voicemail for one week and then erases them. She administers a group of **Lights** assigned to her chain. She calls the **Prayer Chain Lights** in her chain once a month and is a source of prayer and support to them. If the "**Shepherd** of the Day" receives an emergency prayer request, she immediately calls the other **Prayer Chain Shepherds**, and they will call the **Lights** in their chains.

The **Prayer Chain Lights** are the numerous pray-ers who comprise the multiple chains in the Prayer Chain. They will receive a **Prayer Chain Shepherd** for organizational purposes, guidance, and direction. They comprise a **Shepherd's** chain. They call the Prayer Chain voicemail daily, pick up prayer requests and praises, and then pray for them. In an emergency, they may receive a call from their **Shepherd** to pray immediately. One **Light** can form a buddy system with another **Light** on her chain and pray together as prayer partners. No discussion of prayer requests occurs outside the Prayer Chain.

"I am the good shepherd; I know my sheep and my sheep know me" (John 10:14).

Service Opportunity Description for
Prayer Chain Shepherd

Service Requirements:
- Enjoy prayer and have a daily prayer life
- Have a telephone
- Be a prayer intercessor
- Willing to take responsibility for daily checking prayer request line during assigned days
- Organized
- Willing to be discreet and not discuss prayer requests
- Willing to oversee a chain of **Prayer Chain Lights**

Service Responsibilities:
1. During assigned days as "**Shepherd** of the Day," frequently check the ministry message line for prayer requests.
2. Write down the prayer requests and praises. Use the person's name and as many of her original words as possible.
3. Form the message into a succinct prayer request and call it into the Prayer Chain voicemail. Leave the prayer request in the form of a prayer for the **Lights** to pick up. Also, leave praises.
4. Remove any prayer requests or praises that have been on the Prayer Chain voicemail for a week.
5. Oversee a chain of **Lights** assigned to you. Call them once a month to give encouragement and support. Pray with them and hear their own personal prayer requests.
6. If you are the "**Shepherd** of the Day" retrieving prayer requests and there is an emergency prayer request, immediately call the other **Shepherds** to call the **Lights** in their chains.
7. Report any problems or questions to the **Prayer Chain Shepherd Coach.**

Service Duration:
This position is central to the Prayer Chain. We hope that you will enjoy it and serve for an extended time. If your schedule should change and you can no longer perform as a **Shepherd**, we would appreciate you asking one of your **Lights** to replace you.

"I have made you a light" (Acts 13:47).

Service Opportunity Description for
Prayer Chain Light

Service Requirements:
- Enjoy prayer and have a daily prayer life
- Have a telephone
- Be a prayer intercessor
- Willing to take responsibility for daily checking Prayer Chain voicemail
- Organized
- Willing to be discreet and not discuss prayer requests

Service Responsibilities:
1. Call the Prayer Chain voicemail daily and check for new prayer requests and praises.
2. Immediately pray for the requests, and write them down to pray during your prayer times.
3. Do not discuss the prayer requests with anyone outside the Prayer Chain, including the person who left the prayer request. Your job is to intercede and lift the prayer requests to the Lord.
4. This is a service performed in your own home and on your own time frame. We just ask that you do it daily.
5. In case of a crisis or emergency prayer request, your **Shepherd** will call you, and we ask that you pray immediately.
6. If you choose, you can form a prayer partner relationship with another **Light** in your chain.

Service Duration:
We appreciate your willingness to pray for your fellow sisters in Christ. There are so many heavenly rewards in being an intercessor. It blesses the Woman to Woman Mentoring Ministry to have you share this spiritual gift with us, however, praying should never be a burden. If your life situation changes, and it is no longer possible for you to perform this service, please inform your **Prayer Chain Shepherd**.

CHAPTER 14

"Just as there are many parts to our bodies, so it is with Christ's body. We are all parts of it and it takes every one of us to make it complete, for we each have different work to do. So we belong to each other, and each needs all the others ... If God has given you administrative ability and put you in charge of the work of others, take the responsibility seriously" (Romans 12:4,5,8).

When Is It Time to Give Away the Ministry?

You Need to Let Go to Grow

I can hear you now, "Give my ministry away? She must be crazy. I just got it going good, and it is growing faster than I can keep up with!" My point exactly. If you are completing the first year of the ministry and it has grown as ours did, you probably feel as if you are dealing with one of those games we played as kids. You know, the one where you pounded down all the blocks with your hammer, but when you pounded down one block, another one popped up. Just like in the game, as you finish a Coffee and get everyone trained and matched, it is time for another group to have their Mentor Halftime Refresher. Then another Coffee is completing their six months, and a Potluck Celebration needs planning. It never stops, at least you hope it doesn't. How do you keep up with it all and have a life yourself? Or worse yet, not burn out?

You do not keep up with it all by yourself. You need administrative help. You need a team. More than just having someone to help you, you need to be ready to let them take over major parts of the ministry. The ministry needs to be in a position where it can continue to function even if you are not present. No ministry should be dependent on only one person. It certainly cannot grow and may fall apart if that one person becomes ill or moves.

I would advise you to try to find administrative helpers as soon as possible. I tried, but no one came forward, interestingly enough, until I really needed it. Our ministry started in January 1996. On October 20, 1996, we had our fifth and last Coffee of the year.

The Lord Did A Miracle That Day!

I put out my usual plea for administrative assistance. I was overjoyed when 7 women signed up that day to help administratively! We ended our first year with 176 women matched into mentoring relationships, and it was obvious that I could no longer lead it on my own. The Lord knew that the Woman to Woman Mentoring Ministry was going to experience a growth spurt, and I would need each of these 7 women.

The next week I called and thanked them for their offer of administrative service. We agreed on the night of November 26 for our first meeting. On the weekend of November 15-16, Pastor Rick gave a message to the congregation on the need for everyone to have a mentor in his or her life. He also stressed that as Christians, we needed to make ourselves available to mentor a newer Christian.

The church asked me if one of our M&Ms would give a testimony. We found a dynamic mentee to give her testimony, and she brought her mentor on stage and presented her with flowers. Pastor Rick concluded the message by instructing those who wanted to be involved in the Woman to Woman Mentoring Ministry to write *mentoring* on the church registration card and put it in the offering basket. Approximately 500 women turned in response cards!

God knew this was going to happen, because He had put the message on Pastor Rick's heart. I did not know about the message until the week before when they called me to ask for someone to give a testimony. I never panicked though, because I knew the Lord had provided me the administrative help I needed even before I knew I was going to need it. Our God is an awesome God. He knows when you will need help, too.

Next came the time for me to decide what I needed these seven women to do. What part of the ministry was I going to turn over to someone else? How would I be sure they performed the tasks just the way I wanted? What if they forgot something important? What if they did not have time to complete the job? What if they did not take it as seriously as I did? Are these some of your thoughts? The Lord kindly reminded me that this was not my ministry—it was His. I heard Pastor Rick's voice in my ear.

"As your ministry grows bigger, it has to become smaller. If not, your ministry will be like a big snowball that is rolling down the hill, getting bigger and bigger as it picks up more snow while rolling. It will soon be a big ball rolling out of control, until it hits a tree and flies into a million snowflakes."

I knew Pastor Rick was right. After his mentoring message, the phone rang continuously. Our ministry was going to grow fast in the new year. As our first year was ending, I could see the Woman to Woman Mentoring Ministry snowball rolling and getting bigger and bigger as we planned a December Christmas Party, a Mentor Halftime Refresher in November, and a new ministry Prayer Chain. The first weekend in January was a Six-Month Potluck Celebration, and the second weekend in January was the first Coffee of 1997. There was no question that I could not keep my hand in everything any longer. That snowball was picking up speed down the hill, and I could see the trees below. I needed to quickly delegate responsibility.

Saddleback Church has a class called 301 in which church members discover the gifts the Lord has given them to use for Him. At Saddleback we call

Our God is an awesome God. He knows when you will need help.

it your S.H.A.P.E. (**S**piritual Gifts, **H**eart, **A**bilities, **P**ersonality, **E**xperiences). We know that people do best when they are working within their natural gifts and talents. I knew I could not assign these seven women the particular areas of administration I thought would be best for them. They would know their own S.H.A.P.E. and what they were most gifted to do.

I made a list of all the areas where I needed help. Of course, at that point it was *all* areas. With the help of one other woman, I had been doing all the administrative work as well as a good deal of the operational tasks. I prepared a list of administrative positions, and a Service Opportunity Description for each of the administrative areas I had identified. They would be able to see what each area entailed and make a determination as to which one matched their S.H.A.P.E. best.

I had identified more than seven areas of responsibility. At the meeting, I told the women they could choose more than one area if they wanted. We went over all the Service Opportunity Descriptions together, and I suggested they pick an area where they were gifted and felt they would have time to serve. At the end of the first meeting, I had the following positions filled: **Assistant/Apprentice, Prayer Day Shepherd Coach, Financial Shepherd Coach, Prayer Warrior Shepherd Coach, Hospitality Shepherd Coach, Prayer Chain Shepherd Coach,** and **Publicity Shepherd Coach.** In keeping with our "feed My sheep" beginnings, we use the title **Shepherd** for the **Administrative Team** and the title **Coach** to go with our Kickoff Night, Mentor Halftime Refresher, and team building theme. **Coordinators** are in leadership positions on the **Shepherd Coaches**' teams. This works for us, but you can use whatever titles you feel comfortable with.

When one woman said she would be **Financial Shepherd Coach**, another laughed that this was a perfect area for her because she kept her checkbook balanced to the penny. She knew her S.H.A.P.E. The women left the meeting ready to take on their new administrative tasks. I breathed a sigh of relief. The ministry would soon be able to get along without me. Well, maybe not completely.

The first Coffee after the administrative meeting was our largest, with 86 women attending. It was the first Coffee when all I had to do was show up and do my part. I didn't talk to the **Hostess** until the day of the Coffee. Each **Administrative Team** member did her part, and it went beautifully. By the next **Administrative Team** meeting on February 1, 1997, we had grown from 7 to 12 on our **Administrative Team**. I thought that was a prophetic number, and I hoped it would signify the plans the Lord had for us.

Always make it known that you need administrative help, and always be on the lookout for women who show leadership gifts and abilities. As you pray about it, the Lord will bring women forward to help you, but be selective in whom you chose to work on your **Administrative Team.**

I found that I actually did not need 12 administrative positions. Now I have an **Apprentice/Assistant, Training Leader,** and 7 **Shepherd Coaches**, and they each develop a team from the helper servants within their area of responsibility. I learned that if your **Administrative Team** is too big it can easily become a

"As your ministry grows bigger, it has to become smaller."

Chapter 14: When Is It Time to Give Away the Ministry?

committee bogged down with too many opinions, personalities, and conflicts. Yes, conflicts happen even among Christian women! If you are looking for some excellent counsel in leading, look to Jesus! I also highly recommend Bob Briner and Ray Pritchard's books *The Leadership Lessons of Jesus* and *More Leadership Lessons of Jesus*. These books revolutionized the way I lead the ministry.

I learned to lead with the same principles that Jesus used. While I thought my 12 administrative positions were following Jesus' model, these books pointed out to me that Jesus did not have each disciple on His core leadership team. He had 3 close and trusted disciples as His core team, and they were the ones that were with Him when He was making major decisions.

Another lesson I learned was that Jesus handpicked His disciples. He asked them to join Him. Wow! That was a revelation for me! I had been so eager to get administrative help that if someone said they wanted to lead in an area, I gave it to them. I was just happy not to have to be doing it myself. Big mistake! Through God's intervention, I am sure, I literally did scale my team of 12 down to 3 trusted women. Then I built back up again using the principles I learned in the Briner and Pritchard books. Here are a few tips for selecting your **Administrative Team:**

- **Administrative Team** members need to have been involved in the ministry and experienced the blessings of successful mentoring relationships.
- Interview a new **Shepherd Coach** to learn about her spiritual gifts, spiritual maturity, and willingness to assume the responsibility of the position.
- Thoroughly discuss the Service Opportunity Description for the position to be sure she can assume all of the duties and responsibilities expected.
- Pray together and separately for a period of time to discern if you are both comfortable with her taking the administrative role. Don't make a quick decision, and don't be afraid to tell her if you feel this may not be a good fit. Better to do it now; if it is not right it will be much harder later.
- Select women who are willing to build a team themselves and to develop an assistant or apprentice.
- If one of your **Administrative Team** members retires, and she does not have an apprentice, look at the members of her team and see if anyone shows potential for leadership. Go through the same interview process.
- Sit back and watch the Lord work through the women on your **Administrative Team** just as He has worked through you.

Meet with your **Administrative Team** monthly. Have each team member give a report on her area of responsibility. Ask them to make note of items where they need to take action. Initially, I asked each of the **Administrative Team** members to call, fax, or email me each week to let me know the activities in their area of responsibility. None of the pressure comes off you if you are sitting home wondering if everything is being done. That can be as stressful as trying to do it all yourself. I soon realized, however, that this method still kept me at the center of everything and was almost as time consuming as doing it myself! After much prayer I arrived at a method that has worked fabulously. I asked each

Jesus handpicked His disciples.

Administrative Team member to make a list of the things she does to get ready for an event. Then they exchanged lists with another woman on the team and became accountability partners. They served as a check and balance to be sure all was done, and I was taken out of the loop. This helped a great deal in cementing relationships on the team and gave them a sense of it being their ministry.

Thanks to these wonderful women, we now have a fabulous newsletter mailed to the ministry participants by our **Publicity Shepherd Coach,** who also oversees all communication and advertising in the ministry. I have turned over the training to a **Training Leader**. I never handle the donations or spending of it; our **Financial Shepherd Coach** takes care of that.

What do I do, you ask? As of this writing, I am still attending and leading the Coffees, and I am part of Monday's Prayer Day Team. I can see the day coming, however, when I will be able to clone myself, and Coffees will successfully take place without me being present. This should be your ultimate goal, too.

Do not get me wrong. It's not that I don't want to be there. I love the Coffees, and I never tire of seeing the wonder of the Lord at work. You will find though, if you are the only one orchestrating a Coffee, they can only happen when you are available. Unless you have no life at all, quarterly Coffees are about all you can handle. If other women, in addition to you, equip themselves to lead, you could be having an Orientation Coffee every month in different parts of the city or county. Many possibilities will reveal themselves to you as your ministry grows and leaders begin to emerge from the mentors and mentees.

You will notice that I do not have a Service Opportunity Description for you and me. That is because it is always evolving. In the beginning you do a little bit of everything. Then you move into a leadership position where you are responsible for everyone else doing their part. Today my title is the **Ministry Visionary Shepherd,** and I like that much better than being called the *leader* or *director.*

You will do the groundbreaking work in the beginning that turns your vision into a reality. Groundbreaking is a good word for it because it can be laborious and exhausting. But remember the verse from Chapter 13, "In my distress I called to the Lord; I cried to my God for help. From his temple he heard my voice; my cry came before him, into his ears" (Ps. 18:6). When He answers your cry and brings that help, you must rejoice and let them serve!

As I prepared to present to the 86 women coming though the door at our sixth Coffee, I watched chairs being delivered, wiped dry (it was raining), and set up in the living room where we were meeting. Previous to this Coffee, I had always borrowed chairs from everyone I knew. On Coffee day, I would load up my jeep with folding chairs and bring them with me to the Coffee. Arriving at the Coffee, I would begin unloading not only the chairs but the coffeemaker, punch bowl, all the supplies, and the handouts for the Coffee. I would hurry and set up the chairs, show the **Hostess** how to use the coffeemaker and, of course, reload it all after the Coffee. For the sixth Coffee, our new **Hospitality Shepherd Coach** suggested we try to borrow chairs from the church. She made all the arrangements to pick them up at church, set them up at the home, and return them to the church. What a great idea! Why hadn't I thought of that?

In the beginning, I was the one who raced the film to a one-hour developer, picked up the developed pictures, and stayed up until midnight putting the pictures on the Profile Cards. Actually, now that I think about it, I took the pictures, too! First, I gave up taking the pictures. Then I handed over the film developing run. Then someone suggested instant pictures, and the entire process became less stressful and more efficient. Next, I gave up feeling as if only I could put the pictures on the Profile Cards.

It continues to amaze me how the Lord works at teaching me to let go. I received a phone call from the new **Prayer Warrior Shepherd Coach**. She wanted to meet some of the **Prayer Warrior** candidates and since this was her first time, I thought I needed to be at the meeting to show her "how I felt it should be done." She called to tell me they were meeting the next Sunday afternoon. I quickly ran over my weekend calendar—my son's wedding on Saturday, out-of-town guests in my home all weekend—Sunday afternoon, no problem.

She very gently said, "I know you have a busy week with your son getting married on Saturday and trying to finish your book, so you don't have to be there. It is OK if you can't make it. I can take care of it." Of course she could. She and I had talked over this meeting, and she knew why we were having it. I did not need to be there. Are you getting the idea? I had to let go of "my baby." I needed to let it grow and mature and give others the opportunity to grow with it.

Each of the **Administrative Team** still needs my input, and I do continue to think of new ideas for improving our ministry. However, I am *overseeing* rather than *doing* everything myself. I also can now make myself available to help other churches set up their own Woman to Woman Mentoring Ministries.

Following are the **Administrative Team** Service Opportunity Descriptions that I am currently using. After the **Administrative Team** positions you will find five Service Opportunity Descriptions for **Coordinator** and **Shepherdess** positions that are helpful and nice to have, but they are not essential to the operation of the ministry. They would each serve on one of the **Shepherd Coaches'** teams. As more women join the ministry and add their spiritual gifts and talents, you will have more potential to fill these positions. Until then, the **Administrative Team** and the Shepherd Coaches can perform the duties.

You may need to modify these Service Opportunity Descriptions, but use them as a guideline until you develop your own. (With the CD-ROM included in the Leader Kit, you can customize the descriptions for your ministry. Or you have permission to make copies from this book. You will also find a Service Opportunity Description Index on page 4 for your future reference.) Notice that each description has a requirement that they develop an assistant. This is essential to the continued operation of the ministry. If the **Shepherd Coach** leaves the ministry, the assistant can step in. She can also substitute at **Administrative Team** meetings or any other time the **Shepherd Coach** is not available.

I needed to let the ministry grow and mature and give others the opportunity to grow with it.

"Two are better than one, because they have a good return for their work: If one falls down, his friend can help him up. But pity the man who falls and has no one to help him up!" (Ecclesiastes 4:9,10).

Service Opportunity Description for

Assistant/Apprentice

(Administrative Team Position)

Service Requirements:
- Have a heart for women and their issues
- Have an understanding of the instructions the Lord gave to mature Christian women when He had Paul write Titus 2:3-5, telling them to be role models for the upcoming generations of women believers
- Have a desire to see the Woman to Woman Mentoring Ministry reach as many women as possible
- Serve on the **Administrative Team** and attend monthly meetings

Service Responsibilities:
1. Assist with all aspects of the administration of the ministry.
2. Attend Orientation Coffees and assist the **Ministry Leader** with the program.
3. If possible, be part of the **Prayer Day Team** that matches the mentoring relationships.
4. Help make announcements promoting the ministry at various church functions.
5. Represent the ministry when the **Ministry Leader** is unavailable.
6. Help with training as needed.
7. Network the ministry and be a source of information to those who want to learn more.
8. Be flexible to help where needs arise.
9. Help with special projects.
10. Be on the alert for ways to improve or add to the operation of the ministry.
11. Help lead **Administrative Team** meetings.

Service Duration:
As long as the Lord brings new Christian women to our church, there will be a need for a Woman to Woman Mentoring Ministry and women to organize and operate it. However, when it stops being fun and becomes a burden, that is probably the time to take a break. On the other hand, if the **Ministry Leader** receives a calling away from this area of service, the **Assistant** could keep the ministry operating.

"Likewise, teach the older women to be reverent in the way they live, not to be slanders or addicted to much wine, but to teach what is good. Then they can train the younger women" (Titus 2:3-4).

SERVICE OPPORTUNITY DESCRIPTION FOR

Training Leader

(Administrative Team Position)

Service Requirements:
- Experience in setting up and operating training programs helpful, although not mandatory
- Teaching experience helpful, but not necessary
- Willing to coordinate and operate the training program for the ministry
- Have sufficient time in your schedule to take on a job of this magnitude
- Serve on the **Administrative Team** and attend meetings
- Lead a **Training Team**; develop an **Assistant Trainer**

Service Responsibilities:
1. Recruit a team to help with training programs.
2. Follow the *Woman to Woman Mentoring: Training Leader's Guide* for Kickoff Night and Mentor Halftime Refreshers.
3. Develop a calendar of dates and times for each year's training schedule. Training would include a minimum of:
   - Kickoff Night Training
   - Mentor Halftime Refresher for mentors
   - Quarterly training for mentors, sometimes to include mentees and interested women in the church
4. Arrange for meeting rooms.
5. Coordinate publicity of training sessions with **Phone Coordinator** and **Publicity Shepherd Coach**, or both.
6. Arrange for guest speakers when appropriate.
7. Design and print any literature or training materials that will be used in addition to the *Mentor* and *Mentee Handbooks*.

Service Duration:
Hopefully this position is permanent. You will develop a team in the areas where you need assistance. The **Ministry Leader** will also interact and help where and when needed.

"Whatever you do, work at it with all your heart, as working for the Lord, not for men, since you know that you will receive an inheritance from the Lord as a reward. It is the Lord Christ you are serving" (Colossians 3:23-24).

Service Opportunity Description for
Hospitality Shepherd Coach
(Administrative Team Position)

Service Requirements:
- Willing to plan the Coffees, organize helpers, and coordinate with the Coffee **Hostess**
- Flexible; able to stay calm in the midst of chaos
- Able to plan in advance and good at follow-up
- Previous event planning is helpful, but not necessary
- Have access to a computer—helpful, but not necessary
- Serve on the **Administrative Team** and attend monthly meetings
- Lead the **Hospitality Team**: all Coffee and Potluck helper positions; develop an assistant

Service Responsibilities:
1. Find a **Hostess** for each Coffee and Potluck; keep in continuous communication with her.
2. Coordinate with the **Publicity Shepherd Coach** to have fliers made announcing the date and location. These should be out six weeks prior to the Coffee, so give her plenty of notice.
3. Send a letter to the **Hostess** one month in advance along with the Hostess Checklist.
4. Help the **Hostess** obtain any items she might need. Keep her calm and reassured.
5. Work with the **Phone Coordinator** to call everyone registered for a Coffee and reconfirm one week prior to the Coffee.
6. Ask **Servant Coordinator** (if you don't have one you will need to do this yourself) to recruit a **Greeter/Hugger**, two **Registrars**, a **Photographer, Photographer's Assistant, Name Tag Scribe, Hospitality Floater,** and **Resource Guide** for the Coffees. Send out Service Opportunity Descriptions.
7. If extra chairs are needed, obtain in advance and make arrangements for them to be delivered to the Coffee and returned.
8. Attend the Coffee and oversee the helpers and details of the Coffee.
9. After the Coffee, give the **Ministry Relations Shepherdess** the names of the **Hostess** and all the helpers so she can send thank-you notes.
10. Arrange with the **Hostess** for the Six-Month Potluck Celebration and coordinate with the **Publicity Shepherd Coach** to send out the Potluck Celebration Letter one month before the event.
11. Recruit a **Photographer** for the Six-Month Potluck Celebration.

Service Duration:
Once you have gone through the process the first time, you will have the experience to develop a routine. This could be a position for two people to work in together, but it is important that you have good communication. We hope that you will take this position for at least one year of Coffees. It is very rewarding to see how the Lord works at the Coffees and to know you had a vital part in making it all happen.

"Here is a trustworthy saying: If anyone sets his heart on being an overseer, he desires a noble task" (1 Timothy 3:1).

Service Opportunity Description for
Prayer Warrior Shepherd Coach
(Administrative Team Position)

Service Requirements:
- Good at coaching and motivating people
- Organized and consistent
- Have a computer
- Strong belief in power of prayer and impact it can have on mentoring relationships
- Willingness to hold **Prayer Warriors** accountable for their responsibilities
- Serve on the **Administrative Team** and attend monthly meetings
- Lead the **Prayer Warrior Team**: all **Prayer Warriors**; develop an assistant

Service Responsibilities:
1. Recruit three or four **Prayer Warriors** for each Coffee, giving them each the date, location, and time to meet on Kickoff Night.
2. Contact the **Prayer Day Shepherd Coach** after each Coffee to obtain the names and phone numbers of the matched mentoring relationships.
3. Maintain and update the Mentoring Roster.
4. Assign four or five mentoring relationships to each **Prayer Warrior** and prepare a Prayer Warrior Handbook consisting of:
   - Mentoring Roster for their Coffee
   - Prayer Warrior Journal
   - Service Opportunity Description
   - Prayer Warrior Guidelines
5. Attend Kickoff Night and meet with the **Prayer Warriors.** Give them their Prayer Handbooks and go over the procedure for the next six months.
6. After Kickoff Night, follow up with a phone call to see if there are any questions. Discuss with them the importance of their monthly phone calls. This is the only real contact the ministry has with each woman after the matching. Advise them to let you know if they run into any problems or have questions.
7. Let the **Prayer Warriors** know that you will be calling them the second week of every month to see how the phone calls went. Encourage them to call the matches the first week of the month for consistency and to arrange the second and fifth month meetings with their M&Ms.
8. Report back to the **Ministry Relations Shepherdess** any problems you cannot handle.
9. At times, the **Prayer Warriors** function as a telephone chain to get out pertinent information. You transmit information to each **Prayer Warrior** to pass on to her mentoring relationships.
10. You are the **Prayer Warrior** for the **Administrative Team**. Obtain their prayer requests at monthly meetings.

Service Duration:
The most active times of service will be right after a Coffee and the second week of each month. This position is so vital because the relationships feel blessed when they know someone is praying for them and taking time to call. Many times **Prayer Warriors** need a nudge or reminder. Some will be better than others. This should not be a time-consuming job, but it is essential. Prayer works, and sometimes we need that reminder.

172   Woman to Woman Mentoring

"For their prayer reached heaven, his holy dwelling place"
(2 Chronicles 30:27).

SERVICE OPPORTUNITY DESCRIPTION FOR

Prayer Day Shepherd Coach

(Administrative Team Position)

Service Requirements:
- Be able to attend the Coffees, Kickoff Nights and take part in the **Prayer Day Team**
- Comfortable with public prayer
- Serve on the **Administrative Team** and attend monthly meetings
- Lead the **Prayer Day Team**: all **Prayer Day Pray-ers**; develop an assistant

Service Responsibilities:
1. Before the guests arrive at the Coffee, gather the **Ministry Leader**, all the helpers, and the **Hostess** and lead in praying over the chairs and for the Coffee.
2. At the Coffee, mingle among the guests as they arrive and see if they have any questions about the Profile Cards. Make an effort to get to know the guests.
3. Take notes as each woman introduces herself and shares what brought her to the Coffee.
4. Recruit three or more **Prayer Day Team Members** to pray the day after the Coffee.
5. If you did not use instant film at the Coffee, pick-up the one-hour developed pictures Sunday night after the Coffee and attach them to the Profile Cards before the team starts the next morning (or assign someone to do it or to help you do it).
6. Make arrangements for the **Prayer Day Team** to meet on Monday to pray.
7. Lead the **Prayer Day Team** in praying over the Profile Cards.
8. Coordinate the **Phone Coordinator** phoning of the mentors and mentees the week after the Coffee to remind them of the Kickoff Meeting and the time they are to arrive.
9. See that the list of matches gets to the **Publicity Shepherd Coach** for input into the Mentoring Roster and the **Prayer Warrior Shepherd Coach** for the Prayer Warrior Journals.
10. Attend Kickoff Night and assist as needed.
11. Attend the Six-Month Potluck Celebration to see the blessings the Lord has provided through Prayer Day.

Service Duration:
The essential times of service are at the Coffees, Prayer Day, Kickoff Night, the Six-Month Potluck Celebrations, and in recruiting the **Prayer Day Team**. Most **Prayer Day Team** members are fairly loyal and consistent, so this should not change much. We always want to leave the door open for new women to participate in the joy and blessing of the experience.

"Let's have a feast and celebrate" (Luke 15:23).

SERVICE OPPORTUNITY DESCRIPTION FOR

Special Events Shepherd Coach

(Administrative Team Position)

Service Requirements:
- Love to have fun and party
- Be a planner and have some idea of what different events require
- Organized and flexible
- Creative; visionary; thinking beyond what is possible
- Serve on the **Administrative Team** and attend monthly meetings
- Lead a **Special Events Team** developed for the specific event; develop an assistant

Service Responsibilities:
1. Plan events for the women of the ministry for each year. This will require coordination with the **Ministry Leader**.
2. Arrange for the reservation of rooms on the church campus or outside the church.
3. Coordinate with other **Administrative Shepherd Coaches** and **Coordinators** and include them in their area of responsibility. Utilize their team members for specific areas such as hospitality, phoning, advertising, etc.
4. Plan the event program and use ministry resources and helpers.
5. Work with the **Financial Shepherd Coach** to establish a budget and obtain required funds.
6. Be creative!
7. Arrange for special guests or speakers, as needed.
8. Form and supervise a committee to help.
9. Plan Mentoring Ministry events such as a Christmas Party, Spring Tea, Holiday Boutique, or Mentoring Retreat.

Service Duration:
This position will be ongoing and will need to establish a permanent team to help with the events and details. It could be quite enjoyable for the person who likes to coordinate and be part of fun events.

"He will be the sure foundation for your times, a rich store of salvation and wisdom and knowledge; the fear of the Lord is the key to this treasure" (Isaiah 33:6).

Service Opportunity Description for

Financial Shepherd Coach

(Administrative Team Position)

Service Requirements:
- Good with numbers
- Willing to keep the donations and funds and be accountable for their use
- Have an assistant so one person is not responsible for all the money
- Serve on **Administrative Team** and attend monthly meetings
- Lead the **Financial Team**: **Resource Guide**, **Ministry Shopper**, bookkeeper; develop an assistant

Service Responsibilities:
1. Keep account of donations and allot how they are to be spent.
2. Be aware of opportunities to put out the donation basket.
3. Establish a policy for donations at the Coffees.
4. Work with **Special Events Shepherd Coach** to create ways to raise funds and develop creative ideas to use the funds such as t-shirts for the women in the ministry, funding special events, and helping offset administrative costs.
5. Be prepared to give any reports necessary on funds used and collected.
6. Deposit donations in church fund and obtain requisitions when necessary.
7. Research opportunities to buy supplies in bulk or at discounted prices.
8. Make purchases of items as necessary.
9. Obtain a minimum of two quotes before any purchases are made for the ministry.
10. Determine appropriateness of all purchases over $25.
11. Reimburse from receipts for approved purchases.
12. Obtain purchase orders and requisitions to order books from local Christian bookstores for sale at Coffees and Kickoff Nights.
13. Recruit helpers as needed.

Service Duration:
This is an ongoing position but will be busiest around the time of the Coffees or special events. Of course, there is always the planning and research to assure that we are good stewards of our money!

"They will tell of the glory of your kingdom and speak of your might, so that all men may know of your mighty acts" (Psalm 145:11-12).

SERVICE OPPORTUNITY DESCRIPTION FOR

Publicity Shepherd Coach

(Administrative Team Position)

Service Requirements:
- Keep current on ministry activities
- Has access to and is comfortable using a computer
- Organized—there are many facets to this position
- Serve on the **Administrative Team** and attend monthly meetings
- Develop a staff and lead the **Publicity Team**: **Phone Coordinator**, newsletter staff, **Information Table Representative**, develop an assistant

Service Responsibilities:
1. Coordinate with church office for submission of bulletin notices.
2. Develop, edit, print, and mail (with the newsletter staff) a quarterly newsletter.
3. Coordinate with all **Administrative Team** members for announcements of events in their area of the ministry that need publicizing or placement of notices in the newsletter.
4. Design and print (with the newsletter staff) all fliers, announcements, bulletin inserts, Coffee handouts and Programs, letters, and other items of publicity.
5. Keep the Woman to Woman Mentoring Ministry Information Table stocked with current fliers, registration sheets, and ministry representatives.
6. Maintain a current ministry roster of M&Ms.
7. Oversee the **Phone Coordinator** and all phone communication.
8. Look for new opportunities to advertise the Woman to Woman Mentoring Ministry.
9. Be creative!

Service Duration:
This is an ongoing position, because there is always something happening that needs publicizing as the ministry grows bigger and bigger. There are many talented people to help and serve on a team with you. This position will oversee that team and ensure that everything gets out in a timely fashion.

"Is any one of you in trouble? He should pray. Is anyone happy? Let him sing songs of praise. Is any one of you sick? He should call the elders of the church to pray for him and anoint him with oil in the name of the Lord. And the prayer offered in faith will make the sick person well; the Lord will raise him up. If he has sinned, he will be forgiven. Therefore, confess your sins to each other and pray for each other so that you may be healed. The prayer of a righteous man is powerful and effective" (James 5:13-16).

SERVICE OPPORTUNITY DESCRIPTION FOR
Prayer Chain Shepherd Coach
(Administrative Team Position)

Service Requirements:
- Good at coaching and motivating people
- Organized and consistent
- Strong belief in power of prayer and impact it can have on lives
- Willingness to hold the **Prayer Chain Shepherds** and **Lights** accountable for their responsibilities
- Willingness to take responsibility for the Prayer Chain and keep it current and vibrant
- Attend monthly **Administrative Team** meetings
- Lead the Prayer Chain: **Shepherds**, **Lights**, **Assistant**; develop an assistant

Service Responsibilities:
1. Contact all women who offer to serve on the Prayer Chain.
2. Hold periodic meetings for new people to learn how to become members of the Prayer Chain.
3. Be available to answer any questions from the Prayer Chain members.
4. Hold a quarterly meeting with the **Prayer Chain Shepherds** to evaluate the status of the Prayer Chain and any changes and or improvements that need to be made.
5. Maintain an up-to-date roster of the women on the Prayer Chain.
6. Put Woman to Woman Mentoring Ministry events requiring prayer coverage on the Prayer Chain (Coffees, Kickoffs, Potluck Celebrations, openings on the **Administrative Team**, special events, etc.).
7. Submit an article for the quarterly WTW newsletter encouraging use of the Prayer Chain.
8. Activate the Prayer Chain in case of a crisis or emergency prayer request.
9. Be available to encourage, pray for, and coach the **Prayer Chain Shepherds**.

Service Duration:
We hope that you will remain in this position for a minimum of one year. There is a great deal of rapport and team building on a Prayer Chain, and continuity is important. Always be aware of a **Light** who could replace a **Shepherd** when necessary, or add to the chain as it grows.

Woman to Woman Mentoring

"May the Lord, the God of the spirits of all mankind, appoint a man over this community to go out and come in before them, one who will lead them out and bring them in, so the Lord's people will not be like sheep without a shepherd" (Numbers 27:16).

SERVICE OPPORTUNITY DESCRIPTION FOR
Spiritual Shepherdess

Service Requirements:
- Comfortable praying out loud and in front of groups
- Enjoy studying devotional material
- Willing to do biblical research and search for answers to spiritual questions that may arise

Service Responsibilities:
1. Lead in prayer at all Orientation Coffees, training, and meetings.
2. Present the biblical references to mentoring as part of the Orientation Coffee Program.
3. Serve as the spiritual reference and mentor to the ministry.
4. Be sure everything in the ministry is biblically sound and glorifies God.
5. Provide the devotional reading for meetings and training.
6. Serve as a reference to M&Ms with spiritual or biblical questions.

Service Duration:
This is a very valuable and necessary position. It can be held in tandem with another administrative position. This position lasts for as long as the **Ministry Leader** and **Spiritual Shepherdess** feel it is enhancing the ministry.

"For there is one God and one mediator between God and men, the man Christ Jesus" (1 Timothy 2:5).

Service Opportunity Description for
Ministry Relations Shepherdess

Service Requirements:
- Previously served as a mentor in a mentoring relationship
- Able to be on call and flexible
- Compassionate and understanding, but also firm and able to instill a desire to be accountable to the Mentoring Covenant
- Able to be an encourager

Service Responsibilities:
1. Call and talk with mentoring relationships who may have questions or be struggling with their commitment.
2. Answer questions about the Woman to Woman Mentoring Ministry from women who call on the information line.
3. Serve as a "customer service representative" for the ministry.
4. Offer suggestions of ways to enhance and strengthen mentoring relationships.
5. Be prepared to always take the women back to the scriptures and prayer if they are encountering problems.
6. Send thank-you notes to Coffee helpers, hostesses, donators, and others as needed.
7. Attend the **Prayer Warriors'** meetings with their M&Ms to offer encouragement and answer questions.

Service Duration:
This is a key position in the ministry. The women in the ministry will build trust and confidence in this position if they know they are talking to the same person each time. This position does take a woman with a heart for the mentoring relationships and a deep desire to ensure they get the most that God has planned for them in their relationships. We hope you will serve in this position for an extended period of time—until you feel the Lord leading you to take a break or to serve in another area.

"Then he said to his disciples, 'The harvest is plentiful but the workers are few. Ask the Lord of the harvest, therefore, to send out workers into his harvest field' " (Matthew 9:37).

SERVICE OPPORTUNITY DESCRIPTION FOR

Recruiter & Servant Coordinator

Service Requirements:
- Have a computer
- Be in communication with all aspects of the ministry to know when events are occurring or what publications are being distributed that provide an opportunity for recruiting.
- Be organized and not hesitant to ask for help—women who sign up to help really do want to serve.

Service Responsibilities:
1. Make yourself aware of every opportunity for recruiting at all ministry training and events, as well as any publication being distributed. This will require contact with every aspect of the ministry.
2. Keep an ongoing, up-to-date list of the helpers and make that list available to the other **Ministry Coordinators** and **Shepherd Coaches** on the **Administrative Team**.
3. Make sure everyone who signs up for service is called and rotated through areas of service.
4. Make yourself available to help other **Ministry Coordinators** and **Shepherd Coaches** find helpers. You will be the central helper resource person.
5. Within two weeks following the Coffee, call all women who fill out an Opportunity to Serve Profile at the Coffees. If there is not an immediate need for their service, let them know you will call them when one arises.

Service Duration:
This will be an ongoing function. If all **Ministry Coordinators** and **Shepherd Coaches** go through you, then you will know how often someone is being called into service and will have the opportunity to ensure that everyone gets a chance to serve. Therefore, your service could be continual and sporadic. It also requires being current with what is happening in the ministry so you can anticipate opportunities to recruit and know in advance when you need workers for the harvest.

"I will sing to the Lord, I will sing; I will make music to the Lord, the God of Israel" (Judges 5:3).

SERVICE OPPORTUNITY DESCRIPTION FOR

Worship Director

Service Requirements:
- Able to attend the Orientation Coffee and arrive at 1:00 p.m.
- Enjoy leading singing with or without accompaniment.
- Comfortable leading a group of women in singing.
- Available to lead worship for special functions.

Service Responsibilities:
1. Plan and lead the worship part of the program for Orientation Coffees and/or special events.
2. Arrange for any accompaniment that might be required.
3. Arrange for music or words to be printed and coordinate with the **Publicity Shepherd Coach** to put them in the printed Programs.
4. Recruit a team to help when needed.

Service Duration:
This is a very special position for the woman who enjoys leading people into the presence of the Lord through music. It is a special gift, and we would appreciate your talents in this position for as long as you choose. Each Orientation Coffee will need worship for the opening and ending of the programs. Other activities throughout the year also incorporate worship.

"Their voice goes out into all the earth, their words to the ends of the world" (Psalm 19:4).

SERVICE OPPORTUNITY DESCRIPTION FOR
Phone Coordinator

Service Requirements:
- Enjoy talking on the phone
- Good at delegating
- Organized and flexible

Service Responsibilities:
1. Keep an up-to-date roster of all **Phone Communicators**.
2. When an **Administrative Team** member calls with a phoning request, assign the request to one of the **Phone Communicators** in sufficient time to accomplish all the phoning.
3. Be sure all **Phone Communicators** receive a Service Opportunity Description.
4. Follow up with the **Phone Communicators** to be sure phoning assignments are being completed.
5. Be sure that the **Administrative Team** member requesting the phone service receives a report on the results of the phone calls.

Service Duration:
Flexibility is necessary because phone requests can come at various times throughout the month. You can expect a request three weeks before a Coffee, Mentor Halftime Refresher, and Six-Month Potluck Celebration. It is important that you delegate the phoning responsibilities to the **Phone Communicators** and not try to do it all yourself. It is good to develop a team that you can depend on when you need help.

CHAPTER 15

"They overcame him by the blood of the Lamb and by the word of their testimony" (Revelation 12:11).

Who Will Be the First to Testify?

THE CALL TO M&Ms

I have covered a tremendous amount of material in this book, and you may be wondering if it is worth it. If it took this entire book to show you how to start a Woman to Woman Mentoring Ministry, could you ever find the time and energy to actually do it yourself? Yes. The Lord will do the work, but He cannot accomplish it on earth without willing hands and hearts. "For God's gifts and his call are irrevocable" (Rom. 11:29).

You do have to be the one who says, "I will take on this challenge. I will answer the call." Women at your church need the kind of relationships you will read about in the following testimonies. You have two women who were strangers before they met at a Coffee, and the Lord placed them into a relationship that He will be working through possibly for the rest of their lives.

The Lord continually reminds me of the mighty work He is doing in the Woman to Woman Mentoring Ministry through the testimonies at every Six-Month Potluck Celebration, the responses on the M&M questionnaires, the handwritten testimonies in the mail, the women approaching me at church telling me "Their Stories," and the phone calls I receive. This is more than enough confirmation to me that God is changing lives through the Woman to Woman Mentoring Ministry.

Every mentoring relationship does not turn out perfectly or have a dramatic story. That does not mean that they are not successful or that God is not moving in their relationships. Sometimes the impact of the relationship will show up much later in their lives, and other times it is simply two women experiencing growth together in Christ or learning to stick to a commitment they have made. However, you know you are "About His Work" when you hear even one testimony of a husband coming to the Lord, a marriage saved from divorce, or a mentee renewing her faith or finding Jesus for the first time.

Telling you the blessing it has been to women is one thing, but I thought you might like to hear from some of them yourself. When I announced to our ministry that I was writing this resource, I asked if any Woman to Woman M&Ms would like to share "Their Story" with you. Many of them realized that "Their Stories" would be a source of encouragement to you and the women of your churches. They also acknowledged that God gives us experiences and testimonies not just for our own benefit, but to share with others. The following testimonies are in their own words with some named changed.

THEIR STORIES

Some tell "Their Stories" on the M&M questionnaires. Following are comments written on the Six-Month Potluck M&M Questionnaire (form J).

- "I found someone to share my trials, hopes, and dreams. (Someone) who could encourage me in keeping the balance between God and the world."—Mentee
- "I gained a lot of wisdom and was able to have a relationship with a godly woman."—Mentee
- "My mentee was awesome and very sweet."—Mentor
- "I didn't expect to get as much as a mentor vs. being a mentee, but I know that I grew in my relationship with the Lord as much as my mentee."—Mentor
- "I actually could see how our relationship was making an impact in our lives through changes of patience, frustration, and perseverance."—Mentor
- "I was not prepared to experience as much growth for myself as I did—I thank God for all I learned and for the tender care by my Prayer Warrior."—Mentor
- "It was not a perfect relationship, but I was happy with what we made out of it. I am sure this friendship will continue after our commitment is over."—Mentor
- "I came through the door of the Coffee an angry, bitter woman. After six months in my mentoring relationship I have renewed my faith in the Lord. I am at peace. I am a new woman in Christ."—Mentee who went on to Mentor
- "When I came to the Coffee I had already filed for divorce, and I blamed my husband for all our problems. Through the gentle wisdom of my mentor, I began to see that I needed to change, too. It was also about me, and not just my husband. As I began to change, so did our relationship and our marriage was restored. I know this would not have happened without the guidance of my mentor and the prayers of our Prayer Warrior."—Mentee
- "I have been married to an unbeliever for 20 years. Through prayers of my mentor and Prayer Warrior my husband accepted the Lord during our relationship and so did my mother and father!"—Mentee

Some send "Their Stories" through the mail. I received the first handwritten testimony in the mail when I was halfway through writing this material. It was the incentive and motivation I needed to continue and finish writing as soon as possible. I hope that it has the same effect on you in starting a Woman to Woman Mentoring Ministry at your church. I realized that there were so many women out

The Lord will do the work, but He cannot accomplish it on earth without willing hands and hearts.

there, like Mary and her mentee, who just needed a good reason to get together and enhance each other's lives. Mary wrote the following testimony.

Testimony #1

"I simply cannot say enough wonderful things about the Woman to Woman Mentoring Ministry! It has been a true blessing to meet and get to know my sister in Christ. We have shared our ups and downs, our hopes and fears, our sorrows and our joys, but the biggest blessing by far has been sharing our love of Jesus and watching ourselves, our children, and our marriages grow stronger in that love.

I was nervous about our first meeting, but we clicked immediately. I saw in my mentee so much potential and such a giving spirit. When we're not doing things together we talk almost daily, sometimes just to say hi or for no particular reason at all, but our conversations can last for hours! We have so much to talk about! Jesus has greatly blessed our friendship!

This ministry has meant stepping out in faith, trusting God to show the way, and reaching out to someone who needed encouragement, understanding, and a shoulder to lean on. Mentoring reflects the same love and concern Jesus demonstrated time and time again during His life on earth; the same love He continually shows me in my life.

I have watched my mentee and her family fall in love with Saddleback Church and embrace it as their church home after months of church shopping. We go to the midweek service together, attend parenting seminars and women's fellowship activities. We volunteer to help at these events also, and it's much more fun when you go with a friend! Her family is energetic and enthusiastic and will be a blessing to any ministry they enter into.

It has been wonderful to watch her settle into her neighborhood, gain confidence in her parenting skills, and watch her grow spiritually and begin to minister to women in her area in lovingkindness and friendship. She's ready to be a mentor herself now! It's a blessing to watch someone grow and be truly joyful as they reach out to others, spreading Jesus' love even farther.

In September she and I may decide to pursue other mentoring relationships, but we are secure in our wonderful Christian friendship. Being a mentor has been easy because it is so very easy to step out and give when you do it with your heart and mind focused on Jesus. The mentoring relationship has worked both ways; both of us have benefited enormously.

I ask the Lord to richly bless Janet Thompson for acting in faith on such a vital need in our church, and I ask special blessings for everyone involved in this uplifting and encouraging ministry. I pray that as this ministry continues to grow, its members will continue to grow as daughters that God can be proud of now and in the future.

Mary (Mentor)

"The biggest blessing by far has been sharing our love of Jesus and watching ourselves, our children, and our marriages grow stronger in that love."

Another handwritten testimony I received was from our most senior mentor, Ina. Ina was part of the testimony that accompanied Pastor Rick's message to the church on the need for mentors in our lives. As Ina stood humbly on the stage with her gorgeous smile and regal silver hair, her mentee handed Ina a bouquet of flowers. At that moment, every woman in the congregation wanted an Ina in her life! What they did not know was that Ina's first mentoring relationship did not work out. Ina waited out a few Coffees, and then bravely jumped in again. The Lord put this situation in our ministry to use as an example of not giving up.

Ina's letter is also a reminder that older women can feel intimidated by younger women. Instead of realizing the wealth of experience they have to offer, they often fear rejection. You may need to spend extra time encouraging the older women who will be such valuable mentors. Ina has since gone on to be a mentor for the fourth time! Use Ina's testimony to encourage the older women in your church to participate in the Woman to Woman Mentoring Ministry.

Testimony #2

Dear Janet,

How excited I was for all when I received and read your first newsletter. You asked for information from some of us who have found your calling a blessing. Being caught up in a world of youth makes each step I take one of caution; and, as you might recall, Janet, I attended your second Coffee at the insistence of not just one granddaughter, but two. I was the "grandmother"—and I say that with pride—of everyone there that day. As I watched from my car all the young ladies enter your home, I put the key into the ignition to go home. The ever still small voice said, "You were asked twice to come," so I entered your home to be richly blessed.

The young lady (age 54 young) you assigned to me offered me yet another new experience of learning during our time together. The Lord opened a door at a Saturday service to let you learn about my mentoring. Sometime later, a lovely young lady, with her doctorate no less, asked for someone to talk to. You thought of me and a new door opened wide for me to walk through. How God has blessed me, Janet. Thank you for answering God's call.

Finally, something in the bulletin was offered to senior citizens—a dinner. I had been waiting for this. There I met other women who I feel have much to offer in the way of experiences that God doesn't want going to waste. I would like to encourage your "twelve disciples" (*Administrative Team*) to make a plea for those ladies at the next senior event.

Once more, thank you, Janet, for letting God work through you in such a wonderful, profitable way.

Sincerely with love and prayers,
Ina (Mentor)

(Note: We did go to the Young at Heart group and do "The Mentoring Game" skit. They loved it, and some came to the next Coffee.)

Ina had responded to a request I put in our first Mentoring Ministry Newsletter asking for testimonies for this resource. I thought they would all come from seasoned mentoring relationships. It was exciting to receive the following note from an M&M pair that had met at the previous Coffee.

I hope the exclamation points she interjected convey the blessing this mentoring relationship has been for Elizabeth and Naomi. Elizabeth and Naomi truly are a testimony of a pair that only the Lord could have matched with so many things in common that those of us praying over their cards could never have known. I hear comments like theirs all the time. These types of notes give me renewed energy to encourage each and every matched woman to stay in her relationship and experience all that God had planned for her.

Testimony #3

Dear Janet,

Great newsletter! My mentee, Naomi, and I want to respond to your request for testimonies for your book. Although we're part of the newest group of M&Ms, and consequently are pretty new in our relationship, we're both having a wonderful time. We meet weekly at Starbucks for fellowship and coffee, and every week we uncover at least one more thing we have in common. God was truly watching over the ministry women as you matched those pink cards. *(Profile Cards were pink.)* Your prayers and our prayers were clearly heard!! Naomi and I are a perfect match with so much in common that wasn't noted on our cards!

We both started our careers in real estate, we both grew up in neighboring towns (our high schools competed in sports)! She went off to Cal Berkeley while I went off to UCLA. Her small group recently took a long break and may not get back together, and she and her husband were looking for a new small group with the right fit. Guess what?! The small group my husband and I lead was looking for additional members! It even turns out that our husbands attended the same private high school, a few years apart! A fun friendship has been formed thanks to this ministry.

As Pastor Rick talks about bringing new believers to Christ, I want to share that being a part of this ministry has provided me with a great way to share my faith. When people ask, "What did you do yesterday?" or "So what have you been up to?" this ministry is the first thing I share! It's a great way to express my excitement about being a believer. I'm so glad I got involved! Best wishes to you for your book and the ministry!

Much Love,
Elizabeth (Mentor)

"Being a part of this ministry has provided me with a great way to share my faith."

Maria, one of our first mentors, wrote this encouraging note. She sent it to Pastor Doug Slaybaugh at church, and he forwarded it on to me.

Testimony #4

Dear Doug,

Just a brief testimony to let you know how much the Woman to Woman Mentoring Ministry has started to change lives. Janet Thompson is doing a fabulous service for the women at Saddleback. I hope many more women will grow in Christ as this wonderful ministry continues to expand.

Sincerely,
Maria

Some call on the phone with "Their Stories." I mentioned earlier that sometimes I come home to messages on my answering machine from mentors and mentees telling me the glories of their relationships. The following two testimonies are very special to me. They were actually recorded on my answering machine back-to-back.

Ritta is a lovely, 70-year-young mentor straight out of the Titus 2 passage. Ritta is the picture that comes to mind when you think of a mature Christian woman who has spent her life close to the Lord.

Testimony #5

"This is Ritta, Janet. Just calling to tell you what a wonderful time I had Tuesday. I met my gal, and it was instant love. Nobody could have matched us up better but the Lord. And I just thank you so much. We just instantly fell in love with each other and hit it off like crazy. So thanks again, you guys. Bye bye."

Jane's message was next. Remember Jane? I told you her story in Chapter 6. Jane is a beautiful, energetic, and enthusiastic woman. I wish you could hear her message the way I did. You will have to use your imagination, but I think you will feel her energy as you read all the "Ohs!" she puts in to stress her point.

Testimony #6

"Hi, Janet, this is Jane. I was at your Woman to Woman group, oh gosh, I don't know, about three weeks ago. I just want to tell you it's been so wonderful to be a part of that. Oh, my mentor is just a beautiful person, oh and I am just really enjoying getting to know her and the time we have shared together. And I just want to thank you for taking the time out of your life to put something so beautiful together. It's a great job that you have done, and like I said, I am sure that many others as well are enjoying it. Again, thank you."

Some tell "Their Stories." My prayer always has been that we would be developing new generations of mentors. As mentees grow and mature in the Lord, they would be equipped to give back to a younger Christian sister. In the following four testimonies you will see the harvest of four generations of mentors.

The first testimony is from one of the women I mentioned earlier who had difficulty sharing at her first Coffee. However, after six months in a mentoring relationship, Marcy was ready to give back as a mentor herself. She now publicly gives her mentoring testimony along with one of her mentees and one of her mentee's mentee. Yes, you read that right! Marcy went on to mentor three women and two of those women went on to mentor. One of their mentees went on to mentor two women. Did you get all that? Essentially, what has happened is one woman who started out as a mentee started a chain reaction of spiritual growth that has raised up ongoing generations of mentors. That is what it is all about—passing the torch on to the next generation and the next and the next. Each year of the ministry we see yet another generation of women mature as mentors. Your Woman to Woman Mentoring Ministry will experience this same phenomena as "One generation will commend your works to another; they will tell of your might acts" (Ps. 145:4).

It's all about passing the torch on to the next generation and the next and the next.

Many women are apprehensive at first about being mentors. Then they realize that their life experiences and walk with the Lord, even though short, make them the perfect mentor for just the woman the Lord had planned. You do not have to be a Christian for 25 years for the Lord to use you as a mentor. God can do His mighty work when we simply open our hearts and lives to a mentee. If you are one day old in the Lord, you are one day older than an unbeliever or a person that has just this minute given her life to the Lord. This is a transcript of Marcy's testimony that she now gives with Donna and Lisa at our Coffees.

Testimony #7

"My name is Marcy. I am here today to let you know how the Woman to Woman Mentoring Ministry has changed my life. Let me begin by giving you a little background on myself. I accepted Jesus Christ as my Lord and Savior October 1994, at a time in my life when my marriage was falling apart and I realized that I could no longer control my life. You see, this wasn't my first marriage, it was my third, and I didn't want another divorce. My son and I were baptized in February 1995, and I became a member of Saddleback Church in January 1996, after attending classes 101, 201, 301 and completing my S.H.A.P.E. interview. While in church on Saturday night, I read in the bulletin where a woman's mentoring Coffee was going to be held at Janet Thompson's house in March 1996. Since being baptized and becoming a member of Saddleback Church, I felt God talking to me and putting it on my heart to become involved with other women. He knew my life and all the struggles, obstacles, and heartaches I had overcome. Maybe I would be able to help someone else going through similar experiences.

"I have been blessed with so many Christian friends I have met through the Woman to Woman Mentoring Ministry—I will be forever grateful for their love and friendship."

I proceeded to call Janet to let her know that I was interested in attending the Coffee and that with my vast experiences throughout my life, I certainly would be able to mentor another Christian woman. Needless to say, as the day of the Coffee came closer, I began to question myself as to what I was thinking. Walking into a situation where I knew absolutely no one, where I would have to talk about some of those experiences in front of strangers, what a crazy thing I was about to do! You see, I have always had a tremendous fear about speaking in front of a group of people. But in order for me to overcome this fear, I felt I needed to take this step. When Janet began to go around the room, wouldn't you know that she would begin with the woman sitting next to me? This meant I would be the second one to speak. Needless to say, I panicked and admitted to Janet that I wouldn't be able to speak right then. I told her to skip me and maybe I would speak after everyone else had spoken. As the other women began to speak, I realized how many women were also hurting. And before I knew it the last woman was speaking. I knew that if I didn't talk about what was on my heart, the whole purpose of my being there would be lost. So I gathered up the courage and let Janet know that I was ready to speak. I remember asking myself, *What do I have to lose?* since the whole purpose of my being there was to be matched up with another Christian woman.

I realized that if I didn't talk, no one would know anything about me, except for the information I had filled out on the Profile Card earlier. I knew in my heart that for me to verbalize to the others how much pain there had been in my life and that I was still going through, would help me begin the healing process. So I gathered up the courage and began to speak. And I must admit even through all the tears, I did feel a sense of peace and comfort come over me as I revealed my hurts and pains. I knew that everyone in that room was there for a purpose, and it was not to judge one another. I did come to realize, though, that I was not going to be able to mentor another woman. I needed a mentor.

After everyone spoke and we went for refreshments, a woman I had noticed in the group came over to me and shared with me how she felt we had so much in common. We were so excited to meet one another that we immediately began making plans to meet for lunch the next week. From that moment on we have become the best of friends. We have been there for each other through the ups and downs of life. What a wonderful friendship we have, and I will always be grateful to God for putting it on my heart to attend that Coffee. For if I had not, I know without a doubt that our paths would never have crossed. I have been blessed with so many other Christian friends I have met through the Woman to Woman Mentoring Ministry, that I will be forever grateful for their love and friendship.

Well, the Coffee was over and we were to be called by our mentors sometime later that week. To be honest with you, after going home and getting back into the weekly routine, I kind of forgot I was to get a call! But that call did come the following week, and when I answered the phone, I heard the enthusiastic voice of Carolyn and how excited she was to be matched with me. I thought I had died and gone to heaven. I began to wonder why someone would be so excited to get to know me. As we began our relationship, my self-doubt was replaced with inspiration and hope.

We met every week faithfully for six months, which we both committed to do. Carolyn is a very spiritual woman, and I can't tell you how much she was able to give me by spending time with me. Being able to talk to her about my life experiences and share my daily difficulties with her was truly a blessing. She shared her faith in God with me and in doing so my faith became stronger. Those six months changed my life. Before my mentoring relationship, I was quiet and shy, and knowing the Lord as I do now has helped me to become more confident and believe in myself. Our six months ended in September 1996. Another Coffee was scheduled for October. I spoke to Carolyn about my desire, fear, and self-doubt about becoming a mentor at the next Coffee. Her words of encouragement strengthened my desire, and I made that commitment. I can't say that I wasn't scared, but I knew in my heart that this was where God wanted me to be.

The Coffee was a great success, as they all have been, but being there and knowing I was going to have the opportunity to help mentor another Christian woman was so exciting. Everyone spoke, but even at the close of the meeting I didn't have any idea as to whom God would put in my life. So we all went home and waited until the following week when everyone would get together again and meet our mentees and mentors. Well, the time was finally here. The big moment we had all been waiting for. How exciting it was for me to meet the lovely young woman named Donna. She began sharing her life with me. At that point, I knew God most definitely played a part in our being put together. We began to meet one another each week, and she became part of my family. You see, she was only 29 years old. She had lost her mom 6 months before we met. Then her boyfriend of 6½ years left her, even after they had purchased a home together.

Her life was falling apart, and she desperately needed to put it in order, making God the center. She told me her Mom's birthday was in February. I told her that mine was also in February. She asked me what day and I told her. This was my confirmation that God was in control of our relationship, because her Mom's birthday was the same day as mine. She was born in Santa Monica and so was I. She is a Dodger fan and so am I. We even joined the church coed softball team. The similarities are incredible and only God knew what He had planned for us. I can't tell you how much this relationship with Donna has meant to me. I've even seen incredible changes in my marriage and my children. My husband and I

"As we began our relationship, my self-doubt was replaced with inspiration and hope."

> "Had I not stepped out of my comfort zone, I would never have known the joy and fulfillment of being a mentor and seeing how sharing my faith in God would make a difference in someone else's life."

were in a small group for a year. We have now committed to attend Lifemates, which meets once a month at Saddleback. And with continued prayers from our Christian friends, my husband accepted the Lord in January 1999. It is awesome to see the growth in our relationship, since putting God first in our marriage and in our lives.

Had I not stepped out of my comfort zone and gone ahead with my desire to be a spiritual mentor and loving friend, I would never have known the joy and fulfillment of being a mentor and seeing how sharing my faith in God would make a difference in someone else's life. Our relationship will be going on for life, as Donna will always hold a special place in my heart. I have now completed my third mentoring relationship. And with each one, they have greatly strengthened my relationship with God, along with sharing a Christian relationship with another woman and making a difference in her life and mine.

So, if any of you are on the fence about whether you have what it takes to be a mentor, I strongly urge you to take the step and enjoy the reward of seeing the difference you will make in another woman's life and the changes you will see in your own life. Thank you for allowing me to share my mentoring experiences with you."

Marcy is currently in her fourth mentoring relationship. The following is from Donna, Marcy's first mentee. It is the transcript of the testimony Donna now gives with Marcy and Lisa at our Coffees.

Testimony #8

"Hi, my name is Donna. I came to Orientation Coffee #5 in October of 1996, by the suggestion of a lay counselor at Saddleback Church. She told me that this would be a great way for me to meet a sister in Christ who could share with me her walk with the Lord and how she had overcome similar trials. The lay counselor also said that she could definitely see how God would use my experiences someday in the near future to help another woman. This suggestion was very appealing to me and I could not wait until the upcoming Sunday.

I arrived as a very new Christian, with a lot of anxiety, due to the fact I knew no one and did not know what to expect. But that quickly subsided as I entered the door and found a wonderful Greeter who was eager to give me a hug! *Wow*, I thought, *this is just what I need!* As the Coffee proceeded and Janet explained what a mentoring relationship entailed, I grew more and more excited as I looked around the room wondering whom I would be matched with. I distinctly remember how impacting the testimony was on me, and I was very inspired by what God had done in their M&M relationship.

Then the moment came when it was our time as guests to stand up and introduce ourselves individually to say what brought us there and whether we wanted to be a mentor or mentee. As they went around the room, I began to see that I was not the only one hurting and in need of a Christian friend. My time came and I could hardly talk without breaking up, as I began to share how I recently lost my mother in March and had a six-and-a-half year relationship come to an end in September. It was obvious I needed a mentor!!

The day came one week later that I would begin one of the dearest relationships I have ever had. God truly blessed me with not only a wonderful Christian friendship, but He also filled my life with a spiritual mother figure who has guided me in my walk with the Lord. There were many times when I thought the storm would never lift, and Marcy was right there to remind me to take it one day at a time and to keep focused on God. We have shared many hours over cups of coffee at our local Diedrichs, becoming acquainted and standing in awe of the many "God-incidences" there were between us. The one that stands out the most was when we discovered that Marcy's birthday was, in fact, the very same day as my late mother's birthday. Till this day it still sends a chill through me!

Marcy has been there to encourage, support, and grow with me spiritually. And even reminded me how to laugh and smile again, which was something I thought could never be possible again. Then there were the times I was feeling down, and Marcy was always right there with a beautiful card reminding me how much God loves me and to remember how much stronger I had become over the past year. And stronger I did become each and every day as I kept my faith and focused on the Lord and was obedient to what He had planned for my life.

The Lord works in amazing ways, because as I began to serve in the Woman to Woman Mentoring Ministry during the next seven Coffees, He put it on my heart at the end of Coffee #12 to step up and be a mentor. Wow! I thought. *I don't think I'm ready to be a mentor.* But the Lord kept tugging at me to step up, and He would provide me with what I needed to be a mentor.

Well, once again, the Lord was faithful. He equipped me with encouragement and guidance through Marcy, along with providing me with many books on mentoring and growing Christian friendships which put me on my way as a mentor. I am so thankful to my Lord and Savior Jesus Christ for putting it on my heart to take a step in faith, because I again was truly blessed with a special friend and sister in Christ named Lisa. Lisa and I have become acquainted until the wee hours many a night, enjoying our favorite foods, sharing our spiritual journeys, and even going to a Joyful Journey Retreat together this past September. She is one of my best Christian friends.

> *"God truly blessed me with not only a wonderful Christian friendship, but He also filled my life with a spiritual mother figure who has guided me in my walk with the Lord."*

Being a mentor and mentee has thoroughly enriched and strengthened my Christian walk. My life has been blessed and touched by Marcy and Lisa in many different ways, which I will cherish for years to come. It's awesome to see how the Lord works by weaving together His daughters in this ministry to grow spiritually and to support and nurture each other. May your future M&M relationships reap a harvest of blessings as did mine. Thank you." (Note: Donna mentored a second time to a young 18-year-old woman named Sarah whose testimony follows Lisa's.)

Marcy, Donna, and now, Lisa, give their testimonies together at the Orientation Coffees and are often with me when I am speaking to other churches on how to start a Woman to Woman Mentoring Ministry. They all want to encourage women who are considering a mentoring relationship. This is the transcript of Lisa's testimony.

Testimony #9

"My name is Lisa. I'm here to tell you how my mentoring relationship with Donna changed my life. My husband and I moved here to Orange County in August of 1997 from Texas. It was a big step for me. Moving across the country with a one year old and a four year old has its challenges. I was moving away from my mom, my dad, my whole family, and lifelong friends. I knew it would be hard, but I told myself it couldn't be that bad. You see, my husband and I had moved to Germany for a two-year job assignment in the second year of our marriage. I told myself this California move would be a piece of cake compared to living on another continent in another culture altogether. Was I wrong! The big change was now being a mom and not having the family support I had the last four years since my daughter had been born. I was used to having my mom around for help and guidance. Now she was thousands of miles away, and I was very lonely.

Three months after we moved here, the job project my husband was working on was completely canceled. The group was disbanded, and there were layoffs. By God's grace my husband's job was saved. So, here we were still in our temporary corporate apartment, still very much in the transition of a major move, and the whole reason why we had moved no longer existed! Talk about a letdown!!!

In a six-month period, we had moved three times. We still weren't settled. All of what we owned was in storage. We were living out of boxes. I was tired of moving and not having roots. We had searched over several months for a church home and had finally made the decision on Christmas Eve of 1997 to join Saddleback, but I was still searching to be connected, to have friends. I was so lonely!

One night in March of 1998, I was in church when I saw the ad for the upcoming mentoring Coffee. I thought, *I'll just go to the information table and check it out*. When I got there, I was greeted by the most wonderful lady named Lena. I'll never forget how kind and loving she was. She made a big impression on me. Right then and there I decided to sign up. When I got home, I was looking at the map of where the Coffee was being held and discovered it was only blocks from where our new home was being built. To me, that was a confirmation, a nudge from God saying, "Go!"

I remember going to the Coffee and being extremely nervous. I remember thinking, *I'm going to meet an older lady and she is going to be my California mom*. I had gone to the Coffee with the idea of getting a mom replacement. I was totally touched and in tears when I heard Marcy and Donna's testimonies. I remember calling my mother and talking to her about Donna and Marcy, never dreaming that Donna would be my mentor.

I had expected to get a mother/daughter mentoring relationship, but God had another plan. If I've learned anything in this, it is to be totally committed to God and your relationship with your mentor, listen to God's voice, follow His command, and don't give up. "Lean not on your own understanding" (Prov. 3:5).

Instead of just getting a mentor, I got so much more—a friend, a Christian friend who loved and cared for me unconditionally, and showed me the love of Christ when I needed it so much. Donna is the same age as me, and she could relate to me moving as she had done several times, also. I, in turn, could relate to her losing her mom because I had lost my grandmother who was a mother to me. Donna has always been there for me. I can't express how she has touched my life. She is my best Christian friend. She connected my husband and me to a small group at our church. Through that small group and the example of other godly men, my husband accepted Christ, and we were baptized together in December of 1998.

Shortly after being baptized, my husband went through six months of insomnia and was diagnosed with depression. There were many days and nights of tears and despair. He was at a breaking point. He even considered quitting his job without having another job. This was one of the darkest periods in our lives, but it made us stronger as a family. Our faith was challenged, but it did not waiver. After several months of continuous prayer and in developing our complete dependence upon Him, God delivered my husband from insomnia. He also provided an even better job for him—one we would have never imagined! God was faithful to us and provided the love and support of Donna, this ministry, and our church family.

I am so thankful that I did not give up on our relationship because of my initial expectations. If I had, I would have missed out on so many of the wonderful blessings that I have received and continue to receive! I pray that God will touch your life through a mentoring relationship like he has mine. Thank you." (Note: Lisa went on to be a mentor three times!)

"Be totally committed to God and your relationship with your mentor, listen to God's voice, follow His command, and don't give up."

I never tire of hearing these three beautiful women share what the Lord has done in bringing them together and the common thread He wound through their lives. They are a living example of mentoring and the results of women being willing to pour their lives into each other. Each year we have seen another generation of mentees grow into mentors. The harvest has been so plentiful.

Some write "Their Stories" in our Mentoring Ministry newsletter. These testimonies all appeared in the Woman to Woman Mentoring Ministry newsletter, *Beyond Coffee … Encouraging Words for M&Ms*.

Following is the testimony of Sarah, a young 18-year-old woman who was Donna's (testimony #8) second mentee. Someone younger in the Lord can always benefit from our experiences. One of our ladies described it as the domino effect—someone is mentored, then mentors another, and then another, and another, and yet another.

Testimony #10

"Dear friends, last year God blessed me greatly through the Woman to Woman Mentoring Ministry. It was almost exactly a year ago when I decided that I wanted to be part of the Mentoring Ministry. I was blessed with one of the greatest mentors a person could have, Donna. God knew my needs and knew that Donna was perfect for me. At that time I had no idea of the great plans God had and the even bigger role my mentor was going to play.

It was not even a month into our relationship when I felt God speaking to my heart about a mission trip to the Ukraine. It turns out that God wanted me to go. Let me tell you, it is all about God's great timing! My mentor, Donna, became a partner of mine as I prepared for this trip. God blessed me with someone who was there with an encouraging word whenever I needed one, someone who listened to the things I was going through and shared in the exciting and great things that God was doing in my life. When I was in the Ukraine, I could feel the power of everyone's prayers, and I knew that Donna was praying for me.

God blessed me greatly on this trip. I see now exactly why God was calling me to go. I walked away learning so much about myself and about who God is. The Ukraine was a life-changing experience for me and I thank God for blessing me with a wonderful mentor." Sarah (Mentee)

Here is a testimony of a woman who mentored twice and learned that each mentoring experience is new and unique. She also shares her experience that mentoring relationships are two-way relationships!

Testimony #11

"Hi, my name is Bonnie. Entering a second mentoring covenant filled me with as much anticipation and curiosity about the next six months as my

"God knew my needs and knew that Donna was perfect for me."

first relationship had in the beginning. What could God possibly have in store for me the second time around as a mentor? I couldn't begin to imagine the possible blessings God would so graciously pour out on me once again. My first relationship was full of commonalties such as age and profession, but what would the classic Titus generational relationship be like with Lori?

It was evident that God's hand had been the one to make this match. I was a generation older in age, but not really much older in the years spent walking with the Lord. God ministered to my needs through a young woman experienced in teaching junior high and high school. Lori consistently encouraged, supported, and gave me insight into my parenting struggles with my two adolescent daughters.

In return, I supported Lori in her parenting through my experience in teaching kindergarten. It was not always clearly defined who was the mentor and who was the mentee because God was able to weave our experiences and needs together, to use them for the good of the other in sharing encouragement, spiritual truth, and growth through the gift of friendship.

I thank God for the beauty and richness of each mentoring relationship in my life. It's more than a six-month commitment, it's making those friends who forever have changed our lives. Thank you, Jo Ann (Bonnie's first mentee) and Lori, for being the beautiful silver and gold threads God lovingly wove into the tapestry of my life. 'How I thank God through Jesus Christ … for each one of you' (Rom. 1:8, TLB). Love in Christ, Bonnie" (Mentor)

This testimony from Lynn, a mentee from Coffee #15, emphasizes the fact that M&Ms can truly see the Lord doing the matching.

Testimony #12

"I had several friends encourage me to get involved in the Woman to Woman Mentoring Ministry. They were involved within the ministry and couldn't say enough about it. Being a stay-at-home mom who could use help and encouragement in the day-to-day trials, I finally took their advice and went to a Coffee. I was really made to feel welcomed by everyone and my nervous feelings easily subsided. My hopes were to first be a mentee, as I wasn't sure if mentoring would be an area for me to consider.

After hearing each person speak a little at the Coffee, I wondered if this was really the place for me or not. There was only one person that I felt could possibly meet what I was looking for in a mentor, yet I didn't feel I should approach her yet. Instead, I prayed to God asking him to guide the right woman into my life and decided to leave the decision to Him. I felt confident that the heavy prayer for God's guidance over who to match with whom would lead the right person God would have to me.

"It was not always clearly defined who was the mentor and who was the mentee because God was able to weave our experiences and needs together, to use them for the good of the other in sharing encouragement, spiritual truth, and growth through the gift of friendship."

"Our six-month commitment may be over, but I know our friendship will keep on going. I would love nothing more than to have her as my lifetime mentor."

Well, at our Kickoff Night meeting I was greeted by Roxana, who was the only lady I had secretly felt could help me in my needs! God is so awesome! That confirmed for me that this truly would be a special relationship. Roxana and I were committed to meeting weekly. There were only a handful of times that we couldn't meet. From our first meeting, I felt such a connection with Roxana. Each time we met we found more things in common with each other than I thought possible.

We were in the Christmas season when we first met. We realized that both of us had difficulties having joy throughout the season—with all the shopping, baking, special events etc., to keep up with. Roxana came up with the idea of doing a study on joy, in hopes that we would find joy and change our old ways. This was life changing for me. I had so much fun just talking with Roxana on everyday things that sometimes we would put aside our study to fellowship and grow. It was during those talks that I learned so much from Roxana.

We were able to open up our fears, frustrations, and struggles which always challenged me to be a better person. Seeing Roxana go through her daily struggles and handling them in such godly ways was an inspiration for me. Roxana has been such a gift to me from God. She has a great love for the Lord. She has encouraged me, inspired me, challenged me, and is my friend with a listening ear. She has really cared for me and prayed for me. But the one thing I needed most in my life was the example she is as a Christian mom. I have learned more from Roxana in these six months than I ever thought possible. Our six-month commitment may be over, but I know our friendship will keep on going. We hope to continue meeting on occasion and I would love nothing more than to have her as my lifetime mentor.

So to sum up my experience briefly is pretty impossible. I am very grateful to a church family that is so loving and supportive. The Woman to Woman Mentoring Ministry is a great place to feel that love and support. I have grown closer to the Lord because of this ministry, and I am very thankful to be a part of it. I am currently serving as a Prayer Warrior for six women and I am humbled that I could be used by God in this way. I really appreciated my Prayer Warrior through my mentoring relationship and felt God's call to now serve in this area. I look forward to how the Lord will continue to work in and through me." Lynn (Mentee)

This testimony speaks to the heart of the Woman to Woman Mentoring Ministry. It is the story of a young unbelieving woman matched with an older Christian mentor. The Prayer Day Team saw things in common such as they both had a Catholic background and originally came from another country. They were from different countries, but they both had to adjust to a new culture in America. However, when they first met all they could see were their differences. Their testimony depicts the miracles that can happen when we let God do the matching, and M&Ms stick with the commitment even when there are doubts.

Testimony #13

"I was born in a seemingly large city in England. My father is a very strict and disciplined Irish Roman Catholic who was born and raised in Ireland. I am one of three children—two brothers, one younger and one older. Our father, a violent, disciplined person, was very strict with religion. We were forced to pray on our knees and say our prayers every night before bed. If we forgot, we were punished. Every Sunday we were dragged to church whether we liked it or not. The years of physical and mental abuse ended at the age of four when my mother divorced my father.

We never went to church or prayed again. In 1994, I came to the United States to fulfill a dream. My first gift from God was my husband whom I met in April of 1998. We were married 6 months after we met and have been married now for 16 months. Jeff was a believer and had already accepted Christ into his heart. When I first met him, he went to church every week, sometimes twice. My first reaction was, "Oh, he's the religious kind," and I thought he was going to start preaching to me and asking me to go to church with him. After my very strict religious torment as a child, I didn't want anyone preaching or forcing religion upon me again. It was a terrible fear and tension that I didn't want repeated.

We got married in October 1999, and I have literally been blessed by God with this wonderful man whom I married. Our marriage is wonderful, strong, and open, but something was missing in my life and in my heart—there was so much sadness and dissatisfaction. I missed my family in England, but that wasn't it. I found that "missing something" when I joined the Woman to Woman Mentoring Ministry.

Coffee #17 was a great experience. My very dear best friend asked me to go. I wasn't that comfortable going, but something was pushing me to go. I sat in the room listening to everyone speak their turn. I kept thinking to myself, *why am I here?* At that moment, I knew that God was that "missing something." I had been so scared to accept religion again; I was always running away from it. I stood in front of everyone and said who I was and why I was there. I had realized standing there in front of everyone, listening to everyone, that God had planned for me to be there, to let go of the anger, fear, and frustration of my past. He was teaching me that praying was not weird nor was it something you *had* to do. God was telling me to let go of my sins and my past and follow his path.

My experience with my wonderful mentor started out as something very uncomfortable for me. I was about to encounter a six-month relationship with someone whom I didn't know. I was scared because I didn't want to be pushed into something that I wasn't completely ready for. I

"I found that 'missing something' when I joined the Woman to Woman Mentoring Ministry"

"I have my dear husband to thank, my wonderful mentor, and the wonderful Woman to Woman Mentoring Ministry that helped me find Christ."

almost gave up, but I stuck with it and began to enjoy our meetings. She helped me understand that God is a patient and understanding person, and that he loves me no matter what. It was in my time that I accept and learn the things that Christ wants for me to learn and to slowly get to know Him. She shared stories from the Bible and helped me overcome stress and worry, which was the source of my depression.

The most beautiful of all was that she prayed with me. How great it was to pray. I really felt that God was listening. Some days I would pray hard for all the people in need, not just for myself. It felt so strange to pray after all these years, but it felt good and appreciated. I know that God was working through me and slowly helping me, guiding me the way I should go. I attended class 101 and 201, and I finally accepted Christ into my heart on October 24, 1999 in class 101. God was with me every second of that class, and I felt His hand on my shoulder to guide me and assure me that everything was okay.

I have my dear husband to thank, my wonderful mentor, and the wonderful Woman to Woman Mentoring Ministry that helped me find Christ. But most of all I have the Lord to thank for the wonderful gift called life he has given me." Lisa Marie (Mentee)

Testimony #14

"Blessings come in many different ways. God has so wonderfully blessed my life through the Woman to Woman Mentoring Ministry! It all started when I stopped by the ministry table and accepted an invitation to a Coffee that was to be held the following week. Although I was looking to meet Christian friends, the Lord had more than I could ever have imagined in His plans!

After that Coffee we met again (Kickoff Night), and the Lord revealed to me that He wanted me to be a mentor. Me? I have no experience at all! Even more confusing to me was that my mentee would be a young woman in her 20s—she could be my daughter. I asked myself what we could have in common. Although I didn't yet have the answers, but trusting in the Lord, I accepted God's plan for me to become a mentor.

I was to meet my mentee, Lisa Marie, for the first time at a coffee shop. I was very nervous, but I prayed before I left the house, asking Him to go with me and to guide me throughout our first meeting. I felt a lot better after praying, and I left trusting the Lord and feeling confident that everything would be fine. At our first meeting, we talked for a few hours and it was really nice and very relaxing. We had a lot in common after all! The Lord always knows better than we do, I reminded myself.

We started meeting every week after that, and I always looked forward to getting together with this sweet, wonderful woman. We talked about the Lord (even though she had not made a decision to follow

Christ), the Bible, and our lives. We shared a lot of different feelings. There were times when I needed somebody to talk to, and there she was for me, always with understanding and lots of wisdom and good advice. Our relationship was nice, but I wasn't sure if I was doing a good job. I wasn't following all the advise I got from ladies with more experience than me, or following a book about mentoring. I got a message from the Lord telling me that every person is different, and I should follow His instructions, so I did. Many times throughout our six-month contract, I asked the Lord if I was fulfilling His ministry well.

To my surprise, Lisa Marie decided to take class 101. But better yet, she was so pleased to tell me that she received the Lord at that class! I cannot express how happy I was! We took class 201 together, and it was wonderful. Now I was at ease. She received the Lord and that is the maximum!

On one occasion toward the end of our meetings, Lisa Marie enthusiastically approached me, asking, 'Esther, guess what my husband gave me for our anniversary?' I said I didn't know, but I was thinking a diamond, based on her excitement. She said, 'A Bible! I have my own Bible now!' She was so happy! We hugged and praised the Lord! That night I came home from our meeting on cloud nine, experiencing such a beautiful happening in her life. What an amazing God we serve! That night in my prayers I thanked the Lord for guiding me throughout all this, as tears of happiness were flowing from my eyes. That was a day I will never forget as long as I live!

I am pleased to say Lisa Marie goes to church, reads the Bible, prays, and she is an example for many women. I love her with all my heart! We still meet as friends and always have a good time together. Thank you, Jesus, for putting Lisa Marie in my life–she's a blessing to me! That's why I said blessings come in many different ways. Please reach out! Touch somebody and get involved in this wonderful ministry! God's Blessings, Esther" (Mentor)

Do I need people telling me, "Great job, Janet"? No. All I need is the Lord saying to me when we meet, "Well done, My good and faithful servant. You kind of blew the first half of your life, but then you got it together and came back to Me. I gave you the call and you answered, 'Yes, Lord, yes!' "

Just as Mary wrote in Testimony #1, it is "acting in faith on such a vital need in our church." You feel the call from the Lord yourself, or you would not have made it this far into this material. I wrote this resource for you and all the women of your church, I know you have names you will soon add to the list—women in your church who will have "Their Stories."

Chapter 15: Who Will Be the First to Testify?

CHAPTER 16

"Their voice has gone out into all the earth, their words to the ends of the world" (Romans 10:18).

"Therefore go and make disciples of all nations, baptizing them in the name of the Father and of the Son and of the Holy Spirit, and teaching them to obey everything I have commanded you" (Matthew 28:19-20).

What Other Churches Are Saying

THE CALL IN OTHER CHURCHES

Many churches have followed the guidelines presented in this material to duplicate the Woman to Woman Mentoring Ministry in their churches. Some have changed the name but still follow the principles outlined in this text. They tell me that they literally go page-by-page, step-by-step, and, "When something is working this well, why reinvent the wheel. We are so glad you went before us and took the time to write it all down. The material was so easy to follow."

I give all the glory to the Lord for what He has done through me. Many times sitting at the computer I would cry out, "Lord, could you take this cup from me? Why must I sit here day after day writing about something I would rather just be doing?" But I knew the answer to my own question. I knew why He helped me remember every detail of what we did that worked. My husband often laughs that few people are both visionary and detailed. I think he is saying that I defy all the personality studies! As a creation of God, He can break all the man-made rules to make us each unique unto ourselves and to use us in the way He chooses.

I thought it might be helpful for you to hear what some of the churches say about using the *Woman to Woman Mentoring* resources and how they have helped them start their ministries. I surveyed churches from across the United States and Canada to get a representation of various sizes of congregations, denominations, ages of churches, and locations. I hope that you find a church you can identify with, and that their testimony will be an encouragement to you. I asked then to comment on using the resources and to share any additional remarks they might have. All expressed the desire that their experiences would inspire you to start a Woman to Woman Mentoring Ministry in your church.

CHURCH STORIES
Church Size of 200-400

Church:	Hockessin Baptist Church
Location:	Hockessin, Delaware (Suburban)
Denomination:	Southern Baptist
Size:	200
Age:	18 Years
Submitted by:	Jewel Boulet

"This kit was an answer to about five different women's burden. We are all working mothers and very busy. We did not need another meeting or group to go to. Your materials helped us completely organize ourselves. After our two meetings (Orientation Coffee and Kickoff Night), the women were thrilled to realize this was now a relationship journey between two women and the Lord. Several couples decided to stay together longer. Many commented they were closer to the Lord and were glad that they had to be accountable in this relationship.

We have many professional women in our church. Several have never taken the time to be a friend to a woman (too busy competing in the engineering and banking world). After six months of being a mentee, I got to see a professional woman who was insecure about being a friend to another woman blossom in confidence and joy and peace! This time around she was so excited to be a mentor to another woman. Another woman was in a spiritual valley with her 20-year-old son being arrested and convicted of theft. I was thrilled to encourage and mentor her, even if she is older than me. A new group of women are becoming one in the Lord in our church. Thank you!"

"The impact of changed lives through the power of God and the commitment in relationships is so evident in our women."

Church:	New Hope Christian Fellowship
Location:	Vacaville, California
Denomination:	Nondenominational
Size:	250
Age:	5 years
Submitted by:	Donna Stephens

"The *Woman to Woman Mentoring* resources have been most helpful and have assisted us in encouraging women to be part of our Mentoring Ministry. Helping the women to have a plan and direction to obtain their goal in the mentoring relationships has been the greatest benefit. The kit is user-friendly and easily adaptable to our women and the direction I wish to go. The greatest blessing is to see how God has taken the gift in Janet, developed it, and allowed women from all over to grow and fulfill His command for the older to teach the younger. The *Handbooks* are excellent resources and reminders for those in the program to use consistently to help with day-to-day questions and concerns.

"My greatest blessing in our Mentoring Ministry is to watch it double in size. The impact of changed lives through the power of God and the commitment in relationships is so evident in our women. We have watched prayers being answered. One woman who was ready to walk out on her marriage is seeing her husband change and ask her to pray, and they now pray together. Another woman is now ready to go on to be a mentor. She is transformed. When one relationship began, the mentor was not very happy, did not even know why she was doing this, and was quite vocal about it. The mentee with tears in her eyes, said "What about me?" That changed a heart and now the relationship has grown and so much love is evident. The mentor's whole family is involved. This mentee, was a newly-separated woman whose husband had abandoned her and taken one of their sons. God worked miracles in both lives. One woman came and was in such despair, she just needed someone with "skin on." God matched her with a godly woman, and now she is the woman whose husband is praying with her."

Church: St. Luke's Lutheran Church
Location: La Mesa, California
Denomination: Lutheran
Size: 350
Age: 55 Years
Submitted by: Lynda Peimann

"The Kit is complete, thorough, insightful, well organized and made it so easy for me to not feel overwhelmed in starting, growing and maintaining a Mentoring Ministry. The Lord of the Harvest planted the seed within me and then watered it as He brought Janet Thompson into my life, along with her materials, wisdom and insight. God used Janet to cultivate that seed as she 'mentored me' through the resources. The women God brought to our first Orientation Coffee are being touched already as God works and moves amongst His daughters. His sweetness is being evidenced even more within their lives as they fulfill their call of the Titus 2 woman. We already have a waiting list of 27 women for our next Coffee."

Church Size of 600-900

Church: Salt Lake City Evangelical Free Church
Location: Salt Lake City, Utah (Urban)
Denomination: Evangelical Free
Size: 600+
Age: 120 Years
Submitted by: Kimberly Mueller

"After having worked in the business world myself for a number of years, it was wonderful to find a mentoring model that was put together with <u>excellence</u>. Janet

"Many commented they were closer to the Lord and were glad that they had to be accountable in this relationship."

and her staff had taken the time to think through all of the details. I was thankful to find a model that was tried and true so we did not have to reinvent the wheel! The *Woman to Woman Mentoring: Training Leader's Guide* and *Handbooks* were very helpful. We found that we needed to modify the training only slightly based on the size of our congregation and the culture here in Salt Lake City.

I have loved seeing how so many of the mentoring pairs have been matches made in heaven. They comment on how much they have in common, and how God answered prayers when the matches were made. I have also enjoyed seeing the long-term relationships that have continued way beyond the six-month mark."

> *"I have enjoyed seeing the long-term relationships that have continued way beyond the six-month mark."*

    Church: Crossroads Community Church
    Location: Freeport, Illinois (Urban)
Denomination: Assembly of God
    Size: 600-700
    Age: 21 Years
Submitted by: Mary J. Thom

"Ministry to women has been a passion of my heart for many years—probably dating back to when I first got saved in 1973. Over the last several years that passion has become more focused around women mentoring effectively. In the spring of 1998 my pastor and some of our staff went to Saddleback Church for a conference. He brought me back some information about a Women's Mentoring Ministry. I decided to order the *Woman to Woman Mentoring* resources.

I was so excited when I received them! The more I read about it, the more I knew it was an answer to prayer. It was just what I needed to help me start a Women's Mentoring Ministry in my church. We followed the kit very closely and learned a lot from our trial run the fall of 1998.

I found the training materials very helpful, especially when we first started. They were very helpful to us as a ministry in providing a quality experience for the women involved in the Mentoring Ministry. Some of the blessings of the Mentoring Ministry have been new relationships, answered prayer, growth, and maturity in both practical and spiritual areas of need."

    Church: Faith Reformed Church
    Location: South Holland, Illinois (Suburban)
Denomination: Reformed Church of America
    Size: 600
    Age: 35 Years
Submitted by: Marlene Santefort

"I found the kit to be very thorough and helpful. We are using the *Handbooks* and doing the program with 11 mentoring pairs at the 3-month training right now. This is our first group to start and I have two fine coleaders.

I liked the very open-ended program that leaves so much freedom for the mentoring pair to choose what is best for them both to do together. I see God answering so many prayers for the women and us."

>Church: Cedar Grove Baptist Church
>Location: Surrey BC, Canada (Urban)
>Denomination: Baptist General Conference
>Size: 700
>Age: 40 Years
>Submitted by: Betsy Wieser

"It's been exciting to see women relating to each other on a deeper level."

"Finally, a program all laid out giving me the 'how to'! I read several books on mentoring, saw the need, but felt inadequate to start it. It is also both inappropriate and awkward to go to that younger woman and say, "I'd like to mentor you." We are into our second year of using the resources at our church. I've recommended it to many others here in Canada, and I know of at least two other churches in our area using it. Thank you, Janet, for putting this together. The kit gave me the tools to encourage others to do what God had put on my heart.

We found the '12 Steps to Starting a New Ministry' very helpful. Our program is called Women Walking Together, and we run it for five months, doing two a year. It's been exciting to see women relating to each other on a deeper level, and hearing mentors say, 'I wasn't sure I was qualified to do this.' An organized program has given them the encouragement to use what they have learned to help others. Praise God!"

>Church: New Hope Christian Church
>Location: Bartlett, Tennessee (Urban)
>Denomination: Nondenominational
>Size: 800
>Age: 102 Years
>Submitted by: Bonnie N. Walters

"This resource relieved much of the stress of beginning a new ministry. It was encouraging to read not only the successes but the areas that needed improvement. Janet's willingness to be herself in writing allowed us to be ourselves in real life. Her continued advice that this was a ministry of faith that God would orchestrate was the best advice as we came to those moments when we could no longer see what would happen next.

The training resources were invaluable for our first Kickoff meeting and mentor training. We changed several things to better meet the needs of our ladies, but it provided a good beginning. We have had two Coffees now. Each Coffee resulted in matches that have had everlasting results. It is a joy to watch the different pairs grow in their relationships with each other and with Jesus."

Church: Hauser Community Church
Location: North Bend, Oregon (Rural)
Denomination: Nondenominational
Size: 900
Age: 45 Years
Submitted by: Royce Bogs

"The Holy Spirit led Janet Thompson to 'cover all the bases' when she wrote the Mentoring Ministry materials! After praying, and praying, and praying, then poring over the materials, all the questions and situations that I could think of were answered within the materials. These resources are invaluable.

We have just begun our Mentoring Ministry. Orientation Coffee #1 was held at our Ladies' Retreat in November. The 20 ladies who committed to a mentoring relationship are off and running, and most of them had met within the week following Kickoff! It was inspiring to watch the Lord match the ladies and their reactions to their matches. It has also been a great spiritual growth time for this facilitator who likes to have <u>everything</u> planned and likes to have an idea of what the results are <u>before</u> they happen. Although planning is important, prayer is what makes this ministry work as it does—with God revealing His purposes in each lady's life as the Orientation Coffee takes place, as matching takes place, and as the mentors and mentees begin meeting and getting to know each other. We're anticipating continued blessings from the Lord as the ladies continue on in their mentoring relationships. We already have a list of ladies interested in our next Coffee! God bless you, Janet, for your obedience and submission to His will in your life regarding the Mentoring Ministry and its resources that He used you to develop. Lives are being blessed abundantly!"

Churches 1000-4000

Church: San Clemente Presbyterian Church
Location: San Clemente, California (Suburban)
Denomination: Presbyterian
Size: 1000
Age: 60+ Years
Submitted by: Sandy Perry

"The kit is very 'user-friendly!' It seems to cover all the 'what-ifs' and gives a wonderful step-by-step process to follow. Very thorough! The training resources are excellent and very thorough, also.

We are brand new. The kit guided us and pointed out all the essential details, helping our first Coffee run smoothly. We saw the value of telling our stories and sharing at the Coffee. We were blessed by the sharing of the new mentors and mentees, and I think the reason they felt safe in sharing was because we were willing to be vulnerable."

"It is a joy to watch the different pairs grow in their relationships with each other and with Jesus. Entire families are being blessed."

Church:	First Christian Church
Location:	Napa, California (Rural)
Denomination:	Christian/Protestant
Size:	1000
Age:	140 Years
Submitted by:	Joanne Birtcher

"God and Janet were the answer to my prayers. When our Women's Ministry asked me to start a Mentoring Ministry, I had no idea where to begin. Through a friend of a friend I found Janet. Her material was the whole answer, written out in a very easy to follow styleand extremely encouraging. I needed the help the kit and training resources gave to me, and it is so specific. How could she think of all of this and not eliminate anything? God worked His special wonders again.

Our women were so ready for this opportunity—we are now on our second year of the ministry and have... now reached 50 women as either mentor or mentees. Everyone tells me what a wonderful experience it has been. Many mentors have returned because they truly believe in being a Titus woman. I feel so blessed. Thank you, Janet, for making it a great experience."

"Prayer is what makes this ministry work as it does—with God revealing His purposes in each lady's life."

Church:	River of Life Fellowship
Location:	Kent, Washington (Urban)
Denomination:	Nondenominational
Size:	1000
Age:	16 Years
Submitted by:	Sue Brockett

"I had no clue as to where to begin when the pastor's wife handed me the kit. As I read from cover to cover, beginning to end, including all of the forms, Women of the Heart (the name they chose for their ministry) Mentoring Ministry took on life and breath. We now have 15 mentoring relationships after our first Orientation Coffee and are planning our second for January 9, 2000. Praise the Lord!

I wouldn't have had a clue what to do with all those mentors without the training resources! Our second training session is already scheduled. The forms and resources for growing the ministry have been invaluable. The descriptions of every area of service are concise and thorough, giving ladies the 'meat' needed to make a decision of where they can help!"

Church:	Lee's Summit Community Church
Location:	Lee's Summit, Missouri (Urban)
Denomination:	Nondenominational
Size:	1100
Age:	11 Years
Submitted by:	Judy Jipsen

"For the past five years I have researched several different mentoring resources and could never find one that had everything I wanted in a step-by-step method. I happened to be in Louisville, Kentucky in August 1998 attending Southeast Christian Church and saw a brochure on their Woman to Woman Mentoring Ministry. Their Women's Ministry Director, Lynn Reese, was at an information table, and I asked her to tell me more about this. In fact, they were having their first Orientation Coffee that afternoon, and she invited me to come and observe. I did and got so excited to see how the Coffee worked. I was so blessed to have been a part of it. After the Coffee, I asked Lynn for Janet Thompson's telephone number, and when I returned home I called her and ordered the complete set of materials. My training leader loved the *Woman to Woman Mentoring: Training Leader's Guide* and *Handbooks*!

This was September 1998, and it took me 8 months to study it and talk to my pastor, who fully approved. The Lord led me to my team, and I started the process of laying the foundation. I found it was very important not to hurry the process. Janet has done a tremendous job of putting this together and when followed, it works out to be a joyful journey.

We spent a great deal of time in prayer, trusting the Lord to lead us step-by-step. Our first Orientation Coffee was September 1999. We had 35 women attend, and 24 signed up to participate. The process of matching the pairs took about 4 hours. The Kickoff Night was very exciting to watch as the pairs met for the first time. Our women have wanted a Mentoring Ministry for two years, but until I had the proper resources, there was no leading to start one. We will be having our first 3 month training and our second Coffee is already planned. I asked the same team that served at our first Coffee to serve at this one, and they all agreed. They are all so eager to serve.

Thank you, Janet, for being obedient to God's call to write this wonderful resource. Isaiah 60:1 has been a motivating verse to us: 'Arise; shine; … the glory of the Lord has risen on you.' Also 1 Thessalonians 5:24: 'Faithful is He who calls you, and He also will bring it to pass.' The Lord has truly led us all the way and brought it to pass."

"Faithful is He who calls you, and He also will bring it to pass" (1 Thess. 5:24).

Church:	Henderson Hills Baptist Church
Location:	Edmond, Oklahoma (Urban)
Denomination:	Baptist
Size:	4000
Age:	33 Years
Submitted by:	Becky Burns

"In the fall of 1998, the Women's Ministry Team of Henderson Hills Baptist Church began to sense the Lord's leadership in forming a ministry where women could meet in one-on-one relationships. We had many women, especially younger women, asking for and desiring a relationship with a spiritually older

Chapter 16: What Other Churches Are Saying

woman. In January 1999, I was asked to pray about and consider leading this part of our Women's Ministry. The Lord had already given me a special love for women, and I already had the joy of investing my life into the lives of several young women. I knew what a blessing a one-on-one relationship could be.

I, however, did not have a clue as to how to implement this type of ministry for the women of Henderson Hills. I told the Lord that He would have to give me some type of vision as to how He wanted this done. To me it seemed overwhelming! One day our pastor's wife handed me an audiotape that had been given to her by one of our other pastors who had recently attended a Church Growth Conference at Saddleback Church. The tape was by Janet Thompson and the subject was 'How to Start, Grow, and Maintain a Mentoring Ministry at Your Church.' I was so excited that I called her personally, and she was so gracious to talk to me and answer questions. As it turned out, I ordered all the resources.

After the resources arrived, I spent literally days poring over all the detailed information written in these books. I had such a peace and an excitement because I knew the Lord had provided the vision. He had provided a very detailed map to start this wonderful ministry. One thing that I so love about all the resources Janet has written is that you could just tell that she loves the Lord because everything is about Him and not her! The glory is always given to our Lord!

As we began our ministry, these manuals were literally our textbooks. Many of the things we have done exactly as she suggested; then other things we changed and molded to the women of our church, but having that basis to go by was a tremendous blessing! I would strongly recommend Janet's material to any church considering starting a Mentoring Ministry. It is so detailed and helpful, but it is also a blessing to see the Lord on practically every page!

At our first Titus Two Orientation Coffee we had 63 ladies attend and were able to match every woman in a mentoring relationship. We are having our second Coffee in a few weeks and can't wait to see what the Lord will do. I continually refer back to my books from Janet and always learn something new."

You have heard the stories of actual mentors and mentees whose lives have been forever impacted by mentoring relationships they experienced in the Woman to Woman Mentoring Ministry at Saddleback Church. Then you read what other churches are saying about how the Woman to Woman Mentoring Ministry model has been the answer to their prayers. You read their hearts. They were all encouraging you to take the step that they took and let these resources be your map and your guide to offering the women at your church an opportunity to experience a timeless, biblically-based relationship. One more chapter and you are ready to start creating stories and testimonies at your church.

"He provided a very detailed map to start this wonderful ministry."

CHAPTER 17

"Be still, and know that I am God" (Psalm 46:10).

Let Go & Let God!

Do Relationships Always Work Out?

You read some exciting testimonies in the last two chapters. Are you wondering if all the mentoring relationships go great, or if some encounter problems? I would be doing you a disservice if I did not tell you that some relationships do not work out. At the end of the first year, I reflected on some of our problems and tried to learn ways to avoid them being repeated. I realize that nothing this side of heaven will ever be perfect, but, like Jesus, I am sad if even one sheep goes astray. I feel an obligation to the women in the ministry to do as much as I can to help them have fulfilling mentoring relationships. Therefore, much of what we do today in the ministry happens for a reason. I have tried to explain those reasons to you as we have gone along.

As a review, let's look at some of the policies we have established in our Woman to Woman Mentoring Ministry and discuss the reasons behind them. You may want to modify the policies for your church, but they come out of experience, so I would recommend that you establish some along the same lines. I cannot make all the choices for you, but I can tell you what I have learned about a Women's Mentoring Ministry. Some of the policies may seem a little rigid, but they have a purpose. Our ultimate goal is to do everything within our capabilities to assist the women to have the best relationships possible. However, we are all accountable to God, and He can bring good out of any bad situation.

Helpful Guidelines

Policy: Do not match anyone who cannot attend a Coffee, arrives after 2:30 p.m. when the orientation presentation has begun, or leaves before the Coffee is over.

Reason: The late arrivals miss the explanation of mentoring and the expectations for those entering into mentoring relationships. They would not receive a complete orientation into the ministry or mentoring. It is not fair to them or a woman matched with them in a mentoring relationship. Those women who leave early miss hearing everyone share, and may not get a chance to share themselves. They do not hear the closing remarks and instructions. Again, you cannot take responsibility to place someone into a match who has not received a complete orientation.

In the beginning, I did not follow this policy. If a woman could not attend the Orientation Coffee, I sent her a Profile Card to fill out and mail back to me. Then we put the returned Profile Card in with the cards from the Coffee. We would not have a picture of her, and the **Prayer Day Team** would have never met her. Sometimes it worked out and the relationship went fine, but most times it did not. The women who have an opportunity to learn about the Woman to Woman Mentoring Ministry, and learn about each other from the sharing time, are much more committed in their relationships.

Policy: We do not match anyone who cannot attend the Kickoff Night.

Reason: A mentor or mentee missing Kickoff Night would not know the expectations of the relationship or have committed to the Mentoring Covenant. They will not have the guidelines to follow. The mentor would miss the Kickoff Night training. You would not be able to see them meet, pray over the relationship, or introduce them to their **Prayer Warrior.** In the beginning, out of naiveté and inexperience, I mailed the training material to the mentors who missed the meeting. They were to read it and contact their mentees. These relationships never worked. We were not doing them any favors by making exceptions.

We now make it clear on all our announcements that attendance at Kickoff Night is mandatory for participating in a mentoring relationship. Emergencies do and have happened. Again, not wanting to disappoint them, I would make an exception, and again, for the same reasons, the relationship would falter.

Policy: We only match women who attend our church.

Reason: Our purpose, as stated in our Mission Statement, is to unite the women of our church. We encourage them to do church activities together. We hope that they will both feel more a part of the church family.

Policy: Do not place any woman as a mentor who has not answered these questions on the Profile Card:
(1) Dates: Accepted Christ? Attended our church? Rededicated life?
(2) Responded "yes" to all the Statement of Faith questions.
(3) Is there anything in your life today that you feel would interfere with you being a mentor?

If they have left any blanks, phone them and fill in the answers before you match them as mentors.

The women who have an opportunity to learn about the Woman to Woman Mentoring Ministry, and learn about each other from the sharing time, are much more committed in their relationships.

Reason: Those Profile Card questions have a purpose. You want to place the more spiritually-mature woman as the mentor. However, you also want her to examine her life to see if there is anything that would interfere with her being a godly role model.

Policy: All women entering into a mentoring relationship agree to adhere to the Woman to Woman Mentoring Ministry Code of Ethics.

Reason: The purpose of the Code of Ethics is to prevent potential problems. Instituting this code helped prevent some of the challenging relationships.

WOMAN TO WOMAN
Mentoring Ministry Code of Ethics

If I am matched into a one-on-one mentoring relationship and participate in the Mentoring Ministry, I understand and agree to abide by the following courtesies. I realize that I am an imperfect creation, and I cannot honor these expectations by myself. Therefore, I will continuously seek the Lord's help through prayer and petition. With His assurance and strength …

I will return phone calls from my mentor and mentee and any woman who calls me from the Mentoring Ministry—remembering that they are taking time out of their schedules to call and encourage me, tell me they are praying for me, invite me to a function in my honor, or just let me know they care and so does the entire ministry team.

I will call back my **Prayer Warrior** who is on her knees praying specifically for me during my six-month covenant relationship.

I will reply in a timely fashion to every notice I receive that asks for an RSVP, whether or not I can attend.

I will make it a priority to attend the Mentor Halftime Refresher if I am a mentor.

I will consider it the highest honor to be invited to the Six-Month Potluck Celebration at the end of my formal mentoring covenant, and will attend this festive occasion planned just for me.

I will call my **Prayer Warrior**, the **Ministry Relations Shepherdess**, or someone on the **Administrative Team** if I am having problems or have

Chapter 17: Let Go & Let God!

questions about my mentoring relationship. Giving up on the relationship will never be an option.

I will pray and also ask others to pray for me that I can continue to learn His ways and be the Christian woman that would please the Lord. I will strive to be a woman who honors her commitments, thinks of others before herself, and loves her neighbor as herself.

Adherence to these policies and the Code of Ethics has helped in the quality and success of the mentoring relationships. Giving the women the opportunity to meet each other on the Kickoff Night and sign the Mentoring Covenants which we witness, conveys the significance of the commitment to each other.

I also now spend more time during the Orientation Coffee discussing the commitment they are making and the time it will take. I stress that it will not be acceptable to change your mind once you have signed and agreed to the Covenant. I remind them that they will be agreeing to stay in the relationship for six months. We occasionally have women call the day after the Coffee to say they do not have the time to commit. They have also called after we matched them, but before they met. While this is an inconvenience and means you have to do some rearranging, it is better to happen now than after they have already met. Someone is always going to get hurt if one of them breaks the Mentoring Covenant. I never give my approval of someone breaking the Six-Month Covenant. I remind them that:

- As a Christian, they made a commitment to another Christian woman.
- God had a plan and a reason for putting them together, and I encourage them to wait on God and let Him do His work.

If they still choose to discontinue the relationship, encourage them to have a closure meeting together. If you receive a phone call from a woman who wants to break the covenant or is dissatisfied with her mentoring relationship, the first thing I would suggest you do is ask if you can pray over the phone with her. Ask the Lord to give you both wisdom and discernment. This will not only diffuse the situation, but it will bring the presence of God into your discussion. I think it will amaze you how the Lord works out the solutions. We now have a **Ministry Relations Shepherdess**, and she handles most of these calls.

Here are responses we give for some problems presented to us. For additional scenarios, see the *Woman to Woman Mentoring: Training Leader's Guide.*

TROUBLESHOOTING

Problem: My mentee does not return my phone calls. I am ready to give up on her.

Answer: As a mentor, your task is to be a godly role model for the mentee. Numerous times the Lord reminds us as Christians to be persistent and not give

I encourage them to wait on God and let Him do His work.

up. If the mentee did not need guidance, she would not be a mentee. Do not match your behavior to hers. She may need to learn that considerate people return phone calls, so you need to be persistent and keep calling.

Do not think of it as rejection. Think of it as godly persistence and guidance. She could be out of town, sick, or have out-of-town company. When you do get in touch with her, let her know that you worried about her when you did not receive a response to your calls, that you enjoy talking with her, and that communication is vital to your relationship. Ask her to please return your phone calls even if it is to say, "I received your call. I don't have time to talk now, but let's set a time for me to call back."

As the mentor, you are responsible for keeping the relationship going. If you stop calling, that will definitely cause a break in the relationship.

Problem: My mentor or mentee is just so busy. We can never find time to get together.

Answer: The next time you get together, bring out the Mentoring Covenant that you both agreed to and suggest that you take a look at how you are doing with keeping your covenant. The second line says, "We will contact each other once a week and meet a minimum of twice a month." Ask yourselves how you are doing on that. Get out your calendars and schedule your next three meetings. Always bring your calendar when you get together and never say good-bye until you have scheduled the next meeting. Do not get lax on this. Then offer a friendly reminder that we make time for things that are important to us. Think of ways to establish more value in your relationship and make the times you meet more meaningful to you both.

Problem: I have too much going on in my life right now. I need to get out of this mentoring relationship.

Answer: In the first few months, I was much too passive when this happened. I listened to all the reasons, gave a few weak ideas of what to do, and then said, "OK, you call and tell your mentor or mentee that you are breaking off the relationship. You need to be the one to do that."

Now we are much firmer and try to get the person wanting to leave the relationship to be more accountable. Ask pointed questions so that you can find out the real reason behind their decision, and then you can address it for what it is. For example, she might say that as a mentor she does not feel she is making a difference in her mentee's life. Remind the mentor that is not her role. Only God can make a difference, or fix her problems, or change her circumstances. She is to be a godly role model, and breaking a commitment is not a good example of

Think of ways to establish more value in your relationship and make the times you meet more meaningful to you both.

Chapter 17: Let Go & Let God! **215**

a Christian woman. Perhaps her expectations for the relationship are too high. She just needs to relax and let God work through her.

Other times simply ask: "Are the six months that you committed to up yet?" Of course, they will say, "No." Then suggest that you need to talk about what you can do to help her honor her commitment. That usually gets discussion going, and then you have something with which to work.

Problem: My mentee does all the talking. I never get a chance to say anything.

Answer: A good response is, "A major part of being a good mentor is being a good listener. Some women have no one who will listen to them. She may be using you to bounce off ideas. The Lord may be wanting you to become a better listener." You can also suggest the mentor ask the mentee if she would like to have a response from her, or if she just needs a sounding board for her thoughts and ideas.

Problem: I don't understand why we are together. Are you sure we should be matched?

Answer: This is a question you address at the Orientation Coffee. Tell them that they may not be able to see right away what the Lord had planned when He put them together. Advise them to wait and watch. Let go and let God. We turned the matching over to God, and He knows why they are together. To some it is obvious the first night, and to others the Lord may continue to reveal it throughout the six months. As your ministry develops you will have testimonies like the one in Chapter 15 where Lisa was so sure she came to the Coffee to find her California mom and ended up with a best friend instead. Or there may be a relationship like Lisa Marie and Esther, both so apprehensive and yet God had a miracle in store for them. Until you have some testimonies of your own to use for encouraging these struggling M&Ms, use ours to give hope to those who want to give up. Encourage them to give God a chance to show them His plan for their relationship. Some women may be so sure they know what they need, but God has something else in mind for them. There are so many stories of women who continually discover commonalties in their lives as their relationships develop. That is why I encourage the doubting women to, "Wait on the Lord. Our human understanding has limits; His does not. You will be circumventing His plan for you if you do not give this relationship a chance to grow and shine for Him."

The minute I hear of a problem, I start praying for the relationship and for both women to be open and receptive to what the Lord is doing in their lives by placing them together. Sometimes I have an idea of the reason, but only the Lord knows for sure. I put the relationship at His capable feet, and ask Him to change or soften a heart, open and refresh or renew a mind.

Only God can make a difference, or fix her problems, or change her circumstances.

God Is in Control

My prayer is that you are full of excitement and not overwhelmed by all you have read in this book. If God could use me, He can use you! He will be there to help you every step of the way. Like the old joke goes: How do you eat an elephant? One bite at a time! My best advice to you is to start one step at a time. The Lord will be so happy that you are working for Him, that He will guide you. God created the ministry. We are just the facilitators—the eyes and ears and hands and mind that He has chosen to use. We are His vessels, and He will fill us up. This will be difficult to remember when the ministry is growing and people are giving you the praise, or perhaps you have met some road blocks, and you are thinking of giving up. Either way, do not give in to Satan's arrows. Don't let him take you down, and the ministry with you.

Just today I received our church newsletter in the mail. The front page feature article is about the successful growth and blessings of the Woman to Woman Mentoring Ministry. It is a well-written article which I know will draw lots of comments. Seeing in print the path that we have taken since that first call from the Lord to "go and feed My sheep," re-energized me. How timely it was that it should arrive in the mail just before I sat down to write my closing words to you. The Lord is always at work around us. All we need to do is join Him. That is what you and I did, as we said, "Yes, Lord, yes!"

I am excited for you and the women of your church. I have accomplished my goal as I write these closing words. When the days were long and hot, and my shoulders ached from long hours at the computer, I had to keep my eyes fixed on the final outcome. Other women besides ours at Saddleback Church will have an opportunity to enjoy the blessings and fruits of being in a mentoring relationship. You, and the Lord's constant tugging, kept me focused and writing all these months. I have been in prayer for you since the first page. Every time I sit down to the computer, I ask the Lord to speak through me. Let my words be His words and my thoughts His thoughts.

You now have the basics of how to start a Woman to Woman Mentoring Ministry in your church. You can take out of this material exactly what you and the women of your church need to launch your Women's Mentoring Ministry. Start at the beginning and take each step slowly. I know you will want to jump ahead, but remember what the Lord says about patience and waiting. Your ministry, built on a solid foundation, will be around for years. Ask everyone you know to begin praying for you. Your constant prayer request should be for whatever step you are on in building the ministry. Pray a daily prayer for the mentors and mentees that He knows will be joining the ministry. Pray for the helpers He is going to bring to you. Pray for the future mentoring relationships. The Lord gave you this awesome ministry. Remember to always give it back to Him.

Until we meet in paradise, we are all About His Work!

The Lord gave you this awesome ministry. Remember to always give it back to Him.

Forms

PERMISSION IS GIVEN TO COPY THESE FORMS FOR USE WITH YOUR MENTORING MINISTRY.

Discussion

The following pages are forms we have developed for our Woman to Woman Mentoring Ministry. Please feel free to use them for your Women's Mentoring Ministry.

Consider printing the Profile Card (form A) and Orientation Coffee Program (form C) on light colored card stock paper so they will hold up better. You might also print the handouts for the Coffee (forms D, E, F, G, and V) and the Opportunity to Serve Profile (form B) each on a different color paper to eliminate confusion. When you are discussing them, you can refer to the paper color to make them easier for the ladies to locate. We change the color of the Orientation Coffee Flier (form L) for each Coffee. This prevents confusion or having an old flier out by mistake. It is easy to spot the wrong color. Use the Announcement Flier (form K) between Coffees. Keep it the same color, and women will soon learn to look for that color flier with information about the Women's Mentoring Ministry.

It is wise to put the Information and Invitation Letters (forms O, Q, R) on bright colored paper and hope the women put them on their refrigerator or bulletin board so they do not forget the event. The Areas of Opportunity for Service Sign-Up Sheet (form W) should also be on a very bright color that attracts attention.

I have also included a copy of our newsletter, *Beyond Coffee* (form X), to give you ideas of what and how we communicate with our ladies. Remember, this newsletter is from our ministry at Saddleback and contains our information. You will need to customize one for your ministry. A newsletter provides a great service opportunity for a woman who is gifted in and enjoys working with computer design.

The CD-ROM in the *Woman to Woman Mentoring: Leader Kit* also contains all the forms from this section as well as a short promotional video clip. To use the files on the disc, you must have Adobe Acrobat Reader 4.0 or higher and Quicktime 4.0 or higher. These applications are included on the CD-ROM. You can refer to the Read Me file on the disc for complete instructions on how to use these files.

Forms Index
Alphabetical by Title

Form Name	Form Letter	Page
Announcement Flier	Form K	233
Areas of Opportunity for Service	Form V	246
Areas of Opportunity for Service Sign-Up Sheet	Form W	248
Beyond Coffee Newsletter	Form X	249
Coffee Closed Sign	Form H	230
Hostess Letter	Form O	239
Hostess Checklist	Form P	240
How to Get Involved in the Woman to Woman Mentoring Ministry	Form G	229
M&M Questionnaire	Form J	232
Mentor Halftime Refresher Letter	Form Q	241
Mentoring Covenant	Form I	231
"The Mentoring Game" Skit	Form N	236
Mentoring Roster	Form T	244
Opportunity to Serve Profile	Form B	223
Orientation Coffee Flier	Form L	234
Orientation Coffee Helper's Pre-Coffee Review	Form M	235
Orientation Coffee Program	Form C	224
Potluck Celebration Letter	Form R	242
Prayer Warrior Guidelines	Form S	243
Prayer Warrior Journal	Form U	245
Profile Card	Form A	222
Recommended Book List	Form D	226
Scripture Printout—Proverbs 31:1,10-31; Titus 2:1-5	Form F	228
Ways to Show Your M&M You Care	Form E	227

Forms Index
by Form Letter

FORM LETTER	FORM NAME	PAGE
Form A	Profile Card	222
Form B	Opportunity to Serve Profile	223
Form C	Orientation Coffee Program	224
Form D	Recommended Book List	226
Form E	Ways to Show Your M&M You Care	227
Form F	Scripture Printout—Proverbs 31:1,10-31; Titus 2:1-5	228
Form G	How to Get Involved in the Woman to Woman Mentoring Ministry	229
Form H	Coffee Closed Sign	230
Form I	Mentoring Covenant	231
Form J	M&M Questionnaire	232
Form K	Announcement Flier	233
Form L	Orientation Coffee Flier	234
Form M	Orientation Coffee Helper's Pre-Coffee Review	235
Form N	"The Mentoring Game" Skit	236
Form O	Hostess Letter	239
Form P	Hostess Checklist	240
Form Q	Mentor Halftime Refresher Letter	241
Form R	Potluck Celebration Letter	242
Form S	Prayer Warrior Guidelines	243
Form T	Mentoring Roster	244
Form U	Prayer Warrior Journal	245
Form V	Areas of Opportunity for Service	246
Form W	Areas of Opportunity for Service Sign-Up Sheet	248
Form X	*Beyond Coffee* Newsletter	249

Date: ___/___/___

Coffee #: _____

Profile Card

Please fill in all blanks that apply to you.

Tape Photo Here

_____

Name _____ Birth date ___/___/___ Age _____

Address _____ City _____ Zip _____

Home Phone _____ Email _____

Occupation _____ Business Phone _____

❑ Single   ❑ Engaged   ❑ Married (# yr.____)   ❑ Blended Family   ❑ Ever divorced (# yr.____)   ❑ Widowed

Spouse's Name _____ Birth date ___/___/___ Age _____

Children's Ages   (M) _____ (F) _____ Grandchildren's Ages   (M) _____ (F) _____

Stepchildren's Ages   (M) _____ (F) _____ Living with you? ❑ Yes ❑ No

Have attended (*your church name*) since _____ Accepted Christ ___/___/___ Rededicated Life ___/___/___

The (*your church name*) Statement of Faith includes the following essential beliefs.

Please indicate with a check (√) if you are in agreement with each one.

❑ God is Creator and Ruler of the universe   ❑ Jesus is the Son of God

❑ The Trinity (Father, Son, and Holy Spirit are one)   ❑ Bible is inerrant Word of God

❑ Eternal life or eternal separation   ❑ Salvation is God's free gift to us

I want to be a: ❑ Mentor ❑ Mentee ❑ Either ❑ Both

I would like to be matched with: _____

Is there anything in your life today that you feel would interfere with you being a mentor?

_____

_____

Hobbies, Interests, Gifts:

_____

_____

What I desire in a mentoring relationship is:

_____

_____

Please continue on the back of this card and share any personal or background information you feel would be helpful in making a mentoring match. Thank you and blessings!

Form A

222   *Woman to Woman Mentoring: Ministry Coordinator's Guide*

Opportunity to Serve Profile

Date: ___/___/___   Coffee #: _____

Name _____ Home Phone _____

Address _____ City _____ Zip _____

Business Phone _____ Email _____

Please circle one or more areas where you feel led to serve:

Phoning	Photocopying at church office	Hospitality Shepherd Coach Apprentice
Prayer Warrior	Baking (for Coffees, special events)	Information Table Coordinator
Prayer Journal Maker	Coffee Helper	Roving Reporter for Newsletter
Prayer Day Participant	Weekend Church Table Worker	Book or T-shirt Sales (for Coffees, Kickoffs)
Potluck Helper	Singing or Drama	Ministry Shopper
Resource Guide	Prayer Chain Participant	Phone Coordinator
		Photographer

TEAM USE ONLY:
❏ Mentor   ❏ Mentee

TAPE PHOTO HERE

_____

Opportunity to Serve Profile

Date: ___/___/___   Coffee #: _____

Name _____ Home Phone _____

Address _____ City _____ Zip _____

Business Phone _____ Email _____

Please circle one or more areas where you feel led to serve:

Phoning	Photocopying at church office	Hospitality Shepherd Coach Apprentice
Prayer Warrior	Baking (for Coffees, special events)	Information Table Coordinator
Prayer Journal Maker	Coffee Helper	Roving Reporter for Newsletter
Prayer Day Participant	Weekend Church Table Worker	Book or T-shirt Sales (for Coffees, Kickoffs)
Potluck Helper	Singing or Drama	Ministry Shopper
Resource Guide	Prayer Chain Participant	Phone Coordinator
		Photographer

TEAM USE ONLY:
❏ Mentor   ❏ Mentee

TAPE PHOTO HERE

_____

FORM B

FORM C

WELCOME TO THE 20TH
Woman to Woman Mentoring Ministry
ORIENTATION COFFEE

June 1
2:00–6:00 pm

At the Home of
Lori Smith
16 Oak St.
Your Town, USA

Women of All Ages Welcome

WOMAN TO WOMAN MENTORING MINISTRY CODE OF ETHICS

If I am matched into a one-on-one mentoring relationship and participate in the mentoring ministry, I understand and agree to abide by the following courtesies. I realize that I am an imperfect creation, and I cannot honor these expectations by myself. Therefore, I will continuously seek the Lord's help through prayer and petition. With His assurance and strength …

I WILL return phone calls from my mentor and mentee and any woman who calls me from the mentoring ministry—remembering that they are taking time out of their schedules to call and encourage me, tell me they are praying for me, invite me to a function in my honor, or just let me know they care and so does the entire ministry team.

I WILL call back my Prayer Warrior who is on her knees praying specifically for me during my six-month covenant relationship.

I WILL reply in a timely fashion to every notice I receive that asks for an RSVP, whether or not I can attend.

I WILL make it a priority to attend the Mentor Halftime Refresher if I am a mentor.

I WILL consider it the highest honor to be invited to the Six-Month Potluck Celebration at the end of my formal mentoring covenant, and will attend this festive occasion planned just for me.

I WILL call my Prayer Warrior, the Ministry Relations Shepherdess, or someone on the Administrative Team if I am having problems or have questions about my mentoring relationship. Giving up on the relationship will never be an option.

I WILL pray and also ask others to pray for me that I can continue to learn His ways and be the Christian woman that would please the Lord. I will strive to be a woman who honors her commitments, thinks of others before herself, and loves her neighbor as herself.

Hats off and applause to:

Lori–Hostess, Lorna–Hospitality Shepherd, Marcy and Donna–Photographers,
Sandy–Greeter/Hugger, Jane and Lisa–Registrars, our testimonial M&Ms, Sue–Worship Director,
Laura–Spiritual Shepherdess, and our Prayer Chain for bathing this Coffee in prayer.

Thanks to our Lord Jesus Christ who created women
and birthed the concept of mentoring in our church.

224 *Woman to Woman Mentoring: Ministry Coordinator's Guide*

Mission Statement
Woman to Woman Mentoring Ministry

To give the women of *(your church's name)* Church the opportunity to experience joy and growth in their Christian lives by participating in one-on-one supporting and encouraging mentoring friendships. A mentor will be a woman who is a practicing Christian, regularly attends *(your)* Church, and has the desire to let her life be an example and godly role model. A mentee will be an attender of *(your)* Church who is younger in her walk with the Lord. Women of all ages are welcome. The scriptural foundation is Titus 2:3-5, where we are told to teach and guide the next generation of Christian women in how to live the life of a godly woman.

Areas of Opportunity for Service and Who to Call

- Hosting a Coffee in your home or helping at a future Coffee
  Call Lorna . . . . xxx-xxxx
- Being a part of the volunteer pool when needed
  Call Nancy . . . . xxx-xxxx
- Prayer Team for matching Profile Cards
  Call Sue . . . . xxx-xxxx
- Prayer Warriors for six months
  Call Darlene . . . . xxx-xxxx
- To participate in the Prayer Chain
  Call Barbara . . . . xxx-xxxx
- Women's Fellowship Table/Ministry Relations
  Call Jill . . . . xxx-xxxx
- For administrative openings
  Call Janet . . . . xxx-xxxx

Enjoy your mentoring relationships. Keep your expectations realistic and watch the wonders that God will work in both of your lives. We were praying for you before you even came today. The Lord knew you would be at this Coffee, and He has a purpose in everything He does in believers' lives.

Agenda for the Afternoon

2:00–2:30
Greetings, Hugs, Registration, and Pictures
Fill out Profile Cards
Refreshments and Socializing

2:30–4:15
Find your seats. We're ready to begin!

Opening Prayer	Laura
Worship Song	Sue
Welcome and Introductions	Janet
"Go and Feed My Sheep"	Janet
What Is Mentoring?	Janet
What Does the Bible Tell Us About Mentoring?	Laura
Skit	Truly A. Saint, Sue Permom, and Grace Abounds
Commitment to Mentoring Covenant	JoAnn

Stand-Up Break

Testimony	M&Ms
How to Get Involved	Janet
Opportunity to Serve	Jane

Break 4:15 - 4:30

4:30-6:00
Please return to your seats.
Time to Meet you—1 MINUTE—Introductions
Closing Announcements, Song, and Prayer

Form C

Recommended Book List

MENTORING

Becoming a Titus 2 Woman: A Bible Study with Martha Peace by Martha Peace
  Can be done as a study for one or a group.

*Between Women of God: The Gentle Art of Mentoring by Donna Otto
  Based on Titus 2.

*A Garden Path to Mentoring: Planting Your Life in Another & Releasing the Fragrance of Christ by Esther Burroughs

*The Influential Woman: How Every Woman Can Make a Difference in the Lives of Other Women by Vickie Kraft

Women Connecting with Women: Equipping Women for Friend-to-Friend Support and Mentoring by Verna Birkey
  Comes with a study guide.

Spiritual Mentoring: A Guide for Seeking and Giving Direction by Keith R. Anderson and Randy D. Reese

*Spiritual Mothering: The Titus 2 Model for Women Mentoring Women by Susan Hunt

*Women Encouraging Women by Lucibel Van Atta
  About mentoring and discipling women with practical applications at the end of every chapter.
  (Out of print, but worth trying to find at the library.)

Woman to Woman: Preparing Yourself to Mentor by Edna Ellison and Tricia Scribner
  A Bible study for mentors.

ENCOURAGEMENT/HOSPITALITY

A Christian Woman's Guide to Hospitality by Quin Sherrer and Laura Watson
The Personal Touch: Encouraging Others Through Hospitality by Rachael Crabb
Silver Boxes: The Gift of Encouragement by Florence Littauer
We Didn't Know They Were Angels: Discovering the Gift of Christian Hospitality by Doris W. Greig

FRIENDSHIP/GODLY WOMANHOOD

Disciplines of a Beautiful Woman by Anne Ortlund
In the Company of Women: Deepening Our Relationships with the Important Women in Our Lives ... Mothers, Daughters, Sisters, Friends & Mentors by Brenda Hunter, Ph.D.
Things Happen When Women Care: Hospitality and Friendship in Today's Busy World by Emilie Barnes
The Friendships of Women: Harnessing the Power in our Heartwarming, Heartrendering Relationships by Dee Brestin
Treasured Friends: Finding and Keeping True Friendships by Ann Hibbard
A Woman God Can Use: Lessons from Old Testament Women Help You Make Today's Choices by Alice Mathews
Woman of Influence: Ten Traits of Those Who Want to Make a Difference by Pam Farrell

FORM D

226 Woman to Woman Mentoring: Ministry Coordinator's Guide

Ways to Show Your M&M You Care

1. Call just to say, "Hi." (Be careful not to call with only business or to ask a favor.)
2. Plan a fun, out-of-the-ordinary, outing for one of your meetings together.
3. Take her flowers from your yard, just because.
4. Love her family.
5. Take her dinner when she is sick, after a new baby is born, or while she is studying for a big test.
6. Help her with an overwhelming project.
7. Take small presents (homemade are the best) to her children on their special occasions.
8. Cleaning her house when she is sick.
9. Send a note affirming her as a wife, mother, daughter, or friend.
10. Give her a gift certificate for a pedicure in her ninth month of pregnancy.
11. Prayer for her and her loved ones.
12. Print Scripture verses on a pretty card or leave a verse on her answering machine.
13. Be available.
14. Be forgiving.
15. Be accepting.
16. Take a snapshot of the two of you.
17. Create an acrostic with her name (Giving, Available, Intelligent, Loving = Gail).
18. Give an encouragement luncheon (like a birthday party) to help her during a difficult time.
19. Take her a surprise autumn gift—put a pumpkin, bottle of apple cider, and popcorn in a box, drop it on her doorstep, ring the bell, and run!
20. Plan a picnic after church for your families or for one of your meetings.
21. Give her your trust.
22. Offer to baby-sit for her kids so she and her hubby can have a night out.
23. Keep her company when her husband is out of town on business.
24. Send a friendship card when there is no special occasion—just to say you care.
25. Help her laugh when she feels like crying (after you let her cry, of course).
26. Listen.
27. When your recipe makes enough for a crowd and your family doesn't want to eat it all week, take some over to her.
28. Offer to take over cookies when you know she is entertaining or having a meeting at her house.
29. Offer to take care of her animals when she is out of town.
30. Loan her a great book you just finished and give her a bookmark to go with it.
31. Let her know that you appreciate her for being a godly woman and helping to keep you accountable.
32. Take her popsicles and chicken soup when she has the flu.
33. Offer to water her plants or baby-sit her friendship bread when she is out of town.

Proverbs 31: 1, 10-31

¹ The sayings of King Lemuel—an oracle his mother taught him:

¹⁰ A wife of noble character who can find? She is worth far more than rubies.

¹¹ Her husband has full confidence in her and lacks nothing of value.

¹² She brings him good, not harm, all the days of her life.

¹³ She selects wool and flax and works with eager hands.

¹⁴ She is like the merchant ships, bringing her food from afar.

¹⁵ She gets up while it is still dark; she provides food for her family and portions for her servant girls.

¹⁶ She considers a field and buys it; out of her earnings she plants a vineyard.

¹⁷ She sets about her work vigorously; her arms are strong for her tasks.

¹⁸ She sees that her trading is profitable, and her lamp does not go out at night.

¹⁹ In her hand she holds the distaff and grasps the spindle with her fingers.

²⁰ She opens her arms to the poor and extends her hands to the needy.

²¹ When it snows, she has no fear for her household; for all of them are clothed in scarlet.

²² She makes coverings for her bed; she is clothed in fine linen and purple.

²³ Her husband is respected at the city gate, where he takes his seat among the elders of the land.

²⁴ She makes linen garments and sells them, and supplies the merchants with sashes.

²⁵ She is clothed with strength and dignity; she can laugh at the days to come.

²⁶ She speaks with wisdom, and faithful instruction is on her tongue.

²⁷ She watches over the affairs of her household and does not eat the bread of idleness.

²⁸ Her children arise and call her blessed; her husband also, and he praises her:

²⁹ "Many women do noble things, but you surpass them all."

³⁰ Charm is deceptive, and beauty is fleeting; but a woman who fears the Lord is to be praised.

³¹ Give her the reward she has earned, and let her works bring her praise at the city gate.

Titus 2: 1-5

¹ You must teach what is in accord with sound doctrine. ² Teach the older men to be temperate, worthy of respect, self-controlled, and sound in faith, in love and in endurance. ³ Likewise, teach the older women to be reverent in the way they live, not to be slanderers or addicted to much wine, but to teach what is good. ⁴ Then they can train the younger women to love their husbands and children, ⁵ to be self-controlled and pure, to be busy at home, to be kind, and to be subject to their husbands, so that no one will malign the word of God.

HOW TO GET INVOLVED IN THE
Woman to Woman Mentoring Ministry

Attend an Orientation Coffee
Fill out a Profile Card
Attend Kickoff Night
Commit to the Mentoring Covenant and Code of Ethics

What Happens After Today?

1. The day after the Orientation Coffee, a Prayer Day Team will pray over the Profile Cards. They ask the Holy Spirit to help match you into a one-on-one relationship with another woman, unless you matched yourself with someone at the Coffee. We actually encourage you to match yourself, because we invited the Holy Spirit into the Coffee, and God might be speaking to you about someone you meet there. Do not hesitate to put that person's name on your Profile Card for us to consider when matching you. Please pray for the Prayer Day Team as they come to your mind during the matching day. They feel those prayers and need them!

2. You will receive a phone call the week after the Coffee telling you the time in the evening to meet at the church in room *(room number)* on *(date)*. This Kickoff Night will be an opportunity for the mentors to receive some initial training. After the training, the mentees will join the group, and you will all have an opportunity to meet the women you were matched with.

3. There will be an opportunity the evening of *(date)* for mentors and mentees to spend time getting to know each other and to sign the Mentoring Covenants together. This will also be the time to set up your first meeting, so bring your calendar.

4. *Please put the evening of *(Kickoff meeting date)* on your calendar today. You must be able to attend in order to be matched in a mentoring relationship. This is a very important part of getting your mentoring relationship started on the right foot—that's why we called it a Kickoff Night!

*We regret that we will not be able to match anyone who cannot attend the Kickoff Night. If this does not fit into your schedule, our next Orientation Coffee is *(date)* and Kickoff Night is *(date)*. Hopefully, this will work out better for you. Remember, it is all in God's timing.

Orientation Coffee
Closed

Next Coffee
in the month of
(June)

We're so sorry we missed you. God bless.

Woman to Woman Mentoring Ministry

Woman to Woman MENTORING

Covenant

We will make a six-month commitment to the mentoring relationship.

We will contact each other once a week and meet a minimum of twice a month.

We will pray for each other and ask the Lord to deepen our bond of friendship.

We will do things together like work on spiritual disciplines, learn a new skill, attend church functions (retreats, seminars, or women's activities), we will take walks together, go out for a meal or coffee together; and spend time in each other's home.

We will make an effort to keep our relationship ongoing, consistent, and fun; we will always ask God to be a part of it and to bless it.

We will take our relationship seriously and make time for it in our schedules.

We will keep our sharing confidential—just between the two of us—unless we agree it is OK to share with someone else.
We will talk only about ourselves.

We are committed

_____
(Mentor)

_____
(Mentee)

Witnessed By

_____

_____
Date

Helpful Hints

Set a time for your first meeting before you leave Kickoff Night.

Try to find a regular meeting day and time early in the relationship. Bring your calendars each time you get together, so you can easily set up the next meeting time. This avoids inconsistency in meeting.

Talk early on about what you would each like to bring to, as well as receive from, the relationship. When you feel comfortable with each other, share your journey—where you have been, where you feel the Lord is leading you, and how you can encourage and support each other. Uplift each other, and remember to talk only about yourselves.

Pray, pray, pray, pray! Pray together when you meet and for each other when you are apart. Make note of each other's prayer requests so you can see the answers to prayer and give God the praise together. Keep a journal of your mentoring experience. It will be fruitful to your spiritual growth.

FORM I

Forms 231

M&M Questionnaire

Will you please help us?
This questionnaire is completely anonymous and will only be used to help
improve and develop our Woman to Woman Mentoring Ministry.
Your answers will not be shared with anyone. Thank you in advance for your help.

1. Were you a mentor or mentee? _____

2. Approximately how many times were you actually able to meet? _____

3. What types of places did you meet?

4. Were you satisfied with the number of meetings? ❏ Yes ❏ No
    If not, how many times would you like to have met during the six months? _____

5. Now that you have experienced a mentoring relationship, how many months do you think they should last?
    ❏ 3 months   ❏ 6 months   ❏ 9 months   ❏ 1 year

6. Was the relationship what you expected? Please explain your answer.

7. Do you have any suggestions for how we could improve the ministry?

8. Any other comments?

Announcing

An exciting opportunity for *(your church's name)* Church women to be part of this wonderful Woman to Woman Mentoring Ministry

"Mentoring requires no special talent, or God-given quality. All God asks is for us to take seriously the task of mentoring and building up other women."—Lucibel Van Atta

Women of All Ages Welcome

If you feel God's nudge to be a mentor and share in another woman's life by using what God has done in your life to encourage and assist her in the glorious walk of a Christian woman …

or

If you are a woman who has been feeling the need to talk to another Christian woman who has "been in your shoes" and with God's help made it through and wants to support and encourage you as a mentee at this time in your Christian life …

Please call xxx-xxxx to receive more information about this one-on-one Woman to Woman Mentoring Ministry and the date of the next Orientation Coffee.

"But we were gentle among you like a mother caring for her little children. We loved you so much that we were delighted to share with you not only the gospel of God but our lives as well, because you had become so dear to us. … encouraging, comforting, and urging you to live lives worthy of God, who calls you into his kingdom and glory" (1 Thessalonians 2:7-8,12).

"One generation shall praise your works to another and shall declare your mighty acts" (Psalm 145:4, NKJV).

Orientation Coffee

Sunday
June 1
2:00 to 6:00 p.m.

At the home of
Lori Smith
16 Oak
Your Town, USA

Women of All Ages Welcome

Come and learn how as a mentor you can use your life experiences
and walk with God to encourage and assist another woman!

or

Come and learn how as a mentee you can be encouraged and
supported in your Christian walk by another Christian woman!

or

Come and learn both! There is now opportunity for the women of
(*your church's name*) Church to experience the joys and blessings of encouraging each other.
Come join us for coffee and we will share with you how you can become a participant in this ministry.

Please register: Call xxx-xxxx

No childcare
Please arrive promptly at 2 p.m. and stay until 6 p.m.
No one admitted after 2:30 p.m.
To be matched into a mentoring relationship,
please keep the evening of June 9th on your calendar from 7 p.m. to 10 p.m.

Suggested $10.00 donation

Directions
From Church:

Orientation Coffee Helper's
Pre-Coffee Review

The Woman to Woman Mentoring Ministry Administrative Team thanks each of you for serving today and for giving of your time, energy, and love. We do have a few reminders to share with you so that the day will be a blessing to those attending and to you as well. If we are all on the same page, the day should go smoothly and be a lot of fun and a blessing for everyone.

1. First and foremost, please remember that we are all here as servants and followers of Jesus Christ. We have two purposes today: to serve our Lord and to serve the ladies who attend this Coffee.

2. Please be sure that all your efforts and energies today are directed toward our guests. We will have plenty of time to socialize among ourselves after the last guest leaves. Let's be sure while they are here we do not "huddle" or chat among ourselves. This is not the place to catch up on news about each other. That can seem very cliquish, intimidating, and unfriendly to our guests. Please lovingly help each other remember this!

3. Please stay in your assigned positions—especially in the front yard. Between guest's arrival, stay in your spots. Please do not go out front if you are not assigned there. The **Registrar** is responsible for the front area, so give her your cooperation and respect.

4. **Greeter/Hugger** puts up the closed sign and stays out front until 2:45 and then puts up the closed sign.

5. **Registrars** and **Greeter/Hugger** return to the front door at the end of the Coffee to give out favors, bookmarks, newsletters, and hugs.

6. If you are staying past 2:30 please take note of the following:
   - It is essential that you remain quiet during the program. If you do not wish to hear the program, go to the designated room to wait and work quietly. Please remain there until the break. If you did not bring something to do or read, please pray for the ladies attending. If the waiting room becomes too loud, please know that the person asking you to be quiet is only doing so for the good of everyone. Even whispering can be distracting to the guests and a hindrance to the speaker.
   - Please do not read the Profile Cards. These are private and confidential. Only the **Photographers** and **Registrars** handle the Profile Cards.

7. After the opening prayer and welcome, please line up to come out and introduce yourselves.

8. **Photographers**, after the program has begun, please immediately attach the pictures to the upper, right-hand corner in the designated area on the Profile Cards and Opportunity to Serve Profiles. Then pass them on to the **Registrars** for their review.

9. If you stay after the break to hear the guests' introductions, remember that everything the ladies share is confidential and not repeated to anyone (even your husbands) outside the Coffee.

10. Any questions? Let's all pray over the chairs. If you stay for the entire Coffee, please help clean up afterwards, and we will have a closing prayer together before we leave.

The Mentoring Game

Adapted from a skit by Anita Christensen

This is a lighthearted skit which enacts the point you will be making in the Coffee presentation—that you do not have to be an expert or a Bible scholar to be a mentor. It is a takeoff from the old "Dating Game" program aired in the 70s. Each actress will wear a placard around her neck stating her character's name in bold-printed letters. Three chairs should be placed side-by-side on stage left for the three potential mentors. The mentee will sit by herself on stage right, and the host will stand between them, a little closer to the mentee.

Characters: Host—Anita
Mentee—Ima Novice
Mentor #1—Truly A. Saint
Mentor #2— Sue Permom
Mentor #3—Grace Abounds

HOST: Good morning, ladies, and welcome to The Mentoring Game! Today on our show we have three potential mentors vying for the chance to mentor our new mentee who is waiting backstage. So, without further ado, let's meet our mentors! *(Gestures toward the ladies. Pause for a few seconds.)* Mentor #1, please introduce yourself.

#1: Hi, Anita, I'm Truly A. Saint. *(Say this like "I'm truly a saint.")* I became a Christian at the age of four, and by the time I was five I memorized all 66 names of the books of the Bible. In high school I was the president of our church youth group, and in college I was discipled by Campus Crusade for Christ. I have completed the Navigator's Design for Discipleship and Topical Memory System and attended Walk Thru the Bible three times. I know I can teach our mentee a thing or two! *(Big smile as you look around at the audience.)*

HOST: Thank you, Truly! Now, #2, tell us about yourself.

#2: Yes, Anita, I'm Sue Permom *(Say it like "Supermom.")*, and I'm glad I could be here this morning. I was able to get someone to fill in for me at Mothers of Preschoolers, of which I am the chairman. I have seven children. The oldest, who is 15, is watching the other 6 until I can get back to finish up our home schooling lessons for today. Then we have gymnastics, t-ball, and karate before we head off to Bill Gothard's Basic Youth Conflicts seminar tonight. But I know I can squeeze a mentee into my hectic schedule. *(Big smile.)*

HOST: Well, we're glad you could make it, Sue. Now, #3, please introduce yourself.

#3: Hello, Anita, I'm Grace Abounds. *(Tentatively, while glancing at the other two mentors.)* Well, I'm probably not as qualified as our other two mentors, but I would love to have a younger friend over for coffee just to chat awhile. I just want to encourage young women to take each day, one at a time, and to see how the Lord is working in their lives.

The Mentoring Game

(continued—page 2)

HOST: Thank you, Grace. And now, it's time to meet our mentee! *(Gestures to the back of the room.)*

(The mentee enters to background music, walking up to the front of the room sort of self-consciously. She stands beside her chair and looks out at the audience.)

HOST: Audience, please welcome our lucky contestant. *(Pause, then turn toward mentee.)* Tell us your name and a little about yourself.

MENTEE: Sure, Anita, Ima Novice. *(Say it like "I'm a novice.")* I've been married for four years, and I have a three year old and a nine month old, and ... I just became a Christian last year.

HOST: Good for you! Well, Ima, your potential mentors are each seated in a soundproof booth which allows them to hear your questions, but they can't hear each other's answers. So, why don't we get started?

MENTEE: Okay ... *(She looks at her list.)* Mentor #1, I've been very tired lately because I have a very active three year old and my baby still wakes up once or twice in the night. My husband doesn't understand why supper isn't always ready when he gets home from work or why the housework isn't done. After supper, he wants to take the family out jogging, when I just want to put my feet up. What should I do?

(The mentors have been listening attentively. #1 nods her head as if to acknowledge she knows the answer. #2 looks a little disgusted and shakes her head. #3 just listens carefully and looks empathetic.)

#1: Listen, honey, "No temptation has seized you except what is common to man. And God is faithful; he will not let you to be tempted beyond what you can bear. But when you are tempted, he will also provide a way out so that you can stand up under it" (1 Corinthians 10:13). *(She punctuates her answer with an emphatic nod of the head as if to say, "So there.")*

MENTEE: *(Startled)* Okay, ... #2?

#2: Now, Ima, you think you got it tough—try seven kids. What you need is a good dose of vitamins. I happen to have a home business selling nutritional supplements, and I can fix you right up. And how 'bout telling your husband if he thinks he can handle it any better, he should stay home with the kids for a week. He'll sure appreciate you then!

MENTEE: *(Incredulously)* Really? Uh, #3, what do you think?

#3: Wow, Ima, I feel for you. Those preschool years are so tough. *(Pauses to think for a moment.)* I have some ideas which really helped me with meal preparation and housekeeping when my kids were young, and I'd love to share them with you. And ... I was wondering, are you familiar with our church's Mother's Day Out program?

MENTEE: Thank you, #3. Actually, I've been meaning to check out those programs.

FORM N

Forms **237**

The Mentoring Game

(continued—page 3)

HOST: Okay, Ima, we have time for one more question.

MENTEE: Hmmm ... *(She looks over her list of questions.)*. Okay, my mother-in-law keeps comparing me to her other daughter-in-law. Lately, she's been wondering when I'm going to take off the "baby" weight I gained in my last pregnancy. Last week she suggested I get my hair cut and wondered when I last bought myself a new outfit. I already feel frumpy as it is. *(Imploringly)* What can I do, #1?

#1: *(Nods her head to acknowledge she understands the problem.)* Ima, try telling her 1 Peter 3:3: "Your beauty should not come from outward adornment, such as braided hair and the wearing of gold jewelry and fine clothes. Instead, it should be that of your inner self, the unfading beauty of a gentle and quiet spirit, which is of great worth in God's sight. For this is the way the holy women of the past who put their hope in God used to make themselves beautiful." *(This last statement should be said like it's a dig against the mother-in-law.)*

#2: You know, that just gets me! I suppose she has a figure like Twiggy? She should be glad you've blessed her with two beautiful grandchildren. Don't worry about the way you look. The most important thing is your kids. A child's life is now!

MENTEE: Well, she really does love my kids ... I guess I just don't like myself lately. What do you think, #3?

#3: Ima, I think your mother-in-law really cares about you, and she probably sensed how you were feeling. You know, my daughter-in-law and I go out to lunch and shopping together periodically. I wonder how it would work if you took a Saturday, and the two of you went shopping and maybe had your hair done? I think you need to pamper yourself a little, and I bet she would be delighted to come along!

MENTEE: *(Brightening up a little.)* Actually, we do get along very well, and she has great taste in clothes! I think she would be pleasantly surprised if I asked her. That's a good idea!

(Now the host wraps up the show. While she is doing this, Ima, Truly, Sue, and Grace appear to be contemplating what has transpired so far in the show.)

HOST: And now, audience, Ima has an important decision to make as she chooses her mentor. *(Stand behind each mentor and put a hand over her head while the audience responds.)* Who would you choose? Mentor #1? ... Mentor #2? ... or Mentor #3? We'll be back after a word from our sponsor.

(Actresses quickly take their seats. Coffee program continues.)

Note: Observe as the guests arrive at the Coffee, and ask three ladies if they would be willing to play the part of a mentor. Have the scripts already highlighted and give each a sign to hang around her neck. Advise them to put the scripts and signs under their chairs, enjoy the program, and you will call them forward when the skit begins.

(This is also a great skit to do for groups in your church that you are introducing to the concept of mentoring.)

Hostess Letter

Date:

Dear Hostess,

I wanted to thank you for offering your home for the *(date of Coffee)* Woman to Woman Mentoring Ministry Orientation Coffee. You really were an answer to prayer!

I just wanted to clarify a few things with you, and send you a Hostess Checklist that has been helpful to previous hostesses. [Do you need a list of registrants to have for a guard gate? I hope the guards can be flexible, because some women pick up a flier and come without registering or register and then don't come at all. Perhaps you can let the guards know the situation, and they can let in women who say they are from *(church name)*, coming to a Coffee.] (Use bracketed section if it is a gated community.)

As you will see on the Hostess Checklist, the hostess provides coffee, punch or lemonade, and light refreshments. We may have close to *(fill-in number)* women attending. We can always find folding chairs if you need them. There will be a ministry donation basket and we will use the donations to help defray your costs, so please save your receipts and give them to me after the Coffee.

The Coffee volunteer helpers and myself will arrive at 1:00 p.m. to set up. Guests usually start arriving around 1:45, and the Coffee will go until 6:00 p.m. Some women stay after to chat. A good time to block out on your calendar would be 1:00 p.m. until 7:00 p.m.

If you receive any phone calls regarding questions about the Coffee or the Mentoring Ministry, refer them to the Mentoring Ministry phone number at church: *(Fill-in phone number)*.

Thank you again for your hospitality. Please call me at home, *(Hospitality Shepherd Coach or Ministry Leader's phone number)* if you have any questions. I will be in close contact with you as we near the Coffee date. Your willingness to help at this time is a special blessing to the ministry.

About His Work,

Signed by Hospitality Shepherd Coach

Form O

Forms

Hostess Checklist

Here is a check list to help keep you stress free on the big day.

Date of the Orientation Coffee is: __/__/__ Time: 2:00 p.m.–6:00 p.m. Helpers will arrive at 1:00 p.m.

They are: Greeter _____
        Registrar and Name Tag Lady _____
        Photographer and Assistant _____
        Hospitality Shepherd Coach _____
        Hospitality Shepherd Coach's Phone _____

Plan on _____ women. I will call with a firmer count the week before the Coffee.

❏ Do you have enough chairs? Don't forget to count couches, typing chairs, stools, chairs in the kids' rooms—anything on which to sit. If you need additional chairs, call me.

❏ You may want to consider moving a dining room table against the wall if it normally sits in the center of the room. This will give more floor space for walking and sitting.

❏ Do you have coffee and a large coffee pot? If not, call me.

❏ Punch or lemonade is good to serve, also. Do you have a punch bowl? If you don't, call me! A small pot of decaf is good to have, too.

❏ What are you going to serve? Keep it simple because there is not a lot of time for the women to eat. Cookies, bars or loaf cake, sliced fruit, sweet breads or bundt cakes served in slices are all good because they do not require a plate or a fork. If you are going to have something that needs to be on a plate, use paper plates and plastic forks. Make it easy on yourself.

❏ Use paper cups, too. You will need those that can be used for both hot and cold drinks.

❏ We will need two small tables—one for registration (please have pens out on this table) and one for book sales.

❏ It is nice to have background praise music on the CD or tape player. If you need praise CDs or tapes, call me.

❏ We will need a box of tissues handy.

❏ Have you prepared the family for this invasion of women into their home? They will probably appreciate advance notice so they can plan accordingly. Don't forget the dog!

❏ There will be a donation basket out to help defray the costs of your hospitality.

❏ Relax and enjoy the thought of lovely Christian women gathering in your home. I am praying for you. Let's pray that God will truly use your home as a place where women can meet and come together to form relationships that will be life-changing.

Mentor Halftime Refresher Letter

Date:

Dear Mentors,

I often think about you and wonder how you are doing. It is always nice to run into you at church or other functions. Isn't it hard to believe it has been almost three months since we met at (*name of their Orientation Coffee hostess*) beautiful home? The seasons have changed, and I am sure your mentoring relationships are growing with the passage of time.

If you recall, the Mentors were to get together again at the three-month point, and we are almost there. Please get out your calendars and put down this special meeting date. At this session, you will also have the opportunity to address any situations that have arisen for you, ask questions, and share testimonies and blessings. Here are the details.

Halftime Refresher Date:

Time: 7:00 p.m.

Location: (Have it in a room at your church, if possible.)

RSVP to:

Bring: Bible, *Woman to Woman Mentoring Mentor Handbook*, pen.

(Anyone feeling ambitious can bring a treat. We will have coffee and water.)

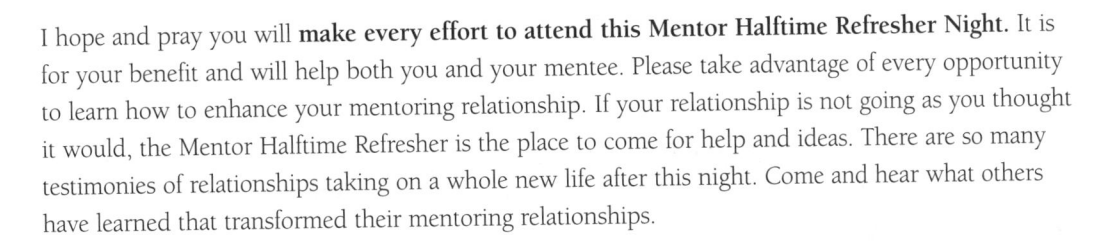

I hope and pray you will **make every effort to attend this Mentor Halftime Refresher Night.** It is for your benefit and will help both you and your mentee. Please take advantage of every opportunity to learn how to enhance your mentoring relationship. If your relationship is not going as you thought it would, the Mentor Halftime Refresher is the place to come for help and ideas. There are so many testimonies of relationships taking on a whole new life after this night. Come and hear what others have learned that transformed their mentoring relationships.

I pray for you often, as do your Prayer Warriors. I trust you are finding being a mentor a reward from God. If not, please come and let's talk about it.

(*Signed by the Training Leader*)

You are invited to a celebration just for you!

It's time for the Woman to Woman Mentoring Ministry's
Coffee # ___ Six-Month Potluck Celebration

Sunday, *(Date)*
1:00 p.m.

at the home of
(Hostess name)
(Hostess Address)
Directions

Special Awards Presentation After Lunch!

RSVP to our Hospitality Shepherd Coach at *(Phone Number)*

Here is what to bring:
If your last name ends in:
(A-E) Salad   (F-J) Hot dish   (K-P) Dessert   (Q-U) Rolls   (V-Z) Beverage

It is hard to believe it has been six months since we all met at *(Hostess name)* beautiful home. This potluck is for you. *(Hostess name)* is opening her home again for us so we can return to where we started and have an opportunity to reflect on our relationships. *(This paragraph will need to be altered if your potluck lunch is held in a different location.)*

The Potluck is the time to bring closure to the initial six-month covenant you agreed to and then take a look at what you would like to do next. It also is a time to renew friendships, hear testimonies and stories, and just fellowship together. You may be planning to continue in your same mentoring relationships indefinitely, or you may be staying friends while each of you moves into another relationship. Mentees, you may feel ready now to mentor someone yourself. We have another Orientation Coffee coming up in *(date)*, and, as always, we pray for sufficient mentors.

Please make every effort to attend this celebration since it is a part of your mentoring experience. Even if for some reason both of you cannot come, please come yourself. We look forward to seeing all of you soon.

About His Work,

(Hospitality Shepherd Coach)

Prayer Warrior Guidelines

Dear *(Prayer Warrior's name)*,

I would first like to sincerely thank you for serving in the Woman to Woman Mentoring Ministry. The Lord has so blessed this ministry, and it is expanding rapidly. In His sovereign way, the Lord spoke to you and encouraged you to be a Prayer Warrior for this Coffee.

Being part of the Prayer Warrior team will consist of calling, praying for, and meeting with the M&M relationships you are assigned. You will call each woman the first week of the month for the next six months. The call is to encourage her, see how she is doing, and learn of any specific areas where she might need prayer. Especially focus on prayers for her M&M relationship.

There might also be occasions when you need to call the women on your list to pass along relevant information about the ministry. You are the ministry eyes and ears to these women. I will contact you the second week of each month to see how your phone calls went, how the relationships are doing, and to answer your questions.

Let me explain the attached forms to you:

1. The Mentoring Roster has the M&M names, addresses, and phone numbers. The *M* stands for the mentor and the *E* for the mentee. Each mentoring relationship will have the same number by it: for example, *11M* and *11E* are in the same relationship. If you have someone with an *EM* by her name, she is a mentee of the woman above her name and a mentor to the woman below. All three women will have the same number by their name (48M mentors 48EM, and 48EM is mentoring 48E). Hope that makes sense. Not all of you will have this situation. You only pray for the M&Ms whose numbers are listed on your Prayer Journal.

2. Your Prayer Warrior Journal lists the numbers of your assigned relationships along the left-hand side. It also contains the months of your M&M's six-month commitment. There is extra space under *Pray* to note the dates you pray for them, and you can use the *Prayer Request* area to note their prayer requests and praises. Call them once a month (the first week), and check the space under *PH* (phone) when you make that call.

3. M&M Meetings: Please arrange two meetings during the six months. The first is to be held in the second month, and it is a group meeting with only your assigned mentors. It is to be a time to pray and check on how they are doing after their first month of mentoring. Remind them to come the following month to the Mentor Halftime Refresher.

    In the fourth month arrange a group meeting with all your M&Ms. This can be a social time and a chance to see how they are progressing with their relationships. Encourage them to all come to their Six-Month Potluck Celebration, and be sure you attend also.

If you have any questions, or anything arises that you need to discuss, please do not hesitate to call me at *(number)*. You can also call the **Ministry Relations Shepherdess** at *(number)* if there are problems with your M&M relationships, and you need her suggestions and input. I pray the Lord's blessings on you as you continue to do His work. I know you will find this a rewarding experience. All these ladies are wonderful and so excited to participate in their M&M relationships.

Thank you again for following the Lord's call to your heart,

(Signed by Prayer Warrior Shepherd Coach)

FORM S

Mentoring Roster

Mentor or Mentee	Name	Address	Phone	Coffee #
1 M				
1 E				
2 M				
2 E				
3 M				
3 E				
4 M				
4 E				
5 M				
5 E				
6 M				
6 E				
7 M				
7 E				
8 M				
8 E				
9 M				
9 E				
10 M				
10 E				
11 M				
11 E				
12 M				
12 E				
13 M				
13 E				
14 M				
14 E				
15 M				
15 E				
16 M				
16 E				
17 M				
17 E				
18 M				
18 E				
19 M				
19 E				
20 M				
20 E				

Prayer Warrior Journal

Mentor or Mentee	Name	Prayer Request	Coffee #	September Pray	Ph	October Pray	Ph	November Pray	Ph	December Pray	Ph	January Pray	Ph	February Pray	Ph
1 M															
1 E															
2 M															
2 E															
3 M															
3 E															
4 M															
4 E															
5 M															
5 E															
6 M															
6 E															

FORM U

Woman to Woman Mentoring Ministry

AREAS OF OPPORTUNITY FOR SERVICE

Administration:

The Lord has graciously used me as the vessel to start the ministry, but I would never presume that He meant for me to do it alone. We now are forming an administrative team. We could use more willing hearts who could help us with the organization, planning, and growth of the ministry in areas such as finances, special events, hospitality, prayer warriors, prayer chain, and publicity.

You will have no doubt if the Lord calls you into this type of commitment, because He will speak very clearly to you.

Call Janet xxx-xxxx

Coffee Hostess:

Open your home on a Sunday afternoon to approximately 30-40 women. Provide light refreshments and seating. A love donation basket will be put out to help with the cost of food and supplies. We can help round up extra chairs, large coffee pots, etc. It is fun and your home is so blessed with the presence of wonderful godly women.

Call Lorna xxx-xxxx

Phoning:

Make phone calls in one or more of the following areas:
 (1) the waiting list to announce the next Coffee,
 (2) one week before a Coffee to remind those who have registered,
 (3) mentors right after a Coffee to announce first training, or
 (4) to inform of other meetings or to disseminate information as the need arises.

Call Nancy xxx-xxxx

Publicity Assistants:

Could entail addressing and stuffing envelopes, collating the newsletter, assembling program handouts for Coffees, and making copies at the church office.

Call Jane xxx-xxxx

HE WILL SPEAK VERY CLEARLY TO YOU

"It is good to give thanks to the Lord, and to sing praises unto Your name, O Most High; to declare Your lovingkindness in the morning, and Your faithfulness every night, ... for You, Lord, have made me glad through Your work; I will triumph in the works of Your hands" (Ps. 92:1-2,4, NKJV).

FORM V

246 *Woman to Woman Mentoring: Ministry Coordinator's Guide*

Woman to Woman Mentoring Ministry

AREAS OF OPPORTUNITY FOR SERVICE
(page 2)

Assisting with an Orientation Coffee

Greeter: Positioned at the front door to welcome women as they arrive and direct them to refreshments and the registration table. Say goodbye to them as they are leaving.

Registrar: Stationed at the registration table to assist with filling out name tags, Profile Cards, and handouts.

Photographer: Takes pictures of the Orientation Coffee and of each woman as she introduces herself. Camera, film, and developing are provided.

Above three call Lorna xxx-xxxx

Prayer Really Works

Prayer Warrior Team: Given 4-5 mentoring relationships to pray for during your personal prayer time. Also assigned mentors and mentees to call once a month to encourage them in their relationships and hear any specific prayer requests. You do need to attend Kickoff Night. You will be provided with a prayer and calling journal.

Call Darlene xxx-xxxx

Prayer Day Matching Team: Participate in the Prayer Team that meets the day after the Coffee to pray and ask the Lord to help with the matching of the mentors and mentees. You will need to attend the Coffee and take notes as the women introduce themselves. Prayer for matching is usually the day after the Coffee and takes the whole day.

Call Sue xxx-xxxx

Prayer Chain Participants: Be a link in a dynamic Prayer Chain that would pray for the needs of the women in the ministry as they arise. You would be instructed how to pass the prayer request along the Chain by phone, immediately after you receive the request. And, of course, you would pray for the requests you receive. This could be a very dynamic addition to your prayer life. All requests are confidential and transferred just as they are received.

Call Barbara xxx-xxxx

Women's Fellowship Table: Answer questions and distribute information to ladies who show an interest in the Mentoring Ministry. You would only need to be there 15 minutes before the normal service you attend and 15 minutes after the service. This is a great way to fulfill your commitment to the ministry.

Call Jill xxx-xxxx

SIGN UP TODAY
(before you leave, if possible)

Woman to Woman Mentoring Ministry

Areas of Opportunity for Service
Sign-Up Sheet

	Position	Name	Phone Number
1.			
2.			
3.			
4.			
5.			
6.			
7.			
8.			
9.			
10.			
11.			
12.			

Form W

Beyond Coffee...

ENCOURAGING WORDS FOR M&Ms

Winter Quarter — **Woman to Woman Mentoring Newsletter**

Dear Sisters in Christ,

I am so excited about our first edition of the newsletter. Doesn't it look great? We hope to keep you informed of all the many blessings the Lord continues to bestow on our ministry. Last year was a year of beginnings for us, and it seems that this is the year of growth. As some of you may have heard, 86 women attended our first Orientation Coffee of this year at the home of Mary Smitts on January 12th, in spite of heavy rain and classes at the church. In anticipation of the growth, the Lord has been gracious to me and brought 12 women to form an Administrative Team. Twelve is a very prophetic number, don't you think? But Jesus did not stop with 12, and neither will I. Jesus' 12 quickly turned into 72, so if you have a desire to become a part of the Administrative Team or serve in any of the many areas of the ministry, please do not hesitate to call. I would like to take this opportunity to thank each and every one of you who have offered your home, your time, your prayers, your servant's heart, and your love.

The Ministry is all about each and every one of you, so if you have ideas or suggestions of how we can make it more meaningful to you, please do not hesitate to call. I really encourage any of you who love to pray to become a Light in the Prayer Chain. Please don't forget to leave a prayer request yourself if you have the need, and let us pray for you or your loved ones. I pray for all of you who have been and are currently in mentoring relationships. I feel the Lord had a plan in each and every one of those. You may not know it now, but you will. My prayer for you is His peace in hectic times.

About His Work,

Janet Thompson

> **Mission Statement:** To give the women of Saddleback Church the opportunity to experience joy and growth in their Christian life, by participating in one-on-one supportive and encouraging mentoring friendships. A mentor will be a woman who is a practicing Christian, regularly attends Saddleback Church, and has the desire to let her life be an example and godly role model. A mentee will be a Saddleback Church woman who is younger in her walk with the Lord. Women of all ages are welcome. The scriptural foundation is Titus 2:3-5, where we are told to teach and guide the next generation of Christian women in how to live the life of a godly woman in Christ.

Who Will Be the First to Testify?

The first draft of the book that will allow other churches to enjoy a mentoring ministry like ours is coming to a close and getting ready for submission. I have several testimonies for it, but I would really like a few more. Hearing a real live story is always so encouraging, just as we hear every Sunday. Your story could be what helps another woman reach for a friend. If you don't have the means to type it out, a handwritten version would be great; or call and give it to me over the phone, and I will type it. I know so many of you have a story about how blessed you have been in your mentoring relationships, both as mentors and mentees. Wouldn't you please take a moment to jot it down? My fax number is (*XXX-XXXX*). Mailing address: (*name and address of your contact person*). Do it right now, while you are thinking about it. Don't worry about how it sounds. Anything from the heart is melodious. Blessings and Thanks!

Phone Numbers of Importance:
Woman to Woman Mentoring
Ministry Information Line:
(XXX) XXX-XXXX
Prayer Chain for M&Ms
(XXX) XXX-XXXX
(press * skips message)

Next Orientation Coffee
March 16th

FOR YOUR INFORMATION
Vital Statistics of the Ministry

Coffee #1	1/96	20 women
Coffee #2	3/96	33 women
Coffee #3	6/96	42 women
Coffee #4	8/96	34 women
Coffee #5	10/96	42 women
Coffee #6	1/97	86 women
Total in ministry after 6 Coffees		**257 women**

Orientation Coffees are held five times in one year. Commitment to a relationship is six months. Potlucks are six months from original Coffee.

On December 8th, 1996, the Woman to Woman Mentoring Ministry had our first annual Christmas Party. The joyful event was held at Dianne Artim's home in Mission Viejo. Many women brought a Christmas dish to enjoy that day, canned goods and gifts for the needy, and lots of Christmas cheer! There was glorious entertainment by Monique Nelson and Gloria Haslam. They played "Selma & Sylvia" in the skit "As It Wasn't Written," a hilarious musical skit about 2 Jewish women who lived 2,000 years ago, around the time of Jesus. The crowd of over 50 enjoyed every moment they performed. Janet did a recap of past, present, and future items about the ministry, and introduced and kicked off our Prayer Chain. The day was a beautiful way to end our first year in the ministry. We look forward to next December's Christmas party!

Women's Fellowship Table
Ministry Relations Shepherdess

Jill–xxx-xxxx

Are you excited about what the Lord has done in your life through the mentoring ministry? Share it with other women at the Women's Fellowship Table before and after one of the weekend services. It is a one-month commitment to volunteer weekly, and we now have four services to choose from! Please call me for more details or to sign up for the February, March, or April slots.

Upcoming Item of Interest
A New Group Forming—M&Ms

This group is forming to nurture mentoring relationships with spiritual guidance, information, sharing of gifts, fellowship, and encouragement. We welcome your suggestions, comments, or questions, about what would be meaningful to you. Enthusiastic M&Ms call Special Events Shepherd Coach Tracy at xxx-xxxx

Have you moved, or do we have the wrong address or phone number? Please call the ministry information line with all changes to demographics. We certainly do not want to miss you!

DONATION ITEMS NEEDED:

- Coffee

- Paper Goods: coffee cups, napkins, small plates

- Portable Microphone System for Orientation Coffees

Call the Mentoring Ministry line.

Thanks!

BIBLE TRIVIA

Write your answer down and look for answers on page 4. Have Fun!

1. Which two Hebrew prophets had a fruitful mentoring relationship?
   _____
   _____

2. Which two Hebrew women did God make houses for? _____

3. Which two sisters of Bethany had a brother named Lazarus and were close friends of Jesus?
   _____
   _____

4. According to Paul, how often are we supposed to pray? _____

5. What Old Testament book begins, "Let him kiss me with the kisses of his mouth—for your love is more delightful than wine"? _____

6. According to Jesus, where is a person's heart? _____

7. What will happen to the pure in heart, according to Jesus? _____

8. Which part of the body tests words? _____

9. The book of Proverbs states, "Give me neither poverty nor riches." What, instead, is requested?
   _____

10. According to Proverbs, what type of person causes best friends to go their separate ways?
    _____

Your Response Is Kindly Requested

You are such a tease,
When you forget your RSVPs.
The poor hostess never knows
If she'll have a crowd or no-shows.

It takes just a moment
To respond to the event.
And yet the worry spared,
Lets the hostess know you cared.

It seems to be a lost courtesy,
And that really worries me.
Christian women could make a difference
By being willing to honor their commitments.

You know if it were you
Who needed to know how many or few,
You'd be pulling out your hairs
Wondering if you had enough chairs!

So when the invitation arrives,
Put it in a spot that cannot miss your eyes.
Then before the week is over give a ring a ding a ling,
And hear your hostess smile as you are RSVPing!

Poetry by Janet Thompson

Woman to Woman Mentoring Ministry
Prayer Chain

To request a prayer: Dial (XXX) XXX-XXX
Press * (to skip pre-recorded message)
Leave your prayer request at the sound of the tone.
Briefly, in 1 or 2 sentences, state the person's first name and what to pray for regarding the person.

If your prayer is a crisis and you need to speak to a pastor:
Dial (XXX) XXX-XXX until 9:30 p.m. to speak to a Pastor of the Day. After 9:30 p.m. call XXX-XXX. Press 9 to have a Pastor of the Day paged.

The Prayer Chain is now growing, and we need volunteers. If you have extra minutes during your day and you'd like to join this heartfelt ministry, please call Barbara, Prayer Chain Shepherd Coach at XXX-XXX.

The M & M Matching Prayer Team Meets!

As everyone knows, after the Orientation Coffees are held, the next phase of the ministry kicks into gear, praying for the matching of mentors and mentees. Early Monday morning, Janet Thompson, Kelly, and Mary arrived to begin our task. Together we invited the Lord to lead us in the privilege of matching the wonderful women who were seeking His way in their lives.

We sat on the rug in front of the fireplace and spread out the cards. In the beginning we looked at obvious clues for matching such as needs/requests listed on the cards, whether married (with children) or single, and even address proximity. But as is typical of the Lord, we had to dig deeper. It was really helpful to review the notes we had taken while women were sharing their hearts at the Orientation Coffee. When we reached a "logjam," we stopped. It was time for prayer and a song to the Lord. Sometimes we just took a break for food or coffee (lots of coffee for Janet).

There was a true sense of joy in the process, and even a measure of laughter as we began to get tired and slap-happy! Since there were more mentees than mentors, we made telephone calls to ask if some would be willing to take on the mentoring responsibility. Not surprisingly, we always got a positive response. It was clear everyone was willing to serve however the Lord was leading them.

As Janet has mentioned at the Coffees, we're not finished until everyone has a deep sense of peace. We thought we were just about through when Mary had to leave at 4:30 p.m., but as we prayed over the last few cards we sensed we needed to go back through the previous matches and pray over them again. Hours went by as we labored over the cards and then the telephone rang—it was Tracey. She prayed with us over the phone and we gained new strength for the last mile. What a blessing to have so many sisters in the Lord supporting each other. Finally, we crossed the finish line and victory was sweet.

There is no doubt that the Woman to Woman Mentoring Ministry is close to the Lord's heart. Each mentor and mentee can be assured that Jesus Christ is Lord in their relationship and is walking with them as they serve Him and each other.

In His love & grace,
Sue
Prayer Day Shepherd Coach/Worship Director
XXX-XXXX

Did You Know We Also Have a Special Events Shepherd Coach?

Since I have been involved with the Woman to Woman Mentoring Ministry, I have been so impressed with the warmth and love of all of you. It gives me such joy to see so many women connect so quickly, sharing their life experiences and friendship. We need guidance, love, and support, of course, but we also need a little fun in our lives. I am the new Special Events Shepherd Coach, and I'd like to plan some fun and interesting events for us this year. There is so much talent in our group, I want to solicit suggestions on what you would like to do to have fun. Field trips? Interesting speakers? Time management? Golf, tennis, or hikes? Please call me at XXX-XXXX or email me at XXX@XXX.XXX and tell me what you think is most fun. Anyone who wants to help plan events with me can also call! I look forward to being swamped with numerous ideas.

Tracy
Special Events Shepherd Coach

Bible Trivia Answers from page 3
1. Elijah and Elisha
2. Puah and Shiprah, the Hebrew midwives (Exodus 1:20-21)
3. Mary and Martha (Luke 10:38-42; John 11)
4. Continually (1 Thessalonians 5:17)
5. The Song of Solomon (1:2)
6. Where his treasure is (Matthew 6:21)
7. They will see God (Matthew 5:8)
8. The ear, of course (Job 12:11)
9. "My daily bread" (Proverbs 30:8)
10. A whisperer (Proverbs 16:28)

Administrative Team Roster and Coordinators

Ministry Visionary Shepherd
Janet Thompson
XXX-XXXX

Spiritual Shepherdess/Assistant
Laura
XXX-XXXX

Prayer Day Shepherd Coach/Worship Director
Sue
XXX-XXXX

Hospitality Shepherd Coach
Lorna
XXX-XXXX

Financial Shepherd Coach
Marcy
XXX-XXXX

Special Events Shepherd Coach
Tracy
XXX-XXXX

Publicity Shepherd Coach/Newsletter Editor
Jane
XXX-XXXX

Prayer Warrior Shepherd Coach
Darlene
XXX-XXXX

Prayer Chain Shepherd Coach
Barbara
XXX-XXXX

Training Leader
Jo Ann
XXX-XXXX

Ministry Relations Shepherdess/Fellowship Table Coordinator
Jill
XXX-XXXX

Phone Coordinator
Nancy
XXX-XXXX

And many, many more that are not mentioned. Call the ministry info line for more information.
XXX-XXXX

Woman to Woman Mentoring Ministry Newsletter • page 5

Areas of Opportunity FOR SERVICE

Opportunity	Call
Ministry Administration	XXX-XXXX
Hosting a Coffee	Lorna
Phoning	Nancy
Prayer Chain Member	Barbara
Women's Fellowship Table	Jill
Newsletter Assembly	Jane
M&Ms Encouragement	Tracy
Greeter (for Coffees)	Lorna
Photographer (for Coffees)	Lorna
Registrars (for Coffees)	Lorna
Prayer Warrior Team	Darlene

Dates to Remember

August 19
Coffee #4

February 23
Potluck

March 16
Next Orientation Coffee

Next newsletter publication will be for the months March and April.

FORM X

Forms **253**

The complete handbook for women's ministry!

Women Reaching Women: Beginning and Building a Growing Women's Enrichment Ministry, Revised

Compiled by Chris Adams

ISBN 0-7673-2593-1

This handbook contains Bible-based help for developing women's leadership skills and starting/building a women's ministry. It includes the latest information written by leading women's leaders. *Women Reaching Women* helps you plan a balanced ministry of outreach, inreach, Bible study, fellowship, and discipleship. New topics addressed in this revised edition include: The Generations in the Postmodern World; Women's Ministry in Smaller Churches; Involving the Uninvolved; Girl's Ministry; and more!

To order this resource: WRITE LifeWay Church Resources Customer Service, One LifeWay Plaza, Nashville, TN 37234-0113; FAX order to (615) 251-5933; PHONE 1-800-458-2772; E-MAIL *orderentry@lifeway.com*; order ONLINE at *www.lifeway.com*; or visit the LifeWay Christian Store serving you.

Ready to take the next step with your women's ministry?

Transformed Lives: Taking Women's Ministry to the Next Level

Compiled by Chris Adams   Foreword by Esther Burroughs

Transformed Lives does exactly what the subtitle describes—it takes women's ministry to the next level! You'll find guidance in how to move women from learning to doing, from being the objects of ministry to ministering to those around them.

ISBN 0-7673-3116-8

This book is organized into sections that emphasize prayer, Bible study, spiritual gifts, service and ministry, special needs, and leadership skill development. In addition, each chapter includes suggestions for adapting women's ministry to the needs of smaller churches.

To order this resource: WRITE LifeWay Church Resources Customer Service, One LifeWay Plaza, Nashville, TN 37234-0113; FAX order to (615) 251-5933; PHONE 1-800-458-2772; E-MAIL *orderentry@lifeway.com*; order ONLINE at *www.lifeway.com*; or visit the LifeWay Christian Store serving you.